Using

America Online with Your Mac

Using

America Online with Your Mac

Gene Steinberg

Using America Online with Your Mac

Copyright© 1995 by Que® Corporation.

Library of Congress Catalog No.: 95-71431

ISBN: 0-7897-0593-1

97 96 95   6 5 4 3 2 1

Interpretation of the printing code: the rightmost double-digit number is the year of the book's printing; the rightmost single-digit number, the number of the book's printing. For example, a printing code of 95-1 shows that the first printing of the book occurred in 1995.

Screen reproductions in this book were created with Collage Complete from Inner Media, Inc., Hollis, NH.

Composed in *ITC Century*, *ITC Highlander*, and *MCPdigital* by Que Corporation.

Credits

To Barbara and Grayson with love and appreciation.

And to my brother Wally, whom I'll miss always.

About the Author

Gene Steinberg is an inveterate desktop computer user who first joined America Online in 1989. He quickly became addicted to the new online service and finally earned positions on its computing forum staff. At present, he is Forum Leader of the service's Macintosh Multimedia Forum, and serves as curator of AOL Portrait Gallery, a library containing photos of America Online members and their families.

In his regular life, Gene has worked at several occupations. He first studied broadcasting in school, and then worked for a number of years as a disc jockey and newscaster. Gene is now a full-time writer and Macintosh software and systems consultant. His published work includes *Special Edition Using America Online* and *Using The Macintosh* for Que Corporation, and feature articles and product reviews for *Macworld*.

Acknowledgments

Although the book you hold in your hands includes my name as the author, it is not a project a sane or almost sane person can do alone. I am grateful for the assistance of many people, working behind the scenes, who made this book possible.

Among America Online's in-house staff, I have special praise for Dave Baker, Lyn Cameron, Jeff Crowe, Betsy Davison, Keith Deaven, Ken Huntsman, Matt Korn, Ann Kort, Pam McGraw, Kathy Ryan, and Deborah Shaw for their ongoing help in making this project a success.

I am also grateful to America Online's Tim Barwick, and my friend (and sometimes co-writer) John Stroud (one of AOL's favorite Mac forum leaders), for getting me involved in America Online's forums to begin with.

A number of experts in the computing industry have provided special assistance in researching several chapters of this book. They include Clayton Cowgill of Supra Corporation (the modem manufacturer), Brian Combs and Ric Ralston of Power Computing (the first official Macintosh-compatible computer maker), Joanne Sperans Hartzell of Insignia Solutions (publishers of SoftWindows), and Pieter Paulson, the computer wizard at Nike, Inc.

Somehow, despite the long hours I spent in front of my computer writing this manuscript, my forums on AOL managed to keep rolling anyway. For that, I must give heartfelt praise to my staff at the Macintosh Multimedia Forum (Rob Sonner, Mark Elpers, Marshall Goldberg, Robn Kester, and Trish Meyer) and my staff at the AOL Portrait Gallery (Debbie DeRosa, Adam Lasnik, Michael T. Lester, Lisa Anna Lind, and Tom Wiseman).

I must give special praise to the team at Que Corporation for putting up with my many eccentricities and for allowing me a great deal of latitude in outlining and writing this book. They include Publishing Manager Jim Minatel, Acquisitions Editor Cheryl Willoughby, Product Development Specialist Oran Sands, and Senior Editor Nancy Sixsmith. Kim Tedrow, the dedicated, fearless technical editor, deserves to be singled out for poring over every word and illustration to verify that it was absolutely correct to the last, minute detail.

And last, I wish to offer a heartfelt, loving thank you to my wonderful, beautiful wife, Barbara, and my extraordinary son, Grayson, for putting up with the long hours I spent chained to the front of my computer so that my work could be done on schedule.

We'd like to hear from you!

As part of our continuing effort to produce books of the highest possible quality, Que would like to hear your comments. To stay competitive, we *really* want you, as a computer book reader and user, to let us know what you like or dislike most about this book or other Que products.

You can mail comments, ideas, or suggestions for improving future editions to the address below, or send us a fax at (317) 581-4663. The address of our Internet site is **http://www.mcp.com** (World Wide Web).

In addition to exploring our forum, please feel free to contact me personally to discuss your opinions of this book: I'm **osands@que.mcp.com** on the Internet.

Thanks in advance—your comments will help us to continue publishing the best books available on computer topics in today's market.

Oran Sands
Product Development Specialist
Que Corporation
201 W. 103rd Street
Indianapolis, Indiana 46290
USA

Contents at a Glance

Getting on the Information Superhighway

Table of Contents

8   From Baby Boomers to Science Fiction: Online Lifestyle and Interest Forums   121

9   Get Advice, Help, and Software from AOL's Computing Forums   137

Introduction

In 1989, I found an interesting offer with my usual collection of junk mail. It was for something called America Online, a service allowing fellow computer users to meet, exchange messages, find software, and look up information covering a variety of subjects.

In that first year, America Online was rather a lonely place. There weren't many members, and, more often than not, I didn't find too much to occupy my attention, though I enjoyed browsing through the service for software to run on my new computer.

I never anticipated the population explosion that would occur.

As this book is written, there are four million members on America Online, making it the world's largest online service (and hundreds of thousands of subscribers are added each month).

America Online has also rapidly expanded its services. There are alliances with major media centers, such as ABC, Simon & Schuster, *The New York Times*, Time-Warner, and others. The simple software was soon expanded to provide many new options—fast download of online artwork, for example, and the capability to connect to a new, uncharted territory, the global Internet.

You have read about America Online in your daily newspaper or have seen reports about the service on TV. It's clear that the online world has made a tremendous impact on all our lives. And you'll see the changes to America Online continue unabated in the years to come.

Who is this book for?

I've written this book for the beginner and the seasoned online traveler. So even if you've just begun to perfect your mouse-clicking skills, you'll find this book an easy way to get connected to America Online and learn the ropes.

And please don't consider me your teacher, nor this a textbook. Think of me as just a fellow computer user, sitting across the room from you, who is there to discuss ways to make your online experience easier and more fun.

You can read this book like a novel, from beginning to end. Or you can focus just on the chapters that contain the information you need right away. The book is written for both kinds of readers, so you don't have to pore through chapter after chapter to find what you want. If it's necessary to read a another part of the book for expanded information, I'll mention it.

Shooting at a moving target

I began writing books about America Online for Que in 1994, and each edition has changed radically from the previous work. America Online, like a large city, is growing and changing constantly. You will find that the service's look and feel will develop and improve over time. Some of the places pictured in this book might look a little different on your screen, too. But the information in these pages will be useful for a long time as a guide to learning about America Online.

As you begin to explore the online community, keep this book at hand. When you have a question or want to learn more about a particular place, you can move directly to that chapter for the information you want.

The online community has, over the years, become my second home. Here, I meet and interact with friends and even conduct many of my regular business affairs. I have made deals and begun work projects with people known only by e-mail.

Indeed, the dream of the information superhighway has, to me, become a personal reality, and I want you to share that dream, too. Let the pages that follow be your starting point on the road to a learning experience that might be unlike any other you've ever had.

The bill of fare

Using America Online with Your Mac is divided into six parts, so you can easily focus on the chapters that interest you the most. Here's the menu:

Part I: Let's Get Going

In the first two chapters of the book, I'll show you how to install America Online's Mac software, set up your online account, and enjoy your first session on AOL. Then I'll give you some helpful hints on setting up the software to run best on your computer. If you run into any problems along the way, there are some hints to solve common connection and software problems.

Part II: Getting Your Feet Wet

Here's where the action begins. First, I'll take you briefly through AOL's 14 departments, then explain how you can meet other AOL members. And then I'll show you what AOL's e-mail, message boards, and online forums are all about. I'll even introduce you to those famous America Online conferences, where some of the most famous personalities from the political and show business worlds have "appeared."

Part III: Having Fun on AOL

In the next four chapters, you'll learn how to locate online information and how to introduce your kids to AOL and the Internet. Then, I'll cover the lifestyles and special interest areas, which cover loads of subjects from health care to *Star Trek*. You'll also get a brief tour of AOL's computing forums and the industry connection areas, where you can contact the major computer manufacturers.

Part IV: Information at Your Fingertips

America Online has tens of thousands of software files available for you. You just need to know where to find them, and I'll show you how in this section. You'll discover a number of resources for online education and reference information. You'll take a quick stopover at AOL's online newsstand, where some of your favorite publications are available. You'll discover handy sources for buying merchandise online at low, low prices and pay a visit to AOL's travel agency.

Part V: Getting on the Information Superhighway

The global Internet network has become the hot new frontier, and America Online offers a full slate of Internet services. In the final five chapters of this book, I'll show you how to send e-mail through the Internet, how to subscribe to mailing lists, and how to participate in the wild, wacky newsgroup message boards. You'll also learn about the newest Internet feature, the World Wide Web, which offers you pictures, text, and sometimes sound to enhance your online visits.

Special book elements

This book has a number of special elements and conventions to help you find information quickly—or to skip stuff you don't want to read right now.

 **TIP** **Tips either point out information often overlooked in the documentation, or help you use your software more efficiently, like a shortcut.** Some tips help you solve or avoid problems.

 **CAUTION** **Cautions alert you to potentially dangerous consequences of a** procedure or practice, especially if it could cause serious or even disastrous results (such as loss or corruption of data).

 **Q&A** *What are Q&A notes?*
Cast in the form of questions and answers, these notes provide you with advice on ways to solve common problems.

 Plain English, please!
These notes explain the meanings of technical terms or computer jargon.

Sidebars are interesting nuggets of information

Sidebars provide interesting, nonessential reading, side-alley trips you can take when you're not at the computer or when you just want some relief from "doing stuff." Here you may find more technical details, funny stories, personal anecdotes, or interesting background information.

1

How to Get Started on America Online

● **In this chapter:**

- **Sign up with America Online**

- **Create your own online address**

- **Take a fast tour of the service**

- **But first, a little history...**

With just a software disk you can start out on your online adventure!. . . . .

So many of our technological marvels had their humble beginnings as toys for hobbyists, engineers, and scientists. When their value was demonstrated to the rest of us, manufacturers found ways to make them faster, cheaper, and better. What was once an incredible achievement became a regular part of our everyday lives. In the 1980s, we had compact disc players and videocassette recorders. For the 1990s, it's the personal computer. There are tens of millions of computers in our homes, offices, and schools. Airplane seats are filled with folks preparing documents or playing games on their laptop computers. Hotels provide special phone jacks so their guests can stay connected via their computers.

As computers spread across our landscape, those of us who bought these new appliances sought out ways to connect to other computer users. We bought those little devices that let your computer talk to a telephone—modems—and we signed up with organizations that let computer users link up together to share messages and receive information.

The history of America Online

The dream of the "information superhighway" wasn't really in many people's minds in 1985, when America Online was founded as Quantum Computer Services. In that year, the Apple Macintosh was just a low-powered niche computer, and Microsoft Windows didn't exist.

Today, America Online is a publicly owned company that offers an online community to well over four million members. The service offers online shopping, information services such as daily newspapers and magazines, and even virtual reference books such as encyclopedias.

America Online is like a huge city, with many people hanging out and communicating with one another on a host of subjects, from the time of day and the weather to the state of the nation and the world. The online experience is unlike any you've ever seen. After you have been introduced to America Online, you'll probably want to stick around.

Here's the easy way to install America Online software

Installing AOL's software on your Mac (or compatible) is easy. In just a couple of minutes, you'll be ready to connect to the service for the first time.

Knowing what you need

To use America Online software, you need a Mac Plus or better running System 6.0.7 or later, with 4M or more of installed RAM and at least 4M of free hard drive space. AOL's multimedia features, including access to the Internet's World Wide Web, require a color-capable Mac with a 68020 CPU or better with System 7.1 or later, and 8M or more of installed RAM.

 **Plain English, please!**

Multimedia is a term that describes the ability to mix pictures, sound, and text on a computer, or even on your home audio system or TV. **"**

Plain English, please!

The **World Wide Web** is a feature offered on the worldwide Internet network that combines pictures, sound, and fancy text into attractive images you can see on your computer screen. Check out Chapters 16 through 20 to learn more about what the Internet is and AOL's Internet features. **"**

In writing this chapter, I'm assuming you are comfortable performing the basic functions of using your computer, such as installing new software from a floppy disk onto your hard drive, performing simple file-management chores, opening applications, and using the mouse. If you need a quick refresher course, review the instruction manuals that came with your computer or operating-system disks. Or get yourself a copy of *Using Your Macintosh* from Que at your local bookstore.

Before you install the AOL software, though, make a backup of your original floppy disk. (You should do this with *all* your software and valuable disks.) Then lock the original disks in a safe (preferably physically separate) place, in case your copies are damaged.

You *do* need one more thing, of course, and that is a Hayes-compatible modem with a speed of 2400 bps (bits per second) or faster.

Plain English, please!

The word **modem** is short for **modulator/demodulator**. It's a device that allows you to send and receive computer data over telephone lines. A modem actually converts the binary 1s and 0s of computer data into sounds (although it usually sounds more like an screech of whistles and hisses to most of us) so the phone lines can handle the information. **99**

America Online has been rolling out its 14,400 and 28,800 bits per second services, and prices for high-speed modems have dropped, so you'll want to buy the fastest modem you can afford. You also can expect even higher speeds to be supported by America Online in the future.

 Plain English, please!

Computer data is expressed in terms of **bits** and **bytes**. There are eight bits in a byte, for example. The bits per second, or **bps**, figure expresses how quickly the modem can send information over your phone lines. **99**

 CAUTION **The descriptions in this book are based on version 2.6 of AOL's** Mac software. As the software is revised, you should expect some of the features and information screens to change too, but the basic setup instructions will still apply.

Ordering your software

America Online (AOL) disks often come free with your new software or computer purchase. Some of your favorite computing magazines also include the software disks from time to time. Lots of disks also are sent by direct mail, so watch for a trim little package with an America Online logo on it.

If you don't have an America Online disk on hand, you can order one by calling 1-800-827-6364. Please tell the operator the kind of computer you have, so you will receive the right software. You will get your disk in a couple of weeks. In the meantime, you can review this book's information about installing your software, establishing your personal online account, and mastering the America Online program.

Even if you already have telecommunications software installed on your computer, America Online uses its own proprietary software to provide the unique graphic environment and efficient performance. You need America

Online's special software to use the service. It does not work with a general-purpose terminal program.

CAUTION **Before you install software on your Mac, restart the computer** (choosing Restart from the Special menu) with extensions off. This is done by holding down the Shift key as soon as you hear your Mac's startup tones and releasing the key right after you begin to see the Welcome to Macintosh screen. Installing with system extensions off ensures that your new software installation goes on without a hitch. (Some system add-ons or extensions, such as virus-detection software, can sometimes foul up new software installations.)

Installing your AOL software

America Online's software is **compressed**, which is a technique used to make files smaller so they take up less room. That way, the software can be supplied on a single 1.4M floppy disk.

TIP **Before proceeding with your software installation, have your** software's registration certificate and your credit card or checkbook handy. Also be sure that your modem has been turned on, and is hooked up to your computer and to your phone line.

Q&A *Help! My Mac is an older model. It doesn't have one of those superdrives (or high-density drives), just a regular 800K floppy drive. It won't read AOL's software disk. What do I do? Is my computer now obsolete?*

Don't despair. Your computer is not obsolete as long as it can run the software you need with acceptable performance. You also can still join America Online. To get disks that will work on your computer, call America Online at 1-800-827-6364 and request a set of 800K floppy disks.

After you've made a backup of your original software disk, you're ready to get the software up and running. Follow these steps:

1 Insert the floppy disk into your Macintosh's floppy drive.

2 Double-click on the America Online icon.

3 Click on the Continue button (see fig. 1.1).

Fig. 1.1
After you double-click on the AOL icon to begin the installation process, this is the screen you see.

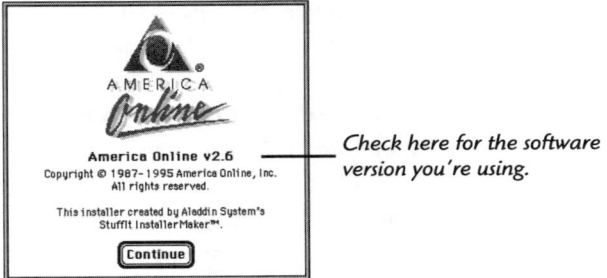

Check here for the software version you're using.

4 The program then asks you to select a destination on your hard drive for installation of your software. Your America Online software gets its own special folder. You can either accept the suggested folder name or pick a name of your own.

After you've decided on the location for the new folder, the installation process continues. America Online keeps you informed of its progress.

In a minute or two, you receive a message that the software has been successfully installed. If you have any problems at this point, you should probably just try to install the software again.

5 Now you can double-click on the AOL application icon to display the screen shown in figure 1.2. You then are guided through the steps needed to adjust the computer to your modem.

Fig. 1.2
Your first welcome message from America Online appears after you double-click on the AOL application icon.

For the next few moments, you see several information windows (see fig. 1.3). As America Online software versions are upgraded, the displays might be different from the ones shown here. Just read the instructions carefully before proceeding. If you have any questions or problems, you can choose Cancel to stop the installation and try again later.

If you've opted for the standard configuration profile, your modem will be checked for a moment or two by the software to see how fast it is. If your modem has status lights, you'll see them flicker on and off (so don't worry). Then you will be connected to America Online's host computer.

Fig. 1.3
This is where you get ready to make your first online connection.

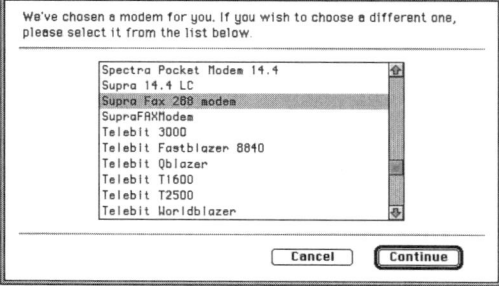

First, we will automatically dial a toll-free number to reach America Online. During this free call you will choose a number in your area that you will use regularly to sign on to America Online.

You probably... –use a touch-tone phone
      –have your modem connected to your Macintosh's modem port
      –don't need to dial a '9' for an 'outside' call
      –don't need to disable call waiting during calls to America Online
      –are calling from the United States

If this is correct, click 'Continue.' If any one of the above does not apply, click 'Special Setup.'

    Cancel   Special Setup   Continue

If you want to check or revise your modem profile, click on Change Options and continue. If you have decided to change your options, you have a few more things to select:

1 Although the software has made choices for you about modem speed and the kind of modem profile it's using, you can change these setups to something you feel might provide better performance (see fig. 1.4).

Fig. 1.4
You can change your modem setup on this screen.

We've chosen a modem for you. If you wish to choose a different one, please select it from the list below.

Spectra Pocket Modem 14.4
Supra 14.4 LC
Supra Fax 288 modem
SupraFAXModem
Telebit 3000
Telebit Fastblazer 8840
Telebit Qblazer
Telebit T1600
Telebit T2500
Telebit Worldblazer

    Cancel   Continue

TIP **AOL software comes with profiles for most popular makes and** models of modems, including Global Village, Hayes, Motorola, Supra, U.S. Robotics, and others. For most users, the default selection should work best. I'll tell you how to choose a different modem setup in Chapter 2.

2 If you decide to change your setup options, you are asked whether you want to install the option to disable Call Waiting when you are online. If you have Call Waiting and someone tries to call you while you're online, the tones you hear in your telephone will quickly dump you from your online connection. You might have to check with your local telephone company, however, before choosing to disable this option because not all services allow you to turn off Call Waiting for a single call.

3 If your online connections are being made from an office, you might have to dial a special number, usually 9, to get an outside line. Be sure to select this option if you need it; otherwise, you can't make your first online connection.

66 *Plain English, please!*

AOL's **modem profile** is a file containing instructions that tell your modem how to talk to AOL's host computer network. 99

Getting a local connection

Now you want to have America Online's host computer find a local connection number for you (see fig. 1.5). As soon as your modem setup has been completed, you are asked to enter your area code so America Online can hook you up to the closest (and thus the cheapest) connection to your area.

Fig. 1.5
This screen appears when you're making your first connection.

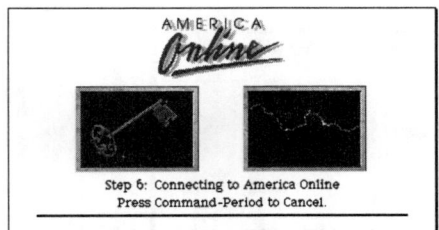

The host computer searches its directory of access numbers for ones that match the area code you entered (see fig. 1.6). If you cannot locate a number in your area code, you have the option to choose another number from a nearby area code. Because America Online is continuously adding new connection numbers, you always have the opportunity to change your connection number later.

Fig. 1.6
This is the screen where
you pick your first local
access number.

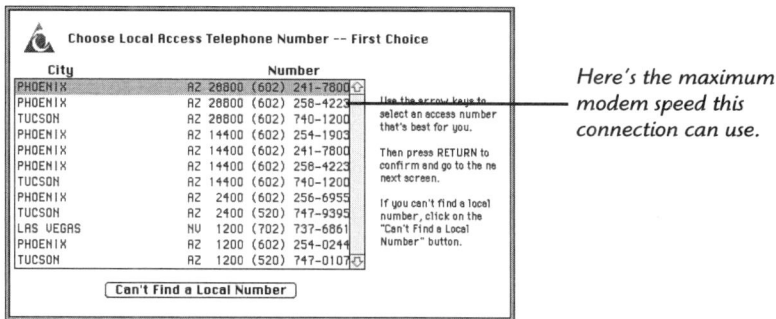

*Here's the maximum
modem speed this
connection can use.*

TIP   **See Chapter 3 for more information about locating and changing**
your America Online access numbers.

You should select two connection numbers if they are available. That way, if
your modem can't make a connection with the first number—perhaps
because the number's busy or because of line noise—you have a second
chance to connect to America Online.

TIP   **Once you've joined America Online, you can always get a new set**
of local numbers. Just choose Get Local # from the pop-up menu of your
AOL software that lists your screen names (you'll find out about those in the
next section), and AOL's friendly host computer will guide you through the
process of creating a new set of connection numbers.

Establishing your online account

From here on, until you log on to the service for the first time, you are guided
through steps that enable you to establish your own exclusive America
Online account and set your billing options. (Now you find out why I suggested that you have handy the certificate that came with your software
disks, and your credit card or checkbook.)

The choices you make now are not etched in stone. If you decide to change
your password or billing information later, you can easily do so in the free
Online Support area.

To establish your online account, follow these steps:

1 First, examine the registration numbers that are on the folder of your America Online software. Enter the certificate number and certificate passwords in the blank Certificate Number and Certificate Password entry boxes (see fig. 1.7). You can use the Tab key on your computer's keyboard to move from one entry field to the next.

2 Click the Continue button.

3 Enter your name, mailing address, and telephone number.

4 Click the Continue button.

5 Indicate how you want to pay for your America Online service. You can choose Modify Billing Information (see fig. 1.8), and then choose from American Express, Discover Card, Mastercard, or Visa. Or, if you prefer, you can have your online charges deducted regularly from your checking account (see fig. 1.9).

Fig. 1.7
Use this screen to set up your online account.

Fig. 1.8
Enter your credit card information here. You can easily change your credit card billing information whenever you want.

Fig. 1.9
You can have your online charges deducted automatically from your checking account for a slight monthly surcharge.

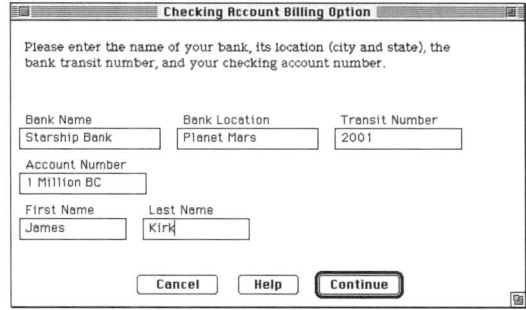

To protect you, America Online verifies all your billing information. If the program encounters a problem in establishing your account, the account is suspended until you are able to update your billing information. This precaution is taken for your protection. After all, you wouldn't want to pay for someone else's online charges.

 **If you are billing your service to your checking account, America** Online may take up to a day or two to verify the account before you can connect to the service. If this is the case, you'll see an onscreen message to that effect.

 **To check your usage bill on America Online, type the keyword Billing**. You are then taken to a free support area where you can check your current bill and make changes to your billing information.

Create your online mailing address

Next, you need to enter your online mailing address—your **screen name**. This is a golden opportunity to be creative. Your online address can contain from three to ten characters (letters and numbers). You can identify yourself on America Online by your first name, an abbreviation of your name, or even a descriptive word or two that expresses your own unique personality traits, such as TheBear.

The online name you choose for yourself is used by your master account, and the host computer checks that name (along with the password you select) every time you log on to America Online. You can add up to four additional names to your online account, for use by other members of your family, or for yourself if you decide to try on a change of clothing from time to time (or you want to use one screen name for business purposes, and one just for fun). Bear in mind that you can use only one screen name attached to your account at any one time. If you want to log on simultaneously with more than one screen name (to allow, for example, your child to hook up to the service), you need to establish separate accounts.

If someone is already using the name you select, you are given the option of using that name plus a number (the number is randomly selected by the computer). You might, for example, be offered the choice of using GeneS12345 if a number of people online are already using the screen name GeneS.

CAUTION **You cannot delete your master account name without deleting** your account, so take as much time as you need to select an appropriate screen name.

As you try to locate an available screen name, America Online searches its database to determine whether someone else already has selected that name. Because America Online is a family-oriented service, names using vulgar language or with a vulgar connotation are not accepted.

After America Online has accepted your screen name, your next step is to select a password. A **password** is your ounce of protection against someone using your account without your permission, so don't use anything obvious, like a contraction of your name.

 Plain English, please!

In the computer world, a **password** is a key that unlocks something, such as your access to an online service or access to a computer network at a typical workplace. This key may consist of letters, numbers, or both (such as UFO, 1234, or UFO23). It is very important to choose a password that would not be easy for others to figure out (a simple name isn't a good idea) but that you can remember without difficulty.

After you've chosen your screen name, you're ready to go out and meet the online community.

 **When you select a screen name and password, write them down** and place that information in a safe place. That way, if you happen to forget your password, you can find it again quickly.

Before you are formally welcomed to the America Online family, you are asked whether you accept the Terms of Service. Carefully read the information displayed. You also can check the text of the terms in the Online Support area. Basically the terms request that you be a good citizen during your online visits, avoid using vulgar language, and other such things.

 **TIP** To review AOL's Terms of Service at any time, use the keyword **TOS** (for Terms of Service). This takes you to an area free of online charges where you can read the terms.

Enjoy your first online session!

Here are couple of quick shortcuts for getting around the online community quickly and getting direct online help.

The first shortcut is the **keyword**, which is a keyboard command you can specify only while you're connected to America Online. You can use keywords to go just about anywhere on America Online, without having to worry about the exact routes for getting there.

To use America Online keywords, press Command+K, and then enter the keyword in the entry field of the Keyword dialog box that will appear on your screen (see fig. 1.10). Press Return or Enter, and in just a few seconds you'll be transported to the place you want to visit. (If the keyword happens to be wrong or is mistyped, you'll get a message to that effect.) I'll give you a thorough rundown on AOL's software in Chapter 2.

Fig. 1.10
A keyword is your magic carpet for quick trips along AOL's information superhighway.

Whenever you're logged onto America Online, you can visit the free online support area to get direct assistance with any problem. To get to the support area, open the Members menu and select Member Services, or just type the keyword **Help**. A window will appear, asking whether you want to enter this free area.

Q&A   *What's a free area?*

It's a special "only" area set aside by America Online to provide support information and assistance to members. Because it's free, you aren't charged for the time you spend online while you're in this area getting the information you need.

Okay, now let's get ready to join the online community.

Leaving the starting gate

The first time you connect to America Online (assuming your computer's sounds are working), you hear a friendly voice intone, "Welcome," and a few seconds later you hear that same fellow say, "You've Got Mail." Yes, when you sign onto America Online for the first time, you indeed find a letter in your mailbox. Just click on the You Have Mail icon, and you see your first letter listed in the directory. Double-click on that directory listing to see the text of the letter on your computer screen. The letter is from Steve Case, the president of America Online. He welcomes you to the service and briefly outlines the special features you might want to examine during your travels.

The first screen you see on your computer, the Welcome screen, is your gateway to all the features offered by America Online (see fig. 1.11). In the middle of the Welcome screen is a list of special announcements, places to visit, and the Top News headline. Just click on the icon to the right of the message that describes something you want to investigate (or on the icon to the left of the Top News Story headline), and you are taken to that area on America Online. The list you see in this Welcome screen changes several times per day as different services are featured and the top news stories change.

Fig. 1.11
This screen is your
America Online
gateway.

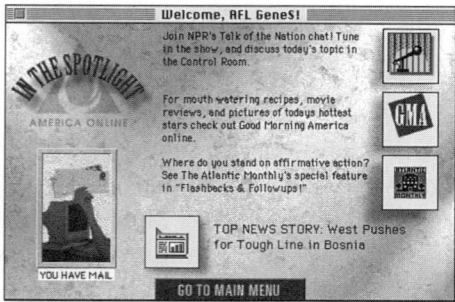

At the bottom of the Welcome screen (also known as In the Spotlight) is a rectangular box labeled GO TO MAIN MENU. When you click on this box, you are taken to the window that lies beneath the Welcome screen (see fig. 1.12), which is your gateway to all the major services on America Online. At the left of the Main Menu screen are three icons. Clicking on In the Spotlight returns you to the original Welcome screen. Beneath it is the icon for America Online's electronic mail center, the Post Office. At the bottom is the Discover AOL icon, which I'll explore further a bit later in this chapter.

Fig. 1.12
America Online's Main Menu is the table of contents to all the major features of the service.

At the left of the screen are the AOL logo, the Discover AOL icon, and your personal mail icon. To the right of those icons are two rows of colorful rectangular buttons, each of which takes you to a different department. These buttons are clearly labeled, and you can click on any one of them now to explore. These departments are discussed in detail in Chapter 3.

For now, I'll just take you on a brief tour of the service.

Beginning a guided online tour

To explore America Online, click on the Discover AOL icon. The Discover America Online screen appears, as shown in figure 1.13.

Fig. 1.13
You can find out all sorts of things about America Online on your very first visit.

You can visit eight different locations, each identified by a unique icon. Clicking once on an icon takes you to the corresponding area on the network.

Before going further, you probably want to click on the A Letter From Steve icon. Every month or two, America Online's president writes a status report on the services, telling about America Online's growth and the new features that are available. He also gives a brief preview of the features you can expect in the near future.

Now you're ready to embark on your tour.

Examining America Online highlights

Using the America Online Highlights icon is a quick way to familiarize yourself with the major features of America Online (see figs. 1.14 and 1.15). The services highlighted change from time to time, so you might want to take this little tour again every so often.

Fig. 1.14

Here you are, at the beginning of your guided tour of America Online.

Fig. 1.15

This screen explains one of the featured America Online services for users of Macintosh computers, the Macintosh Operating Systems forum.

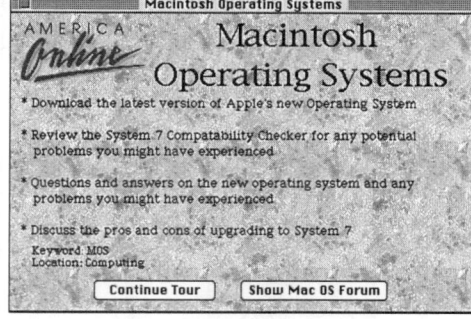

 **TIP** **The stops along the tour change from time to time, but each** window provides information about a specific area on America Online. These areas, called **forums**, are discussed in more detail, beginning in Chapter 3.

For now, you can either click the Continue Tour button to go on with the tour, or the Show button, which transports you directly to the area you are reading about. If you decide to visit one of these forums, you can take the tour again later.

When you've gone through all the forum windows, a screen appears letting you know you have completed the tour. You then are returned to the Discover AOL area.

After you've completed your tour, spend some time poking around the service on your own. At each new location, you can check things out or move on. Literally thousands of services are available to you, covering many interests. This book lists only some of the highlights because new services are added almost daily. You will find every online visit an adventure of discovery and enjoyment.

 **TIP** **If you're watching your budget, type the keyword Clock. You then** see an onscreen clock that shows the amount of time you've been online.

Setting Up Your AOL Software

● **In this chapter:**

● Quickly set up your modem to connect to AOL at top speed

● Solve problems connecting to AOL

● Customize your America Online software

● Adjust the software for top performance in viewing pictures

Here are hints and tricks for getting the most out of your AOL time . . . .

When you first drive a new car, you get comfortable before you take it out for a spin. You adjust the seats, the rearview mirror, the side mirrors, and maybe the steering wheel (if it's adjustable). When you install new software, you'll also want to learn ways to fine-tune it to perform to your taste. With America Online's Macintosh software, you can make several adjustments so the software works exactly the way you want.

 **TIP**   **If you have a problem using your America Online software and you need** an immediate answer, press command+/ or select Help from the Apple menu.

A quick and easy modem setup guide

When you call up America Online, you usually hear that little box next to a desktop Mac (or the one inside your PowerBook or Duo) squawking and squeaking during the connection process. I admit it sometimes sounds intimidating, because that device (your modem) doesn't always adhere to the concept of plug-and-play. But AOL's Mac software makes using your modem easy.

Before you connect to America Online on a regular basis, you'll want to take a moment or two to be sure your modem is set up properly. When you first install your America Online software, the software examines your modem

The Fastest Way to Launch

If you're a System 7 user, follow these steps to instantly access your America Online software, even at startup (it's the method I use myself):

1 Make an **alias** (a small file that is a reference to the original file) for your America Online application icon. Highlight the AOL icon and select Make Alias from the File menu at your Finder desktop).

2 Take the AOL alias and place it inside the Startup Items folder (in the System folder).

Now America Online launches whenever you boot your Mac. Another alternative is to place the AOL alias in the Apple Menu Items folder for quick access from the Apple menu.

In the pages that follow, I'll cover ways to set up your AOL software for best performance. And you'll get some helpful hints to make your online visits more enjoyable.

and sets a default modem profile for it. If you buy a new modem, you'll want to change these settings. Or you might want to change your connection numbers to the America Online network.

 **TIP** **A selection of updated modem drivers is available for download** from America Online's Member Services area (keyword: **Help**). To access these drivers, first click on the Members' Online Support icon in the main Member Services window, and then click on Technical Help. Sometimes, modem makers will supply an AOL connection file with their own software (so you want to check out the files they give you).

To change your connection settings, follow these steps:

1 Click on the Setup button in the main America Online window to display the screen shown in figure 2.1. (You can change these settings only when you're not logged onto the America Online network.)

The left side of the window sets up the program to try connecting with AOL.

Pull down this menu to choose a connection service.

Fig. 2.1
You can quickly and easily make changes to your connection setup.

Choose the maximum modem speed allowed by your service.

Enter the numbers to dial out and to cancel call waiting. Use a comma to pause dialing.

Pick your modem from this menu.

Tell the computer where to find your modem.

The right half is set up for the Second Try.

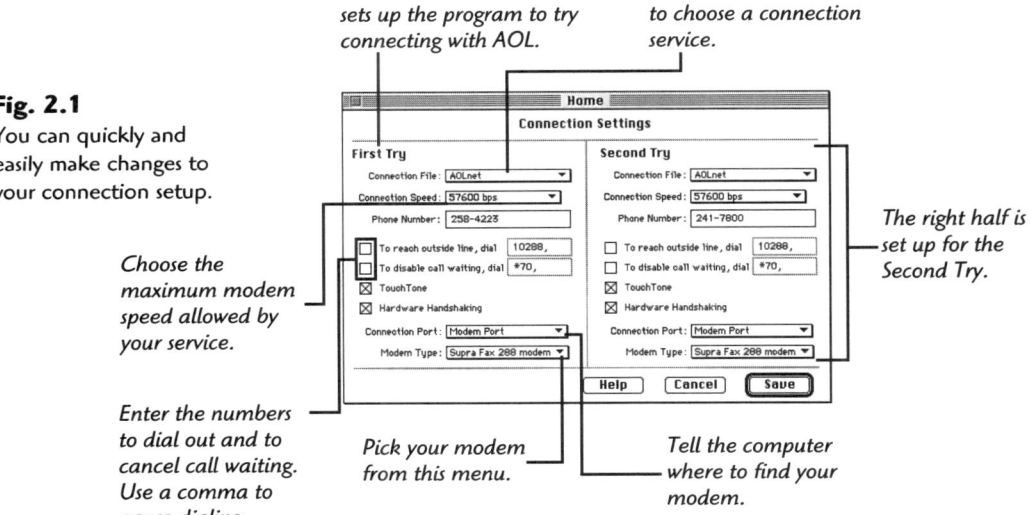

You can set up two connection profiles. Your America Online software uses the one on the left, First Try, when trying to make your initial connection to the network. If the connection doesn't succeed for any reason—usually due to a busy communications port or noise on the line—America Online attempts the Second Try.

TIP   **To change the phone number you are using for any reason—if** you've moved to a different location, for example—just log onto America Online. Then type the keyword **Access**. You are asked whether you want to enter this free area. Press Return or click on Yes. You then see a window with a list of options for finding an access number. For now, just double-click on Search. You see a window with a space for you to enter the area code you want to check. When you enter that number, America Online checks its online phone directory and produces a list of phone numbers for the selected area.

2 Changing online numbers is easy. Just type the new number in the Phone Number box. When you change the number, you also might need to change the Connection File, which represents the service America Online uses to connect you to its network. When you get a list of phone numbers from America Online for your area, you see such names as AOLNet, SprintNet, or Tymnet attached to the phone numbers. In the Connection Settings window, simply pull down the menu at the right of the Connection File label and select the correct name of the service provider.

3 America Online's phone directory also lists the connection speed supported by each phone number. You need to choose a connection speed from the Connection Speed pop-up menu that's the same or higher than the speed at which you're connecting. In other words, choose at least 14,400 bps if you're going to use a 14,400 bps access number.

4 The next four check boxes control how the software uses your modem to dial the service. Some businesses have special phone lines that require a "dial-out" code. Usually this code is 9, but you can change that number if necessary. Some hotels also use 9 as their dial-out prefix. If you need to dial a special number to reach an outside line, check the To Reach Outside Line box.

5 If you have call waiting service, you need to disable it when you make your online connection because the tones that sound in your telephone when someone is trying to reach you can interrupt your connection and end your AOL session prematurely. The number listed in the To Disable Call Waiting check box, 1170, is for rotary telephones. If you have touchtone service, the number is usually *70. To be certain of which number to use, call your local telephone company. Sometimes the ability to disable Call Waiting for a single phone call is an optional service.

6 If you have a touchtone phone, check the TouchTone check box (it's checked by default).

7 The fourth check box, Hardware Handshaking, is needed for a high-speed modem, such as a 9600 or 14,400 bps (or even faster) model. If you're using one of these models, check this box. If not, you can leave this option off.

66 *Plain English, please!*

Hardware handshaking is simply the method a modem uses to talk to another modem. High-speed modems are usually equipped with a special cable that lets you use this feature, which is necessary for efficient high-speed connections. If your modem doesn't come with a cable, you can buy one for ten dollars or so at almost any computer supply store. 99

8 The Connection Port option enables you to tell the software which jack your modem is hooked up to. The default setting is Modem Port. If you're using the Printer Port instead (perhaps for a network modem), select that option from the pull-down menu.

9 The final option enables you to indicate the make and model of your modem. If a modem profile isn't listed for the model you have, you can stick with the one your America Online software picks for you when you first install the software. If you are experienced in the arcane science of modem connection strings, you can even set up your own custom profile. Or you can just search AOL's Technical Help area for a modem file that fits the one you have.

Q&A

Wait a minute! The only options I have available are Internal Modem and Printer/Modem Port. What gives?

If you're using a Macintosh PowerBook model, your choice of available ports may be different. If you have an internal modem (a unit installed inside your PowerBook), the Internal Modem choice is the one to make. For an external modem, use the second option (or whatever external modem choice is available in your AOL setup box).

I just bought a new V.34 (28,800 bps) modem, and it still connects at 2400 bps. Why?

Getting a high-speed modem is half the battle. To log onto AOL at high speed, you need an access number that supports that capability. You can search the full listing of numbers while online via the keyword **Access**.

How do I know I'm connecting at high speed?

Just look at your AOL software window when logging on. Step 3 shows the speed at which you're connecting.

Help! My modem won't dial AOL.

If you've been able to connect to AOL before, something might have changed in your setup. Here are some steps to follow:

1 Switch off your modem and turn it back on again. Sometimes the modem's firmware will freeze due to a software defect or a previous connection problem. When you turn the modem on again, it's the equivalent of restarting your computer, and often has the same result.

2 Try another telecommunications program, such as Microphone, White Knight, Zterm, or a similar program. If another telecommunications program can successfully make your modem dial out, the problem is definitely related to the way your AOL software is set up (review the steps described earlier in this chapter).

3 Make sure the dial prefix or string is correct.

Click the Setup box while logged off. Be sure that the correct Modem Type is selected from the pop-up menu.

Help! I can't find a nearby phone number in my home town or in the place I'm visiting. What's the best way to get onto AOL?

America Online's telephone access networks are always being updated, but there are some parts of the U.S. without a nearby local access number. If you run into such a situation, you have another choice: an 800 number that America Online has established to help you get high speed, 28,800 bps access, to its network. The number is 800-716-0023. I want to add that this phone number carries an hourly surcharge (check AOL's Access area for the latest price), but that charge is apt to be less than you'd pay for most long-distance phone calls.

How to fine-tune your AOL software

The next thing you want to do is set up your America Online software preferences. This is how you adjust the program so it looks and feels the way you want it to. Even if everything looks okay to you at first glance, it's worth the effort to try out a few settings just to see whether you can adjust things a bit better.

To set up preferences, choose Set Preferences from the Members menu, or press Command+= . The Preferences dialog box appears, with a list of Preference Categories on the left side. When you choose one of these categories, a list of options appears on the right side of the dialog box.

Setting most of your preferences involves the same steps. You click on an option to select it, and you see a checkmark appear next to that option. You click again to turn off an item, at which time the checkmark disappears (see fig. 2.2).

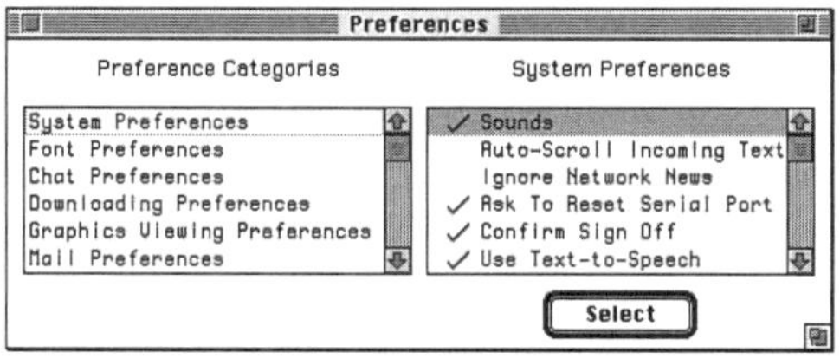

Fig. 2.2
You can toggle Sounds— and other settings—off and on.

The following sections describe some of the settings you can change in the Preferences dialog box. I'll focus just on the essential settings, the stuff you'll want to adjust for best performance during your AOL visits. The other settings that I won't describe here can be left alone most of the time (but they are clearly labeled, so you can try them out if you want).

Setting system preferences

When you first see the Preferences dialog box, you have the option of changing your regular system preferences, which affect the way AOL software runs on your Mac. These options are described in the paragraphs that follow.

Sounds

One of the most attractive features of America Online is its voice messages. When you begin a session, you hear a friendly Welcome voice. And when you log off, you hear the same voice bid you good-bye. But if you work in a busy environment, you may want to turn these sounds off.

Just click on the word Sounds in the Preferences dialog box to toggle off the sounds. (The checkmark next to Sounds should disappear.) If you want to restore the sounds, click on the word again to restore the checkmark.

Auto-Scroll Incoming Text

If you turn on this feature, you'll see text items scroll on your computer's screen as they are received, and you'll see the bottom of the text window when the text has finished displaying. The best setting (with this feature off) just shows the beginning of the text, as many lines as can fill a single text window. But you can still scroll through this text by using your computer's scroll bars at the right side of the text window.

Ask To Reset Serial Port

This is an option you only need to disable if you are using a program such as Apple Remote Access or fax software, and intend to run FlashSessions on America Online (which I'll describe in more detail in Chapter 5). If another program is using your Mac's serial port, America Online's software will give you the option to reset the port so you are able to log on. Otherwise, the other communications program takes over the serial port to do its stuff.

Plain English, please!

AOL's **FlashSession** feature lets you hook up with America Online auto-matically to send and receive electronic mail and files attached to your mail. This feature helps you save on online charges by reading and writing e-mail before you actually connect to the service.

Use Text-to-Speech

The option I'm now describing is only available if you have an AV or Power Macintosh with Apple's PlainTalk software installed and activated using the Speech Setup Control Panel, or if you've installed Apple's Speech Manager software. Otherwise, the choice isn't shown among the list of available preferences. The option lets you attach voices to chats and instant messages (and text windows as well). With this feature, AOL can literally read online text back to you.

Speak Unknown Users

An unknown user is a member for whom you've not set up a default voice as yet. With this option selected, all instant messages or chat room discussions will be spoken aloud and audible through your Mac's speaker. If you don't select this option, you will only hear voices for those members for whom you've selected a voice (I'll explain how to do that shortly).

Allow Simultaneous Speech

If you receive two instant messages at the same time, the voices will overlap. This may seem a bit annoying to most, but if the messages are synchronized, you might get a cute audible effect (perhaps an online chorus).

Set Up Default Voice

This option lets you establish a default voice for text that's being read. Figure 2.3 shows how it works.

The default voice you select here will apply to all spoken text selections when the Speak Text option, in the Members menu, is turned on. To apply a specific voice to an individual member, choose that member's name after clicking on the People icon in a chat room, and then click on the Speech button. You'll read about this in more detail in Chapter 4.

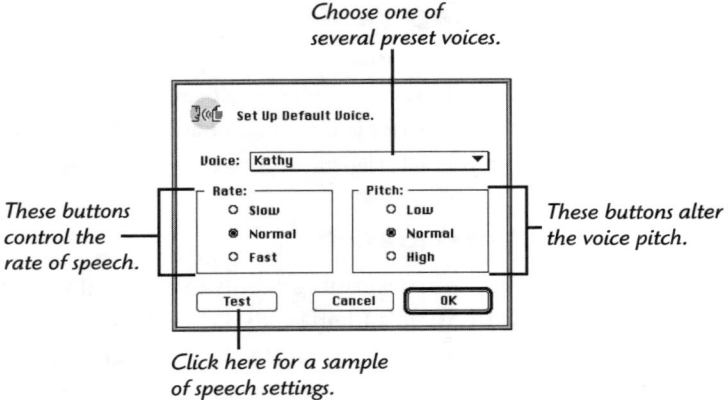

Choose one of several preset voices.

Fig. 2.3
Choose a default voice from the list of those available. The list of voices depends on the version of Apple's speech-making software you're using, and whether it comes with extra voice files.

These buttons control the rate of speech.

These buttons alter the voice pitch.

Click here for a sample of speech settings.

Setting font preferences

When you choose Font Preferences from the Preferences dialog box, you see five options on the right side of the dialog box. You can select a separate font, and you can select the size and color for system messages, chats, e-mail, and instant messages. Simply double-click on the option you want to change, and you see a display with two pop-up menus (see fig. 2.5). The pop-up menu on the left lists all your installed fonts. The one on the right displays your size options. You also see a sample display showing just how your chosen font will look. After you've made your decision, click on the Change Font button. To select the final option—to ignore text colors—simply double-click on that choice, and you'll see a checkmark appear to the left of this option.

 Plain English, please!

> A **font** is a collection of letters, numbers, and other symbols that are all in the same style. When you get a new Mac, a small number of fonts are already installed on your computer. You can find more fonts in AOL's software libraries or from software dealers. **99**

America Online uses the same fonts that are automatically installed on your Macintosh when you load your system software. The normal selections are Geneva and Monaco because they're easy to read on your computer screen. If you're not happy with these selections or want the display to be a little larger or a little smaller, make your selections here. Although you might want to stick with your standard system fonts, feel free to experiment with any other font you've installed on your Mac, in case you like something else better.

TIP **Choose a monospaced font, or fixed-space font, such as Monaco** or Courier, to display your messages online. That way, material that is formatted with tabs lines up clearly onscreen.

CAUTION **America Online software uses your standard Macintosh system** fonts by default, such as Chicago for menu-bar titles, Geneva and Monaco for text display, and New York for the sign-off screen and some text windows. These fonts are automatically installed when you load system software onto your Mac, so don't remove them.

You should leave the Ignore Text Colors option alone. If you turn on this feature, custom colors used in e-mail messages that you receive won't be shown. If you don't have a color screen, or you want to speed up screen display of long messages, it's a good idea to select this option.

Setting chat preferences

Chats and **conferences** are often the most enjoyable experiences on America Online. You can have your chat window display text double-spaced so it's easier to read (the normal mode is single-spaced). You also can decide whether you want to hear sounds that other members might send. And you may want to consider adding voices to chat text, as described a bit earlier in this chapter, if you have a Macintosh that supports PlainTalk software (such as an AV or Power Mac) or has Speech Manager software installed.

 Plain English, please!

A **chat** is an online meeting, where folks can talk to each other by entering text onto the computer screen. A **conference** is a more structured meeting, where members sit in "rows" online and interact with each other or with those presenting the conference. You'll learn more about these activities in Chapter 5.

Bear in mind that you can't hear a chat sound on your computer unless you have installed the same sound. But America Online's sound libraries are huge, so you're bound to find just about any sound that any other member might send. See Chapter 10 for more information on locating a file in America Online's computing and software libraries.

When you click on Chat Preferences, your options appear at the right of the Preferences dialog box.

Setting downloading preferences

Many files you **download** from America Online are **compressed** to make them smaller and thus shorten the time needed to get the files to your computer (thereby reducing your online charges). America Online software includes a tool to automatically decompress files you've downloaded. The supported compression formats include StuffIt, AppleLink Package, and several PC formats. By default, as soon as you end an America Online session, all files you have just downloaded (if they're saved in a compression format that's supported, of course) are decompressed automatically. You should keep this compression option checked. It makes the process of using your downloaded files much easier. If you don't have enough disk space to store all these files, or if you want to decide later whether you want to use these files, just turn this option off.

 Plain English, please!

> To **download** a file means you are transferring that file to your Macintosh's hard disk drive.

 Plain English, please!

> **Compressing** a file is a process that reduces the size of a file using a software algorithm. The reverse process, in which the file is restored to its original size, is **decompressing**. When you make a file smaller, you shorten the time it takes to transfer the file to and from your Mac, thus reducing the amount of time you spend online.

The second option is Delete Compressed Files, which enables you to delete the original file automatically after it's been decompressed. This option is one you ought to use with caution, because having it on protects you against the rare occasion when a decompressed file might become damaged somehow.

Your final download option is Confirm Download Later, which produces a reminder window whenever you choose the option to add a file to your download queue. If you don't want to be reminded about this each time you choose a file to download, turn this option off. I'll describe the features of the Download Manager in more detail later in this chapter (and in Chapter 10).

Setting graphics viewing preferences

America Online's software will open text documents or stuffed documents. You can also open, view, and print files created in several graphics formats, such as GIF, JPEG, and PICT. If you have Apple's QuickTime software installed (version 2.0 or later), you can open and play QuickTime movies. This is a special advantage, because there are literally thousands of graphics files available for you to download in America Online's huge software libraries. You can download photos of fellow AOL members, weather maps, your favorite movie and TV stars, and much, much more.

 Plain English, please!

Apple's **QuickTime software** is a system extension that enables your Mac to create and view multimedia movies. QuickTime comes on all new Macs, or you can download a recent version from AOL's software libraries.

The Auto-View Graphics option allows graphics files to appear on your Mac's screen as you are downloading them. You'll see the image drawn on your screen and a progress bar showing the status of your image-file download. The neat thing about this feature is that if you decide you don't want the file after all, you can just cancel the download before it finishes. This is one option I suggest you leave on.

 **Q&A** *Why am I getting a message that the media tool is not installed every time I launch AOL software? What's a media tool?*

AOL's Mac software can play QuickTime movies (that's Apple's system extension that lets you create and play multimedia productions), but you need to have version 2.0 or later of QuickTime software installed. If you don't have QuickTime (or you've installed an older version), you'll get the message about the media tool not opening. A **media tool** is a little software module that comes with your AOL software to play these movies. If you don't really want to play a QuickTime movie, this is nothing to worry about.

QuickTime is installed on all new Macs; if you don't have a copy, you can download recent versions from AOL's software libraries.

 **TIP**   **If a graphics file is very large, America Online's software may not** have sufficient memory to view it and you'll receive a message to this effect. You can usually get around this by closing all open document windows and then trying to open the graphics file again. If that doesn't work, give America Online's software additional RAM with the Finder's Get Info command. To make this change, first make sure you've quit the program. Then click once on a program icon to select it (not twice, which will actually launch the program), and choose Get Info from the Finder's Special menu. Then enter the new RAM figure in the bottom list field of the Get Info window. An additional 500K or so is often enough to get you much better performance.

The last option, Use Mac System Colors, just defaults the color rendering of the image file to the standard Macintosh color palette. There's no need to switch off this option, unless you've done some serious customizing of your Mac's color settings.

Setting mail preferences

Because electronic mail, or e-mail, is such an important feature of your America Online software, several options appear when you select Mail Preferences in the Preferences dialog box.

 Plain English, please!

Electronic mail (**e-mail**) is, for many, the most important feature of any online service. It allows you to compose messages on your computer and send them, via your online service, to another member (or even, via the global Internet, to a member of another service). You'll learn more about e-mail in Chapter 5.

- If your mailbox is filled when you log onto America Online, or if e-mail is sent during your online session, you hear that same friendly fellow who says Welcome tell you You've Got Mail. If you don't want to hear his voice (even though he seems like such a nice guy), turn off the Male Voice Announcement option.

- Whether you've turned the voice announcement on or off, you probably want to keep the second option active. The Mail Waiting Notice puts up a little flashing mailbox at the upper right side of your Mac's menu bar. If you don't want to be disturbed, just turn this option off.

- When you send e-mail, your America Online software automatically closes the e-mail document window at the moment the e-mail is sent (transferred to the host computer). If you want to keep your e-mail message onscreen, turn off the preference to Close Mail After Sending.

- The next mail preference is designed to keep your screen from getting cluttered, especially if you get a lot of e-mail. As you click on the arrow to go to the next or to a previous message, the message you have open is automatically closed. If you prefer to have all those windows stay open despite the clutter, just turn off the Close Mail On Next/Previous option.

- When you choose to send your e-mail while offline, or at a later time, you normally click on the Send Later icon at the left of your e-mail message form. You will receive a confirmation that you've set your e-mail for later shipment (and the choice to activate a FlashMail session). Turning off this final option keeps this confirmation message from appearing.

Setting members' preferences

One of the most exciting experiences you can have online is getting an instant message. The usual preference is for America Online to display a little flashing Instant Message (IM) notice at the upper right side of the menu bar on your screen when you get an instant message. If you have e-mail waiting, the IM display alternates with the Mailbox icon. If you don't want to receive this notice, turn off the Instant Message Notice option.

The second preference is just for convenience. By default, whenever you get an instant message, that message window is brought right to the front. But this choice might be a bit disturbing if you're doing something else online. In that case, just turn off this option. If you've left your IM notice options on, you won't miss a message.

 *CAUTION*   **Leaving on the option to bring an instant message window to the** front has downsides. If you happen to close another document window at the very same moment that an instant message window appears on your screen, you may close the instant message window too (and there's no way to bring it back). My suggestion: turn off the option to bring an IM window to the front.

And, finally, your IM's arrival is punctuated by a cute little musical sound. I like it, and I'm happy to hear this kind of sound. But maybe you don't, so here's your chance to become a music critic and turn it off.

You have another way to set options with your America Online software, and that's the Personal Choices command in the Members menu. That option groups all of your settings, from program settings to Parental Controls, into a convenient graphical interface. As for Parental Controls, it's a convenient method to control the access of your child to America Online and the Internet. I'll explain what that's all about in Chapter 7.

3

Getting the Hang of It: AOL's 14 Departments

● **In this chapter:**

- **The major departments of America Online**

- **Find your way around the Welcome screen**

- **Consult the Main Menu—a roadmap to AOL's territory**

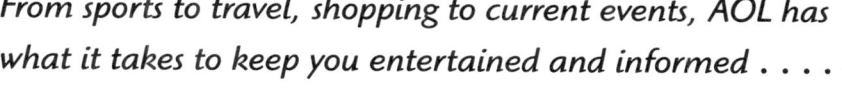

From sports to travel, shopping to current events, AOL has what it takes to keep you entertained and informed . . . .

You've installed your new AOL software and learned a little something about the features that are offered. I've also helped you fine-tune the software so you can get the most out of your AOL time. Now let's have a look at some of the services AOL offers. I'll flesh these out in the later chapters of this book.

A brief look at AOL's departments

Now that you've signed onto America Online and learned how to use the software, it's time to do more than just stick your toes in the water.

Every time you log onto America Online, you'll see the Welcome screen (see fig. 3.1), also known as In The SpotLight. This screen shows the current major highlights and informs you that you have e-mail waiting.

Fig. 3.1
See the current highlights and check your mail when you first log onto America Online.

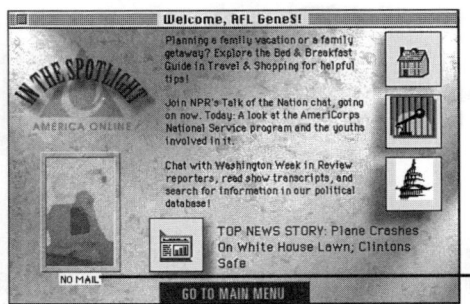

You'll know right away if you have mail waiting for you.

In this chapter, I'll dig deeper beneath the In The Spotlight window to the Main Menu and beyond, where you'll explore the various virtual neighborhoods, known as **departments**, of America Online (see fig. 3.2). The Main Menu is located just beneath the In The Spotlight window when you first log onto America Online. The fastest way to bring the menu to the front is to click on the shaded GO TO MAIN MENU rectangle at the bottom of the Welcome screen.

Use this icon to send
and receive your mail.
Keyword: **Post Office**

Click on this icon to
return to the first
Welcome screen.

Fig. 3.2
The Main Menu is
your gateway to all
the major features of
America Online's
virtual city.

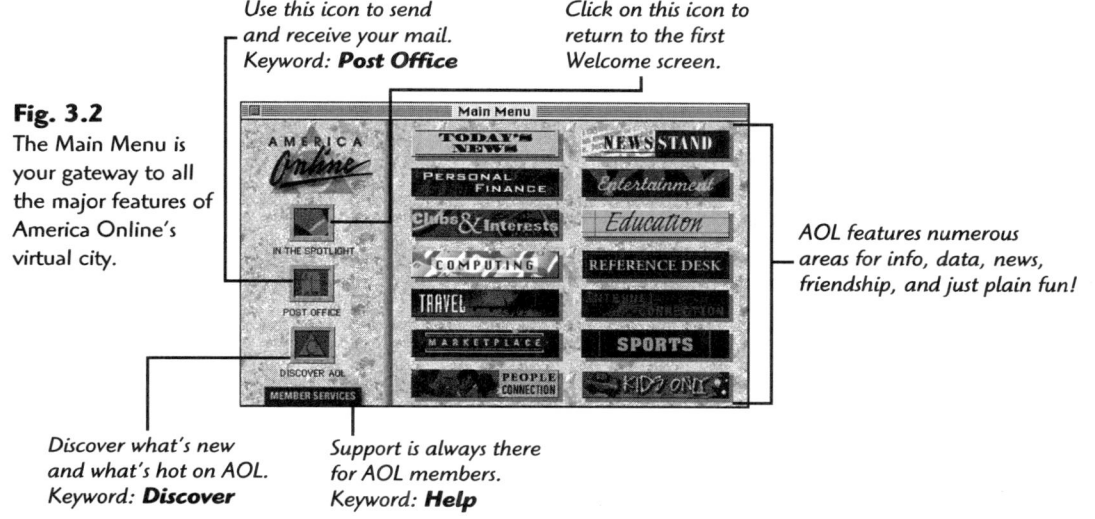

AOL features numerous
areas for info, data, news,
friendship, and just plain fun!

Discover what's new
and what's hot on AOL.
Keyword: **Discover**

Support is always there
for AOL members.
Keyword: **Help**

Each of the 14 online departments shown in figure 3.2 is identified by a major topic of interest. A department contains a number of forums, folders, services, and other areas related (sometimes loosely) to that topic. I'll tell you more about those areas later in this book. For now, I'll just scratch the surface.

TIP **If you've closed the Main Menu during your online session, you** can bring it up again by simply selecting the Go To menu and then choosing Main Menu.

TIP **Almost every part of America Online can be reached by pressing** Command+K and typing a simple keyword. Most keywords are intuitive, such as typing **Computing** to reach AOL's Computing department or **Entertainment** to reach AOL's Entertainment department. If the keyword you choose isn't valid, just click on the Search button in the keyword window, and you'll see a list of likely prospects.

If you visit an online area regularly, you can include that area (and up to nine more) in your list of Favorite Places. To add an area, simply choose Edit Favorite Places from the Go To menu, enter the name of the area followed by its keyword, and then save your changes. From then on, just type the Command key plus the corresponding number (from 1 to 0) while online and you'll be quickly transported to the area you chose.

Today's News

Keyword: **News**

Here's your online daily newspaper. In addition to providing the top news of the day, the Today's News department (shown in fig. 3.3) has special sections: US & World, Business, Entertainment, Sports, and Weather. You can also use the search window, called Search News, to locate stories about a particular item of interest.

 **TIP**   I'll describe this area in more detail in Chapter 12.

Fig. 3.3
Stay on top of the fast-moving events with America Online's Today's News department.

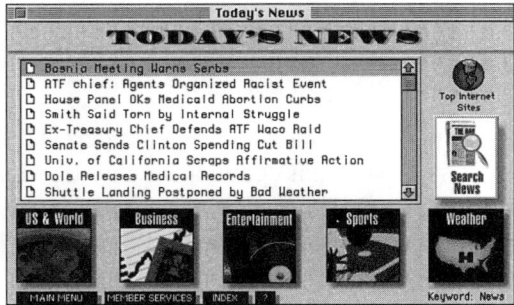

Personal Finance

Keyword: **Finance**

Consider this department an extension of Today's News. The Personal Finance department lets you delve more deeply into all aspects of handling your personal finances, from reviewing the day's business news (and how it may affect your income and investment strategies) to seeking out the profile of a company you may want to add to your stock portfolio (see fig. 3.4). A glance at the main Personal Finance department window shows lots of information resources.

 **TIP**   Personal finance topics are covered in Chapter 13.

Fig. 3.4
A vast storehouse of business news and advice awaits you in the Personal Finance department.

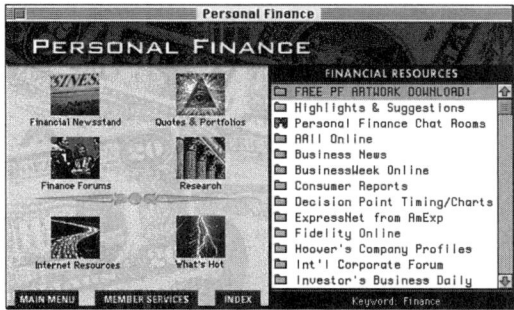

Computing

Keyword: **Computing**

Because we all use our personal computers to connect to America Online, the Computing department, shown in figure 3.5, is one of the most popular places to visit on AOL. You'll find lots of information and huge software libraries for your Mac, and if you have to cross platforms on occasion, you'll also find DOS, OS/2, and Windows files. In addition, many of the major computer manufacturers have fully staffed support areas on America Online. Go to these support areas to get quick solutions to problems with a specific product or advice on how to use that product more effectively.

 **TIP** I'll tell you more about the Computing department in Chapter 9.

Fig. 3.5
The Computing area is one of AOL's most frequently visited online departments.

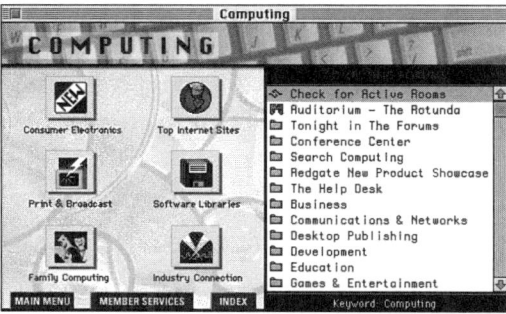

Travel

Keyword: **Travel**

As the name implies, travelers gain gratification in the areas that comprise this department (see fig. 3.6). One of the principal services of Travel & Shopping is *EAAsy Sabre,* American Airlines' computerized travel center. You can book flights on any major airline, reserve rental cars and hotel rooms, or just check schedules and prices during your EAAsy Sabre visit. You can plan an entire itinerary simply and quickly with EAAsy Sabre.

Fig. 3.6
Book a flight or learn about your favorite tourist spot in America Online's Travel department.

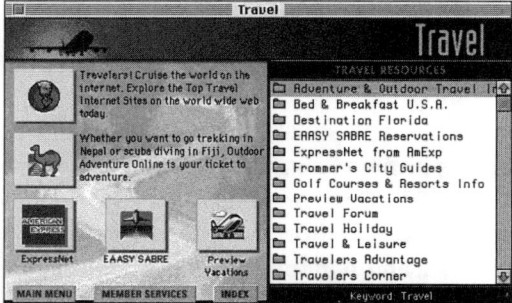

Travelers' Corner brings you information from other wayfaring souls who have already braved the far corners of our country and the farthest reaches of the globe. The Weissmann Travel Reports bring you accurate and enticing reviews of all sorts of places, including such categories as Exotic Destinations, United States Destinations, and International Destinations. You can order the Weissmann Travel Reports through America Online; they are the same reports used by thousands of leading travel professionals when they counsel clients.

 **TIP** I'll cover all this and more in Chapter 15.

Marketplace

Keyword: **Marketplace**

The Marketplace is your AOL center for shopping galore! Whether you're looking for America Online goodies such as T-shirts and coffee mugs, wanting to buy or sell a car, or looking for computer training aids, AOL's Marketplace department (shown in fig. 3.7) offers you these things and more.

TIP **Many of the services offered are explained in more detail in** Chapter 14.

Fig. 3.7
Go shopping and find some bargains while on America Online! When you first reach this department, you may see a special Spotlight screen showing new features, but the Marketplace is just a click away.

The Newsstand

Keyword: **Newsstand**

America Online's Newsstand department offers a vast amount of information about the world today, and the news is as current as it gets (see fig. 3.8). In some cases—such as with *TIME*, *The New York Times*, *The San Jose Mercury News*, and many other daily, weekly, and monthly publications—the information is on America Online before the publications themselves hit the streets.

Fig. 3.8
The corner newsstand was never quite like this.

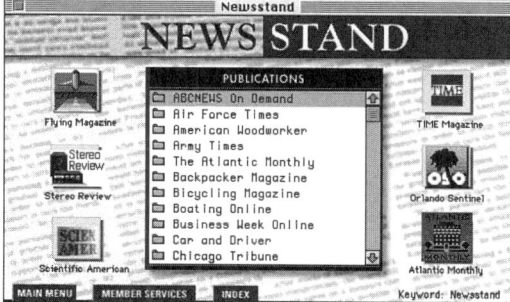

TIP **There's so much more in AOL's Newsstand than I can possibly** mention in this section, so I'll cover it in more detail in Chapter 12. I encourage you to explore this immense area of America Online, not only to absorb the day's news but also to expand your own knowledge about the world and current events.

Entertainment

Keyword: **Entertainment**

Movies, television, books, political and funny-pages cartoons, *Disney Adventures Magazine*, RockLink, the Trivia Forum, and LaPub—these are just a few of the Entertainment department features that draw huge numbers of AOL members. Almost no other online department has the continuous drawing power of the Entertainment department. Both children and adults frequent Entertainment for its culturally diverse content. Be sure to stop by during your travels across America Online (see fig. 3.9).

Fig. 3.9
Here you can see just a small portion of AOL's Entertainment department.

As you explore the Entertainment area, be sure to stop by LaPub for a virtual thirst-quencher served by one of LaPub's congenial barkeeps.

TIP   **You may even find time to bounce on their trampoline or soak in** the hot tub! (I'll explain what *that* means in Chapter 4.)

Education

Keyword: **Education**

Do you need help with that homework assignment, or do you want to take some special courses on a particular topic? You can do these things and more in America Online's active Education department, shown in figure 3.10. Pay a virtual visit to the Library of Congress or the Smithsonian Institution, sign up for a correspondence course, or get information about the next round of college board examinations.

TIP **For now, I'll refer you to Chapter 11 for more information.**

Fig. 3.10
Sign up for a special course or visit a museum during your visit to the Education department.

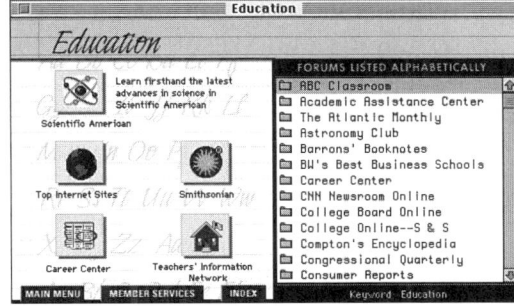

Sports

Keyword: **Sports**

When America's national pastime, baseball, disappeared in the summer of 1994 due to a players' strike, the importance of sports in our lives didn't diminish one iota. We simply talked about the football season instead. America Online's Sports department, shown in figure 3.11, is a repository of the latest sports news, plus discussion groups and regular conferences on your favorite sports. And sometimes you'll be able to converse, through cyberspace, with some of your favorite sports figures.

Fig. 3.11
If you open your newspaper to the Sports section first, you'll want to make regular stops to this online area.

Kids Only

Keyword: **Kids**

I really haven't discussed special places for kids yet on America Online, so I'll remedy that right now. As shown in figure 3.12, young people have lots of special and very friendly places to visit on America Online. *Disney Adventures Magazine* is on hand with a special forum. There's a kids' version of *TIME* to explore, and also special Kids Only versions of America Online's most popular clubs, such as the Astronomy Club and the *Star Trek* club.

 **TIP**   **I'll cover all this in more detail in Chapter 7.**

Fig. 3.12
Kids have a special area to call their own on America Online.

...and More

By now you realize that America Online's departments contain vast areas to explore, and this chapter has highlighted only a few of them.

One of the remaining departments, People Connection, is among the most popular areas on America Online. I'll cover it in depth in Chapter 5. All 14 America Online departments are described in the remaining chapters.

As you read through this book, you'll also find chapters devoted to other important online features, such as e-mail, the Internet (including the World Wide Web), AOL's forums and how to get the most value from them, and much more.

For now, just look around and get comfortable with the general layout. When the time comes to explore your chosen areas of interest, the later chapters will guide you through your journeys of discovery.

The Easy Way to Meet People Online

● In this chapter:

- ● Make yourself known to the rest of the online community

- ● View other members' online profiles

- ● Discover when your friends are online

- ● Follow proper online etiquette while meeting other members

- ● Find other members with similar interests

At any time of the day or night, thousands and thousands of folks like you are connected to America Online. Let's make contact! . . . . ▶

One of the most enjoyable parts of becoming an America Online member is the ability to meet others with similar interests, whether computer-related or not. A number of resources are available to aid you in your quest for meeting other online members. You find out about these features in the following paragraphs. But first, you want to learn how to introduce yourself to others.

Give yourself an online profile

Every member of America Online has at least one screen name. You can create up to five screen names to use when the mood strikes you, or for use by other members of your family. Every member also can create an online profile for each of those online names, for other members to view. Your first step toward meeting people is complete when you fill out your own online profile.

Besides the expected information, such as your real name, screen name, and location, you can enter personal information about yourself to indicate your interests to others. Hobbies, favorite quotes, your occupation, and computers you use are some of the entries you might want to provide for your profile. A complete list of the data you can enter is shown in figure 4.1.

Fig. 4.1
To create or change your profile, choose Edit Your Online Profile from the Members menu of your America Online software.

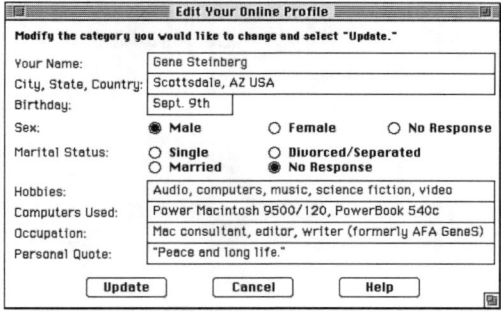

CAUTION   **The first time you create a profile, it defaults to include your full** name. You are free to change it to anything you want to have appear there. AOL will respect your privacy.

As you look at the Edit Your Online Profile screen, make a note to yourself about which entry you want other people to see when they look up your profile. You might or might not want to reveal certain information, such as your gender, real name, marital status, and so on. Fill in only the information you would not mind telling a stranger. In figure 4.2, for example, I listed my city, state, and country information as a region rather than display specific information about my residence.

If you do not want to reveal your gender, be sure to click on the No Response button on that line. (If your name happens to be Pat, you could sure keep 'em guessing!) Also click on No Response for your marital status if you want that information to remain undisclosed.

TIP   **After you learn how to look up other people's profiles, take some** time to look through a few other members' entries for ideas.

The remaining four fields are your basic "essay" answers. Here is where you tell other people about yourself as a person in a few pithy sentences instead of simply stating factual information.

If you've reviewed your completed profile and are satisfied with it, click on the Update button to finish the job and move on to more exciting online activities.

Q&A   *Whenever I try to check a profile, or open an AOL forum or message window, I get a message saying the system is busy. What's wrong? Is it me or them?*

This is a common problem. Your online session involves communication between your Mac and AOL's host computer. If the lines of communication are clogged, you'll see a message that the system is busy (or that the host failed to respond, if you're using an older version of AOL's software). The problem may be at AOL's end; its host computer network is indeed busy. It may be due to a problem with your local AOL access number, or it may be due to a system glitch.

When this problem happens, try the following:

1 Log off America Online immediately and then try to reconnect.

2 Try another access number.

   If you cannot get back online, choose Get Local # from the Locality pop-up menu on your AOL log-on screen; and click the Sign-on button to have AOL help you select new connection numbers from your home town.

3 If the connection problem continues, try logging on again at a different time. The evening hours on AOL are prime time for the service, just as they are on the major TV networks, which means higher numbers of users are online.

4 If you still keep getting those busy messages, use the AOL keyword **System Response** to access an area where you can get further assistance, and report your problem to AOL's customer service.

TIP **If you have several local access numbers to choose from, you can** create separate Locality profiles for each pair of phone numbers (see Chapter 2). That way, if you cannot get connected or get poor performance from one number, you can select a different set of numbers from the pop-up menu at the right of the Locality label.

If you have second thoughts about revealing yourself, you might prefer not to complete your online profile. In this case, click on the Cancel button. Your profile is not saved, and your entries vanish. If you want more information about the Edit Your Online Profile screen, click on the Help button to get additional information.

Q&A *How come when I try to get a member's profile, I get a message that there isn't a profile online for that member? I know their membership is still active; I get e-mail from the person.*

An AOL member doesn't have to make an online profile. Some choose not to do so, perhaps because they just want to preserve their privacy as much as possible. Their wishes should be respected, and the lack of a profile shouldn't reflect upon how you judge a fellow AOL member. You can also decide not to have a profile displayed, if you wish.

Find and meet other AOL members

Meeting people on America Online has had some interesting outcomes over the years since the online community was launched. The syndicated television program, *The Jerry Springer Show*, has spotlighted a number of AOLers who met and married. America Online users often inhabit the various People Connection rooms, such as the Flirt's Nook and Romance Connection, in search of friendship, camaraderie, and, yes, even love.

Locating other America Online members

On busy evenings in recent weeks, America Online has had literally thousands of members in "interactive areas" at one time! But as you stare at the Welcome to AOL screen, you aren't able to see any of these people. It's akin to entering an office building; you need to know where the people are and go there before you can meet anyone. At first, everyone is behind "virtual" closed doors, and those doors are soundproof. Your first step to finding other people is to open these doors and look around. By far, the easiest place to find other members is in the People Connection area of America Online. The People Connection department houses most of the non-computing-related chat rooms where members like to congregate and socialize. Are you ready to take a peek into one of these rooms?

First, select Lobby from the Go To menu (or simply type **Command+L**). You are immediately transported to the Lobby of America Online's People Connection, as shown in figure 4.2. This window represents a place in which up to 23 people can gather and get to know one another by chatting. (If the Lobby is full when you enter, the room expands to additional rooms, and the room name has a number after it, such as Lobby 3.) The mechanics of chatting involves typing what you want others to see in the small box in the lower portion of the chat window, and sending it by clicking on the Send button or pressing Return on your keyboard.

If you're new to the online world, don't worry about starting a conversation right away; just hang around the Lobby and watch what other members type to each other. While you're waiting, chances are that someone will say hello to you (it'll show up in the chat window). Don't worry about sending a reply if you aren't comfortable; no one will mind. (Experienced online visitors call it lurking, but don't get the wrong idea about the word. It just means you're hanging out.)

Fig. 4.2
America Online's
Lobby in the People
Connection area is one
place you can chat
with other members.

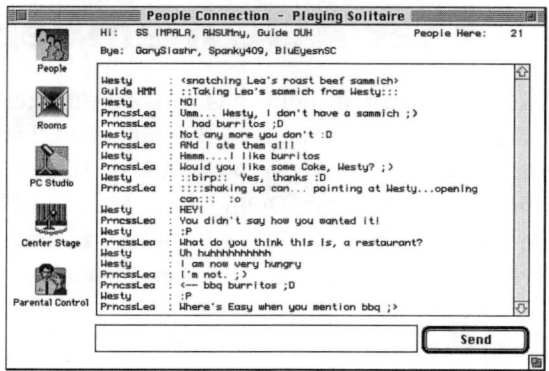

Look at the Lobby screen shown in figure 4.3. This window contains some items of interest apart from the text you type and the text other people have typed. For one thing, now that you've located some people online, you can find out a little more about them.

Viewing other members' profiles

If you want to view another member's profile, you need to know the member's screen name or be in the same chat room with that member. The Lobby is as good a place as any to start.

Members' screen names are shown at the start of each line as it is displayed in the chat window of the Lobby. At the top of the chat window are two lines of text titled Hi and Bye. These lines show you the people who have most recently entered the room and those who have recently left. You might have noticed your own screen name on the Hi line as you entered the room. As more people enter, their names appear at the start of the Hi line, and the earlier names disappear.

You also have a way to view a list of everyone in the chat room and practice finding out about other people by clicking on the People icon in the upper left portion of the chat window. The resulting window contains a list of all the America Online members currently in that room, as shown in figure 4.3.

TIP **Use the keyword Help or select Members' Online Support from** the Go To menu to view and search the member directory from anywhere at any time.

Fig. 4.3
The People in this Room list tells you which members are currently in the chat room with you; it's updated as people enter and leave.

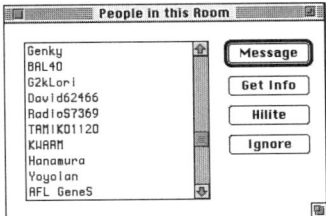

Now you can find out about someone! Select any of the names shown in the list, and click on the Get Info button on the right side of the window. If the person you selected filled out an online profile, you see it in just a few seconds. If that member has not filled out a profile, you receive a message indicating that there is no profile available. In that case, try using some of the other names in the list until you find someone who has provided profile information. Depending on how much information the selected person provided, you see one or more lines of information in the profile window.

Finding a member online

As you become more comfortable using the conference rooms and People Connection rooms of America Online, you will most likely begin to recognize some of the regulars. Perhaps you also know someone who uses America Online and want to find out if that person is signed on at the same time as you.

America Online provides a fast, easy method of locating people using the service. Select Locate a Member Online from the Members menu, or press **Command+F** and type the screen name of the person you want to locate (see fig. 4.4).

Fig. 4.4
Select the Locate a Member Online option to find a member.

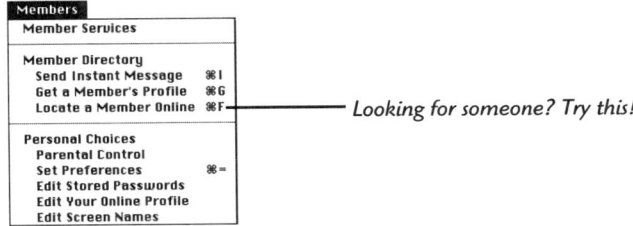

If a person you seek is online when you attempt to find him or her, the America Online host computer tells you that the person you want to find is online but not in a chat area, or you can receive the name of the chat or conference room where the person is. If the person is not online, the software tells you.

Getting involved in the People Connection

Of all the areas where people congregate, the People Connection's Lobby is far and away the place you find most of the people who want to talk. On a busy evening, you can easily find thousands of people in the various lobbies in the People Connection.

Entering the Lobby

You might be saying to yourself, "Hey, wait a minute—didn't you say earlier that only 23 people can gather in a room at one time?" Well, yes, that's correct, as far as it goes. What happens after the 23rd person enters the Lobby is that a new room is automatically created to hold the 24th and all the other people soon to follow. That room is called Lobby 1; after it reaches 23 people, other rooms follow it with names like Lobby 2, Lobby 3, and so on (see fig. 4.5).

Fig. 4.5
The People Connection's Lobby area is a busy place; people are constantly coming and going.

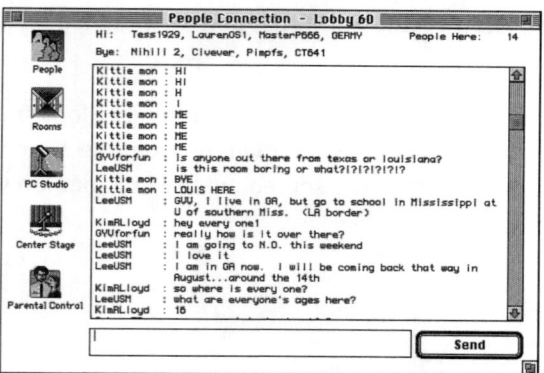

The People Connection Lobbies are usually bustling, crowded areas—think of Grand Central Station. Often people are leaving for other People Connection rooms with specific themes or to go to Computing & Software conference rooms to discuss the latest industry news. Private rooms are also available (more about that later).

As with most public areas in real life, the People Connection rooms have their own etiquette and rules of conduct. First and foremost is TOS, or Terms of Service. TOS is America Online's equivalent of real-life laws. Take some time during your first sessions to acquaint yourself with TOS. Use the keyword **TOS** to go to AOL's free help area and look over the Terms of Service, which are displayed in separate text files, according to category. Spend a few minutes reviewing the contents of this area. (After all, it's free!) By making this effort now, you will feel more comfortable visiting the public area rooms for the first time, and you'll have a greater understanding of how things work on America Online.

The contents of each TOS topic can be saved or printed by using the Save or Print commands from the File menu of your AOL software.

Briefly, the most important parts of TOS state that you are expected to be a good citizen when you visit America Online. You are expected to refrain from using vulgar or abusive language and to respect others in the same way you expect them to respect you.

Hang out at LaPub

Just about every town or city has a neighborhood hangout, where folks gather at the end of the workday to just relax for a while and perhaps talk with some friends. That's the idea behind AOL's LaPub (see fig. 4.6). To get to LaPub, type the keyword **LaPub**, or enter through the Online Games Forum or Entertainment Forum.

Fig. 4.6
LaPub is a pleasant gathering place.

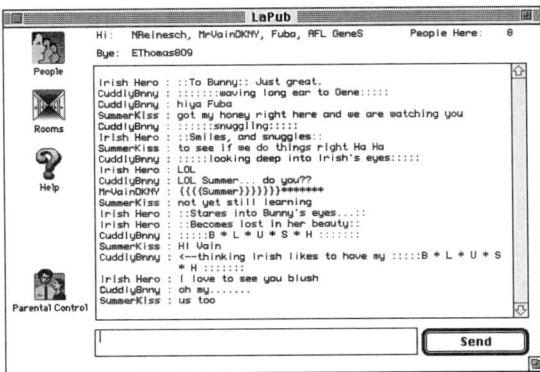

This is one of the liveliest of the People Connection areas ever seen online anywhere. The best part is that you don't have to drive anywhere; just sit in your most comfortable chair with the one-eyed monitor of your favorite computer in front of your face. Most likely, you will have at least one free "online" beverage of your choice offered on your first visit. Accept it, and enjoy!

LaPub is more than just a place to chat with members and partake of the occasional festivities. In addition to the LaPub chat room, you find a special area, the LaPub Cellar, offering files uploaded by other LaPub patrons (see fig. 4.7).

Fig. 4.7
The LaPub Cellar is a collection of marvelous and entertaining files, including pictures of the regulars, sound files, and transcripts of notable LaPub events.

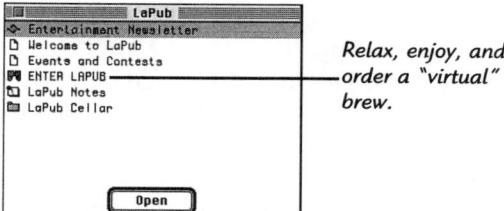

Relax, enjoy, and order a "virtual" brew.

Visiting private chat rooms

If you're like many of the People Connection's regular visitors, you'll eventually meet someone online with whom you want to communicate further. You want more privacy than the public People Connection rooms are able to offer, but in a fashion more convenient than instant messages and e-mail. (Instant messages and e-mail are discussed in more detail in Chapter 6.)

Here's what to do:

1 Go to the Lobby in the People Connection.

2 Click on the Rooms icon on the left side of the Lobby chat window.

3 Click on the Private Room button that is located next to the list of rooms.

4 When you see a request to enter a room name, do so. Remember this room name so that you can send it in an instant message or e-mail to those members you want to join you.

5 Click on the Go button; you are magically transported to that room.

TIP **If you don't want someone to accidentally stumble into your** private room, you should choose a name that cannot be guessed easily (or by accident)—something known only to you and your friends.

Private rooms look and feel exactly like any chat room, such as the Lobby or forum conference rooms. The only difference between a public chat room and a private one is that the name of the room does not appear in any of the People Connection room lists. To join another member already in a private room, you must first know the exact name of that room (or take a very lucky guess, which is why you want to be careful about selecting the name).

Entering the Center Stage Auditoriums

The People Connection staff have also invited some extremely popular celebrities to pay a visit. AOL has featured such personalities as Bob Hope, Mick Jagger, and Terri Hatcher (star of ABC's *Lois and Clark*).

Because the regular People Connection rooms hold only 23 folks before another room is automatically opened, a solution was needed for events that would be more popular. Another problem was that with so many people in one room, so many comments and questions would be typed by members wanting to talk to the guests that tracking the conversation with the guests could be next to impossible.

Many of AOL's forums have chat rooms structured just like those in People Connection, except they hold 48 members (so my instructions about the Lobby apply to these rooms as well).

To solve the dilemma of seating capacity, and to make the sessions more structured to handle a larger audience, America Online and People Connection came up with a unique interactive concept: the AOL Auditoriums. Figure 4.8 shows the screen for one of a number of auditoriums that have been established. At any one time, several online conferences may be in progress.

Fig. 4.8
One of the People Connection Auditoriums, where thousands can gather. Here show biz veterans Phyllis Diller and Bob Hope hold court.

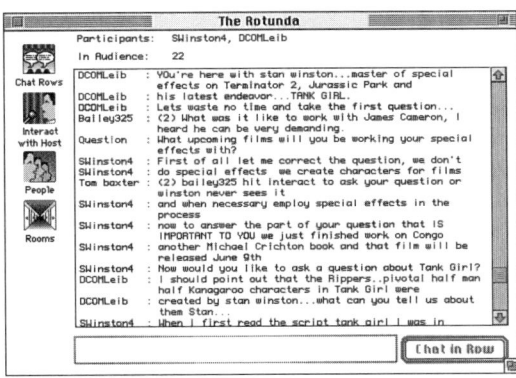

The Center Stage auditoriums are America Online's largest gathering places; each room is capable of accommodating thousands of guests for fun-filled game shows and special events.

When you first enter a Center Stage auditorium, the service reminds you that only those in the same "row" as yours can see the text you type to the screen. If you find that the typing of members in the same rows is distracting or inconvenient to your concentration, you can turn off that feature. Just click on the Chat Rows icon; then click on the Turn Chat Off button in the window that appears (see fig. 4.9). When the Chat feature is turned off, you can enjoy the event while seeing only text that appears from the "stage"—text from your hosts, guests, and contestants.

Fig. 4.9

More chat controls for the Center Stage Auditoriums are found in the Chat Rows window.

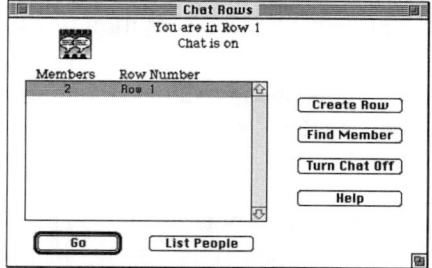

From this window, you also can look for other members who might be online (so you can tell them what a great time you're having on Center Stage), list people in your chat row or any other row, and create a new chat row.

You also can highlight selected speakers or contestants. **Highlighting** causes the conversations of the selected people to appear in the chat window in bold type, so that you can follow the progress of the event more easily. First, click on the People icon on the left side of your Center Stage window. Then click on the Who's Onstage button. Last, select on the stage the individual you want to highlight, and choose the Hilite button .

Entering the AOL Portrait Gallery

The Gallery might turn out to be one of your favorite places online because there you get to place faces with the screen names of people you meet online. To find this interesting area, use the keyword **Gallery**.

TIP **Many areas besides People Connection hold regular chats and** conferences. Look in Computing forums for other chat schedules (see Chapter 9).

The Gallery is a collection of photos that are put in computer-readable form and uploaded for all to see. Thousands of America Online members have already uploaded their portraits or sent their photos to the Gallery's staff to digitize for free. As you get to know some of the regulars online, chances are good that you'll be tempted to find out what they look like, and the Gallery is the place.

A separate library is also included in the Gallery for family-album types of pictures. Perhaps you should gather your own clan's photos and send them to the gallery. If you have a scanner (or access to one at the office), you can scan your own photo and upload it in GIF or JPEG format directly to The Gallery's software libraries, or submit your photo to be scanned and up-loaded for you by the Gallery's staff. The address to which you should send your photos for scanning is listed in the library.

To make viewing these photos easy for all America Online users, regardless of type of computer, the Gallery photos are provided in GIF and JPEG formats.

Plain English, please!

GIF (Graphic Interchange Format) is a cross-platform image format that offers a high-quality image with a small file size that keeps your download time short. **JPEG** (Joint Photographic Experts Group) is a standardized image-compression mechanism that's tailor-made for either full-color or gray-scale images of natural, real-world scenes. It works beautifully for photos (but not so well for text). A JPEG image is smaller than one in GIF, but yields a higher quality image. **,,**

The very latest versions of America Online's Macintosh software allow you to watch a photo gradually appear on your screen while it's being downloaded to your computer, just as we've shown in figure 4.10. To view the photo files after you download them, simply choose Open from the File menu and then select the file you wish to see. Once the file is opened (or has appeared on your computer's screen right after the download process is over), you'll be able to print it the same as any other document.

TIP   **If a photo has been uploaded with the newest version of AOL's** software, you'll be able to see a thumbnail or small version of the photo when you view the file description in the Gallery's libraries. Thumbnails are not available for photos sent using older versions of AOL's Mac and Windows software. A thumbnail lets you preview the image before you download it, so you can decide whether or not to retrieve the file. But if you don't see a preview, don't assume there's anything wrong with the image or your software. It'll take a while before older image files are updated and replaced with newer ones.

Fig. 4.10
As you download a file from The Gallery, the photo begins to display on your computer's screen. The complete photo is shown when the download is finished.

Using abbreviations and shorthand symbols

This section provides a partial list of some of the more popular abbreviations and shorthand symbols you might see while online in the People Connection, in chat rooms, or on message boards. They have grown out of the need to show what cannot be shown when online—facial expressions and body language.

Online abbreviations

Often when chatting, America Online members will shorten long phrases into a few letters so that they can be typed quickly. Here are some of the more common online abbreviations:

Abbreviation	What it means...
LOL	Laughing out loud
ROFL or ROTFL	Rolling on the floor laughing
AFK	Away from keyboard
BAK	Back at keyboard
BRB	Be right back
OIC	Oh, I see
IMO	In my opinion
IMHO	In my humble opinion or In my honest opinion
TTFN	Ta-ta for now
TTYL	Talk to you later
NIFOC	Nude in front of computer
GMTA	Great minds think alike
IHTBHWYG	It's hard to be humble when you're great
<g>	Grin
GA	Go ahead

Online shorthand

When you're communicating with others online via instant messages, chat rooms, or e-mail, it's often difficult to convey body language and tone of voice. As a result, some brilliant individual invented online shorthand—keyboard symbols that convey human expression. Tilting your head toward the left will help you to see most of the symbols; for example, the characters :) form a sideways smiley face. Here are some common (and, well, not so common) examples:

Shorthand	What it means...
[ ]	A hug, repeated as needed for degrees of enthusiasm, such as [[[[[[[[ ]]]]]]]]
:)	Basic smile
:(	Frown
:/	Ho-hum smile
;)	Winking smile
:D	Smile with a big grin
:*	Kiss
8)	Wide-eyed smile
B-)	Wearing glasses
:>)	Big nose
:-)8	Well-dressed
%-)	Cross-eyed
#-)	Partied all night
:-*	Just ate a sour pickle
:~'|	Has a cold
:-R	Has the flu
:-)'	Tends to drool
P-)	Getting fresh
|-)	Falling asleep
:-D	Talks too much
O:-)	Very innocent
M:-)	Saluting (symbol of respect)
-=#:-)	Has wizard status
M-):X):-M	See no evil, hear no evil, speak no evil
>:-(	Sick and tired of reading this nonsense

Shorthand	What it means...
|-O	Bored
:-@	Extremely angry
:-o	Shocked
:-(O)	Yelling
. .	Lying down

5

How to Stay in Touch with Other Members

● **In this chapter:**

- **All about e-mail and instant messages**

- **Join conferences and chats on America Online**

- **The lasting power of message boards**

- **Run your online sessions automatically**

- **Save information to read offline**

Getting to know your America Online neighbors will become your favorite activity in cyberspace . . . . ●>

O n any given evening, there are thousands of members in the various chat rooms of People Connection, computing conference rooms, and other online gathering places. Although you can't see e-mail, millions of such messages fly across cyberspace at all hours of the day and night.

Test the waters: how to write e-mail

You can start writing your e-mail message on America Online with a single, simple step—by selecting Compose Mail from the Mail menu bar item. The resulting message form, shown in figure 5.1, is the jumping-off point for all your original e-mail. Later, we show you how to reply to e-mail without using a new mail form.

When you first conjure up a new e-mail window, the cursor is automatically positioned within the To: field of the form. Although it seems presumptuous, most folks actually do begin composing electronic mail by first addressing it. If this does not suit your tastes, simply press your Tab key to move the cursor to any of the other fields contained in the e-mail window, or click in the desired field with your mouse.

America Online is unflaggingly insistent about a few things regarding its e-mail system. You must include at least one To: address, a subject, and a message. Seems rather Orwellian, but it does make sense. After all, receiving a blank message is like picking up the telephone and finding no one on the other end.

Fig. 5.1
You can use the Tab key to move from one field in America Online's e-mail form to another, to speed up preparing your letter.

Click here to send your message.

Address your message.

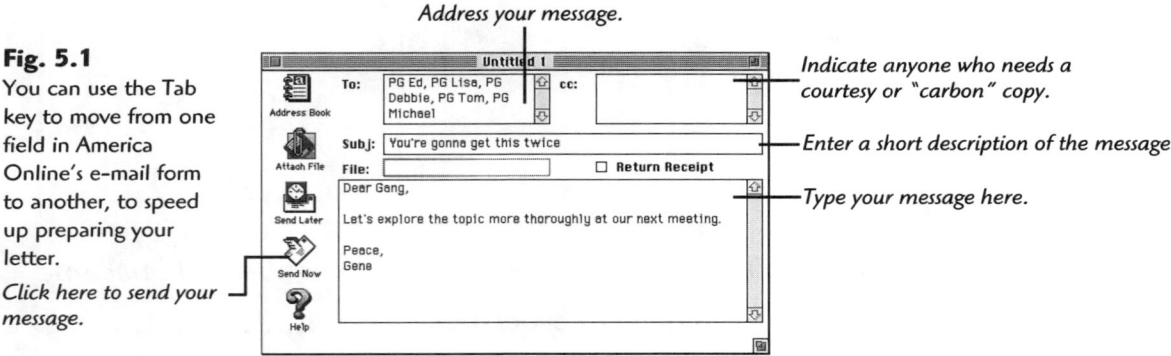

Indicate anyone who needs a courtesy or "carbon" copy.

Enter a short description of the message.

Type your message here.

The address fields of the e-mail window can contain literally hundreds of electronic mailing addresses. If you send a message to more than one person, each person's screen name must be separated by a comma or a Return. When you use the Return key to separate multiple names, the window list is easier to read than when separated by commas. In the example shown in figure 5.1, the To: field shows names separated by commas, whereas the CC: field uses the Return key.

CAUTION   **While the Return and Enter keys often have the same function in** many programs, it doesn't always work that way with AOL's software. So, when you're manually ending a line in your e-mail message, you use the Return key. When you press the Enter key, you're actually sending your message on its way. Be careful before you press Enter!

If you've entered any addresses in your AOL Address Book, you may also click on the Address Book icon to select names for this e-mail.

TIP   **The use of your AOL Address Book is described later in this chapter, in the section titled "Setting up AOL's rolodex."**

Plain English, please!

AOL's **Address Book** is simply a list of the screen names of your favorite online friends and business associates.

Now, move to the Subject field and let the recipient know what your message is about (without making him read it to find out!). This step is both convenient and considered normal e-mail etiquette.

Next, move the cursor to the message body, and compose your message.

How to send e-mail

Once your e-mail is composed, it's easy to send it along its merry way. Click on the Send Now icon on the left side of the e-mail window. The mail is sent immediately, along with any attachments you may have enclosed.

TIP   **File attachments are discussed later in this chapter, in the section** titled, "Sending files with e-mail."

Plain English, please!

Attachments are files that you can connect to your e-mail, so that they can be sent at the same time you send your e-mail message. This is an important feature that separates AOL from some other online services (where files must be sent as a separate piece of e-mail). **99**

If you composed your outgoing e-mail offline, or signed off while composing it, you may choose to use the Send Later feature that saves the outgoing mail on your hard drive. You can send your saved mail manually on your next online visit, or automatically during your next automated mail session, using AOL's marvelous FlashSession feature. Please note, however, that if you enclosed an attached file, you cannot move or delete the file you're sending until after your mail transfer is done.

 Plain English, please!

By **offline**, I'm referring to the ability to write e-mail while not logged onto America Online. **99**

TIP   **Learn about the cool FlashSessions in the section titled "Using** FlashSessions to automate your online visits," later in this chapter.

How to receive e-mail

This is the easy part! All you have to do is log on to AOL and, if you have mail, the happy guy that lives inside the AOL program tells you, You have mail (that is, assuming that you have your Mail Sounds turned on in the Member Preference settings). A special mail icon is also displayed on the Welcome screen (see fig. 5.2).

Fig. 5.2
When you have e-mail in your mailbox, AOL's handy "welcome" voice announces it to you and puts up a notice on the opening screen.

—You have mail!

You can click on the icon directly above the You have mail message on the Welcome screen. You can then double-click to open each piece of mail as you wish. You may also click on the Next arrow icon on the mail form to advance to the next message awaiting you (see fig. 5.3). The Previous arrow lets you move backwards through the mail. The left and right arrow keys on the keyboard are equivalent to clicking on the Next and Previous arrows.

Fig. 5.3
The Read e-mail form. Note the navigating arrows in the lower corners, which you can use to move from one message to another.

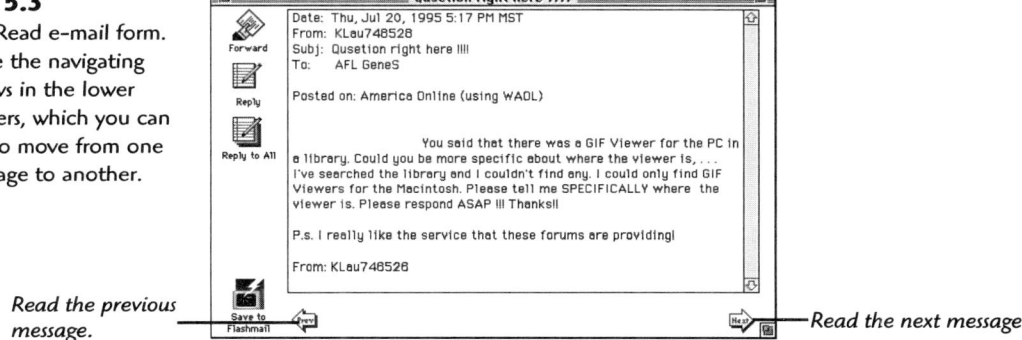

Read the previous message.

Read the next message.

**TIP**   **If you want to send a letter you just received to another online address with your added comments, click the Forward icon.**

Here are some other AOL e-mail features:

- As you read each piece of mail, a checkmark is placed in front of the item as it appears in the New Mail window. If you do not read all your mail in one session, the pieces that have the checkmark do not show up when you next open the New Mail window. Only those items you have not previously read appear there.

- The Ignore button is functionally the same as reading mail, except no Read Mail window opens. Of course, the person who sent you the e-mail will know that you ignored the message.

- The Delete button removes the message from your list of incoming mail, unread. Of course, the person who sends you e-mail will know, in checking the message status, that you have deleted the message.

- The Keep As New button allows you to keep the message among your list of waiting mail, even after you've read the message. It's useful if you want to use that message as a reminder of an upcoming event or as a specific bit of information you want to review the next time you visit America Online.

Sending files with e-mail

America Online's e-mail system allows you to **attach** files from your computer to a piece of e-mail (the online equivalent of stapling separate items together). When you send your e-mail, you also send the files you attached to it.

To attach a file when composing e-mail, simply click on the Attach File icon, and use the accompanying dialog box to select the file you want to attach (see figs. 5.4 and 5.5). You may also choose to compress the file you attach by checking the Compress Files option before you click the Attach button. If you elect to attach more than one file, the AOL software automatically compresses them.

Fig. 5.4
In the AOL e-mail form, the Attach File icon is located in the upper-left margin.

Click here to select the file(s) to attach.

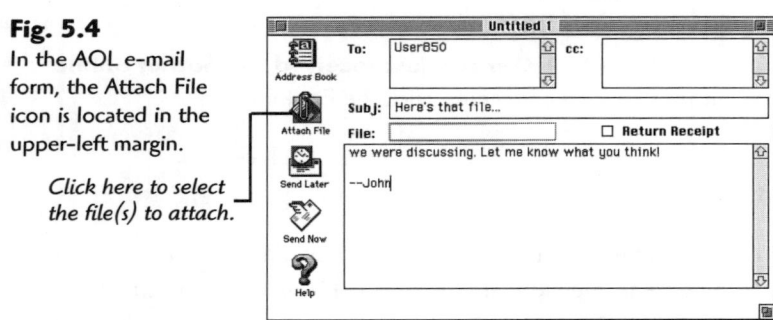

Fig. 5.5
Selecting files to attach is easy in this split window.

Pick the files you want to mail.

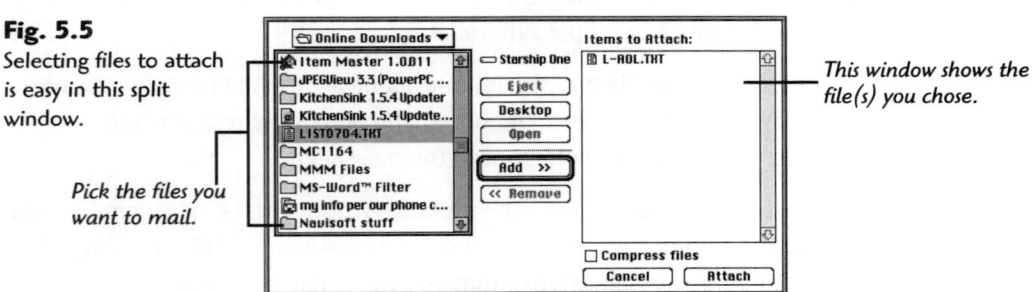

This window shows the file(s) you chose.

66 *Plain English, please!*

Compression is a process that uses a software technique to shrink a file so that it's smaller in size. The compression scheme used by AOL, based on Aladdin Systems' StuffIt software, will let you expand the file back to its original form when you disconnect from AOL (it's an option in the program settings or preferences that's turned on by default). The file you attach must be on a disk drive connected to your computer or on a mounted network drive, and you must attach the file before you send the e-mail. The recipient sees two extra buttons at the bottom of the received e-mail window, Download Now and Download Later. Selecting the Download Now button transfers the file from America Online's host to the recipient's computer. Selecting Download Later marks the file for your Download Manager to transfer at a later time (see fig. 5.6). 99

Fig. 5.6
Here's an e-mail window containing an attached file. Notice the Download Now and Download Later buttons.

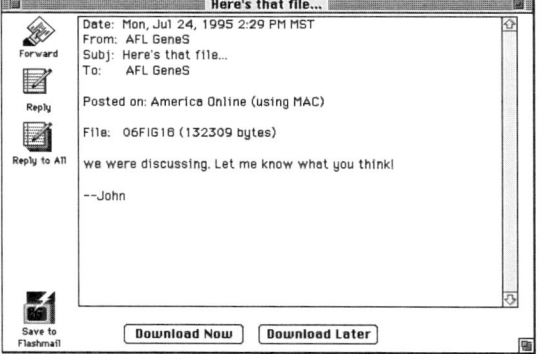

When you send attached files through e-mail, you are charged only for the time needed to send your message and the attachments to the AOL mail-processing area. Similarly, the recipient of the attached file is charged for the time needed to transfer the file from AOL's host to his or her computer. Because this costs money on both ends, it is a good idea not to send unnecessarily large files through e-mail.

Use file-compression whenever possible, and if you believe other AOL members could make use of the file, consider posting the file to a forum library instead of sending it in e-mail. By posting the file to a forum, you are not charged for the connect time spent sending (uploading) the file to AOL's host.

 **TIP** **If you are transferring a GIF or JPEG image file to another AOL** member, compression is probably not going to provide much benefit. These files are already internally compressed and won't get much smaller.

 **TIP** **The Attach File icon changes to Detach File after you attach a file** to your e-mail. If you decide not to send the attached file, but you still want to send the original e-mail message, you can click on Detach File to break the link between the unsent e-mail and the file (and you can still attach a different file to your letter before it's sent).

Saving and printing for posterity

After reading each piece of your e-mail, you have a few options. The first is to simply click the close box of the window, which sends the mail into oblivion. (Well, not quite; you can always find and read mail you've previously viewed from the Check Mail I've Read menu item, found on the Mail menu.)

Another option is to save mail to your Flashbox, a file stored on your hard drive that can hold tons of saved e-mail. To save to your Flashbox, click on the icon just above the appropriately worded Save to Flashmail legend. You can retrieve this e-mail item at any time, whether you are offline or online, by selecting Read Incoming Mail from the Mail menu.

 Plain English, please!

AOL's **Flashbox** is a mailbox that's created on your computer's hard drive when you install AOL's software. As I'll explain later in this chapter, this mailbox (or file folder, which is what it looks like) is filled with e-mail you receive during a FlashSession.

You can also save your e-mail as an individual file. America Online has two special file types for e-mail—one for outgoing mail and one for incoming mail. By selecting Save As from the File menu you may choose to save your e-mail as one of these types of files or as plain text. Saving your mail as plain text allows you to view or change the contents of the e-mail in any text processor, such as your favorite word processing program.

One useful feature found in AOL is the ability to save selected text to a file. If you ever want to save some text from any of AOL's text windows, not just e-mail, simply select the text with your mouse, and then select Save Selected Text As from AOL's File menu (see fig. 5.7). This feature is especially handy for saving addresses or lists contained in e-mail that you want to open or import into other applications.

Printing your e-mail

To print a hard copy of your e-mail, choose Print from the File menu. This works the same way as in almost every other application that supports printing. Remember, however, that if you changed printers since the last time you printed anything from AOL, you first need to select Page Setup to verify your printing options.

Fig. 5.7
It's easy to save selected text from an incoming e-mail message.

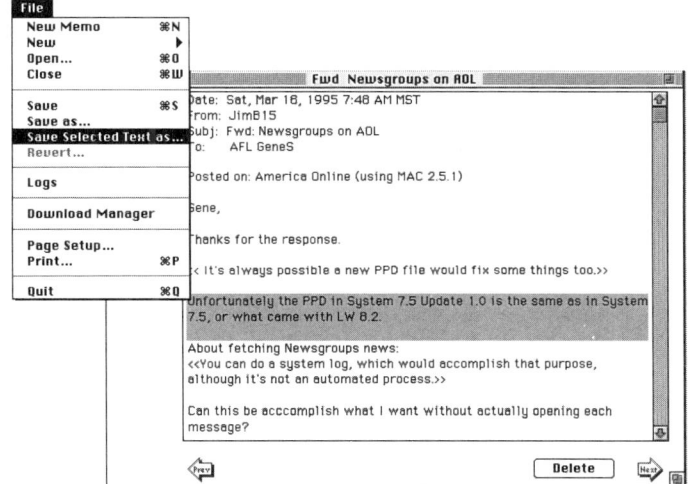

CAUTION  **If you are using a Macintosh and do not have a printer selected in** the Chooser after you start your AOL program, you will probably not be able to print a text window; you'll just see a little flicker from the File menu when you choose the Print or Page Setup functions. Log off America Online, selecting the Quit rather than Sign Off option. Then select your printer, launch America Online's software, then log on again. You should now be able to print normally.

Setting up AOL's rolodex

Your America Online Address Book is the best way to store mail addresses that you use regularly so that they are available at the click of a mouse. Use this feature to build a file card system to keep track of your online friends.

Suppose that you have an online friend named Jesse Dunn. Her screen name on America Online might be Ogyr, and you exchange e-mail with her often.

You'll probably find it more convenient to store her name in your Address Book rather than manually typing it each time you compose mail to her. To do this:

1 Select Edit Address Book from the Mail menu.

2 Click on the Create button. A new address entry form appears on-screen.

3 Type the name of your friend in the Name field; for example, type **Jesse Dunn**.

4 Type the screen name of your friend in the Account field; for example, type **Ogyr**.

Now, the next time you want to send a piece of mail to Jesse, open a new mail window, click on the Address Book icon on the left side of the window, and click on her name.

 **TIP** **As you meet new friends and associates online, be sure to add** their names to your Address Book. That way, you won't lose track of your online contacts.

Keeping those FlashSessions short

If you click on the Options button while the Mail Incoming item is selected, you can instruct the AOL software not to download files that might be attached to incoming e-mail. This is a real money saver when you receive a large file attachment while you are in a hotel room paying exorbitant phone charges for even a local call. Would you want to have your FlashSession download the latest version of the Mac operating system at that time? No, that would not be a good thing, would it?

And, remember you can still retrieve that e-mail up to five days after it's first read, so if you have a faster AOL connection at home than on the road, you can still get the file at that time (at a reduced online cost).

Using FlashSessions to automate your online visits

FlashSessions let AOL's software do the logons for you at the times you set (so you don't have to be at your computer), and send and retrieve all your e-mail and attached files. And, by automating your sessions, you can save money by making your visits more efficient (you cannot visit forums this way yet, but that may come in the future).

Setting up FlashSessions involves a few brief steps, and you can even schedule these sessions for any or all your screen names on your account (see fig. 5.8). You can elect to do one-way e-mail transfer, read-only, or read and download e-mail and their attachments, or any combination of the above. In the next few pages, I'll cover all of your choices in setting up these automatic AOL visits.

Fig. 5.8
The FlashSession manager window is used to quickly schedule your automated sessions.

 **Q&A** *I want to reduce my online billing. Is there any way to forward e-mail sent under one screen name to another screen name?*

As of this writing, you can't. So you may want to schedule your e-mail sessions to include only those screen names where the messages you receive must be answered as soon as possible, and schedule sessions with the other accounts less often.

First, you have to decide what you want to do during a FlashSession. Turning off Files Incoming prevents the downloading of files that may be listed in your Download Manager. Selecting Mail Outgoing and turning it off causes your AOL software to not send any of the e-mail you may have sitting in your outgoing FlashMail box waiting to be delivered to AOL. Turning on the Mail Incoming item causes the AOL software to receive any e-mail you may have waiting the next time a FlashSession takes place.

Turning off Automatically Download Attached Files lets you decide when and if you want to download attached files. You have the ability, for five days after you read the e-mail, to download its attached files manually. Even easier, you can push the Forward icon on the e-mail form with the attachment and send it to yourself. Turn on the Automatically Download Attached Files option before the next connection, and the file will be downloaded at that time.

Okay, let's schedule your FlashSessions

Now that you've decided what you want to do during an AOL FlashSession, it's time to decide when you want to do it, and what screen names you want to run these sessions for. You've selected the FlashMail options in the previous section, and all that remains now is to set up the FlashSession schedule and enter the passwords for the screen names used during these sessions.

If the FlashSession window is not already open, select FlashSessions from the Mail menu. Click on the Schedule FlashSession icon and look at the new window (see fig. 5.9).

Fig. 5.9
Use the FlashSession scheduling window to tell AOL's software when you want it to run your automatic sessions.

Now all you need to do is follow these steps:

1 Tell the software at what hour you want to have it begin connecting automatically, using a 24-hour clock. For example, 18 means 6 p.m. local time.

2 Select the 30-minute period of that hour in which you want the connections to begin. You can select one of two different settings that are automatically 30 minutes apart. The actual minutes, 01 in this example, vary from user to user, so that not everyone's AOL software is trying to make automatic connections at the same time every hour.

3 Select the interval period between your online connections now. You set the period from a pop-up menu just below the Starting At time, and you may select every half hour, every hour, two hours, four hours, eight hours, or once per day.

4 Check the boxes to indicate what day or days of the week you want the FlashSessions to occur. (Fig. 5.9 shows all seven days.)

5 Select the screen name you want to use for FlashSessions. Check those names, and then review the form carefully.

6 Once you're satisfied with your settings, select the Starting At check box. This step actually enables the FlashSessions to begin automatically, according to the schedule you set. If this check box is not selected, no automated sessions take place, regardless of other settings in this window.

7 Click the OK button to close this window and to store the settings you made.

How to store your passwords

This feature allows you and your family members to enter and store passwords for your screen names. This is necessary so that you do not have to be present for scheduled FlashSessions. Otherwise, you have to enter your password manually each time before you log on to AOL. Remember that if you store your passwords, be sure that no unauthorized persons have access to your machine.

 *CAUTION* **When you save a stored password with your America Online** software, anyone who has access to your computer can log onto the service with your account, and use online time that will be charged to your monthly bill. Before using this option, be certain your computer is not easily accessible to others without your permission. You may want to consider, for example, using a security program to prevent unauthorized access to your computer.

To store your passwords:

1 Enter the FlashSessions window.

2 Click on the Enter Stored Passwords icon, and check the boxes in the FlashSessions column next to the screen names you set to connect during FlashSessions.

3 Enter your passwords in the fields next to the checked screen names. Notice as you enter your password that asterisks appear instead of the characters you type. This feature prevents others from looking over your shoulder and seeing your passwords on-screen.

4 Click the OK button to save your settings.

America Online's internal log-in calendar is now working and connects to the service at the times you scheduled. To turn off automatic connections, select the FlashSessions menu item, click on the Schedule FlashSessions icon, deselect the Starting At check box, and click OK.

Using instant messages for one-on-one meetings

Instant messages are used for two-way, immediate, private, person-to-person communication. It's the method that's closest to actually talking to someone online. To send an instant message while online, select Send Instant Message from the Members Menu. You see a new window in which to address and compose your message (see fig. 5.10).

Fig. 5.10
The sender's Instant Message window.

Instant Message		
Name:	AFL GeneS	
Hi, are you busy? Can I talk to you about a problem I'm having with System 7.5?		
Send		Available?

If you receive an instant message, respond to it by clicking on the Send button, entering your reply in the lower portion of the Instant Message window, and clicking on the Send button.

 **TIP** **You can press the Enter key on the numeric keypad, rather than** clicking the Send button, to send your instant message. You cannot use the Return key to send your message because this key starts a new line in your message text.

You can have a two-way conversation with any AOL member by leaving the Instant Message window open after you send a response. When a new message arrives from your friend, it appears in that window. (If your online sounds are turned on, the arrival of the message follows a pleasant musical tone.) The actual conversation appears in the upper text field, while the responses you type appear in the lower portion of the window. You can hold numerous instant message conversations simultaneously.

As with other types of text windows in AOL, you can print or save the Instant Message window's contents by selecting Print or Save from the File menu in your menu bar.

The elements of online forums

America Online's meeting places, called **forums,** are places where staff and members focus on a specific interest. There are more than a dozen forums, for example, in the Macintosh side of the Computing department (see Chapter 9). For a list of these forums, there is a Mac AOL Text Map in the Help Desk Software library for you to open, save, and read. Find that area by entering the keyword **Beginners** (see fig. 5.11).

Fig. 5.11
The America Online Macintosh Help Desk is a place where beginning AOL members can receive help for common questions about the service.

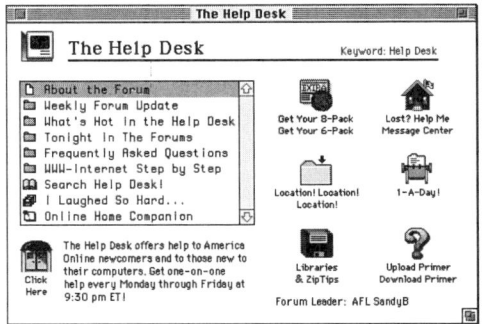

A few thoughts about instant messaging

Using instant messages is a simple and unobtrusive process. If you are typing in a different window at the moment an instant message arrives, for example, you can automatically send the incoming instant message behind the top window with your next keystroke, provided you turn off the option to bring instant messages to the front (in your AOL application preferences, as I described in Chapter 2).

If you choose to let instant messages come to the front in your AOL settings, just be careful. If that message comes through while you're closing another text window on AOL, you may close the instant message by mistake, and lose the message in the process because it can't be retrieved (unless you know who sent it and can ask him or her to send it again).

All the forums have their own chat rooms, software libraries, and message areas configured to focus on the special interests of that forum.

Where the action is: using forum message boards

The message areas are where members and AOL staff leave messages about the forum's field of interest. One advantage of message boards is that you are not constrained to communicating only with members who are online at the same time as you. When you leave a message, you can wait several minutes, hours, or even days before checking back to look for responses. In that sense, a message board isn't terribly different from an announcement you put up at a neighborhood community center.

 Plain English, please!

A **message board** is an online area that contains short statements in text form from members or AOL staff about a particular topic. A message may be a request for information and help, or an opinion about a hot issue that's under discussion. **99**

Over the next few pages, I'll describe how message boards are set up and the simple methods involved in posting messages in them. You'll find many of the steps are very much the same as writing up your e-mail message, except that you have to think of a wider audience when you put something in a message board.

Switching between computing platforms?

It is very common for personal computer users to have a Macintosh at home and a PC at work (or vice versa). In some work situations, both computing platforms are supported. Since America Online offers both Macintosh and Windows software, it's good to know that the Macintosh computing forums are available to users of the Windows version of AOL software and PC and Windows forums are available to Macintosh users. But the special artwork you find in a forum isn't generally shown if you enter that forum from a computing platform other than the one it covers.

For that reason, I've written a separate book for Windows AOL users: *Using America Online with Windows 95* (from Que Corporation), which describes the Windows-specific issues.

Before posting anything in the computing forums' message boards, you should learn about the forums and what their topics or subjects cover. To do this, you need to explore. Most forums have a Forum Update file you can read online to find out what is new. For an example, check out the Weekly Forum Update file in the Macintosh Communications Forum; the keyword is **MCM** (see fig. 5.12).

Fig. 5.12
The Macintosh Communications Forum is an area where you can get help in dealing with modems and general networking issues.

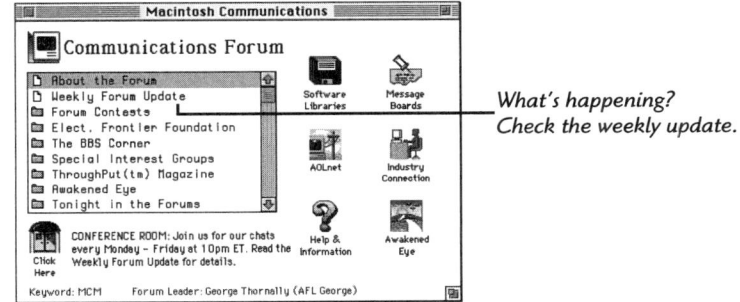

What's happening?
Check the weekly update.

Q&A *I want to leave a message in an AOL forum, but I don't know the difference between Post and Respond.*

Some of the message boards on America Online are **threaded** (organized by topic rather than by date). If you want to respond to an existing message, you click on the Post Response icon that is available on your screen when you access such an area. The Add Response icon indicates that you just want add a message without responding to a particular topic.

In AOL's regular message boards (which cover most of the service's message areas), to **post** means your message will be added to the ones already posted, in date order (and without regard to whether you're answering another message or not).

CAUTION **Before you respond to a message, read the other responses first.** It's possible that the message has already been answered, or your question has already been dealt with by another member. And don't type your message in ALL CAPS (like that!). It makes it difficult to read, and it's also the online equivalent of shouting (which isn't terribly polite).

How to find the forum messages that interest you

Once you've located a forum that covers topics you want to know about, focus on getting to the messages you want to read. First, click on the Message Boards icon, which brings up the window shown in figure 5.13, or one very similar to it. You see the general subject matter of the forum described briefly.

Fig. 5.13

This is a typical introductory message for a computing forum. Although the formats are similar from forum to forum, you'll find the content of the messages may differ substantially.

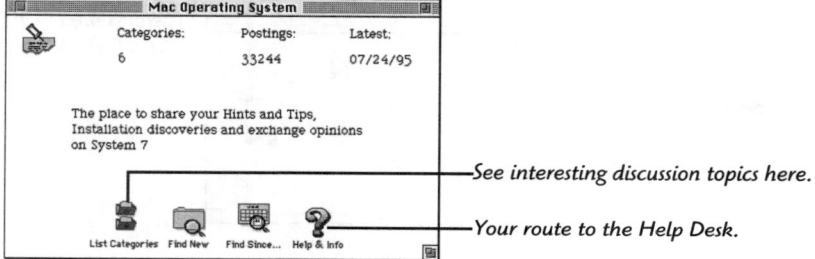

—See interesting discussion topics here.

—Your route to the Help Desk.

You have four icons at the bottom of the window, one of which takes you further along the road to finding messages you want to read. The Help & Info icon gets you to the Macintosh Help Desk. For now, let's click on the List Categories icon, which opens a list of discussion topics (see fig. 5.14).

Fig. 5.14

The forum messages shown here are divided into folders, each of which represents a topic.

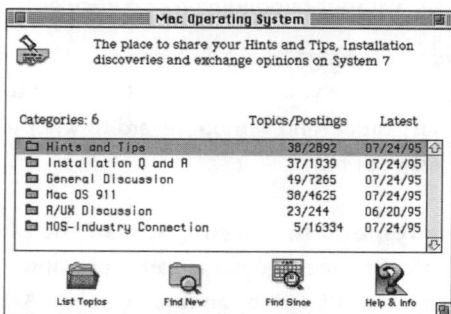

Each forum divides its message boards into a group of overall topics that relate to the forum's field of interest. If you're looking for a particular type of message, check here for the general category. To get to the next step in your message-reading process, click on the List Topics icon (see fig. 5.15).

Fig. 5.15
Here's a list of
discussion topics in a
typical computing-
oriented message
board.

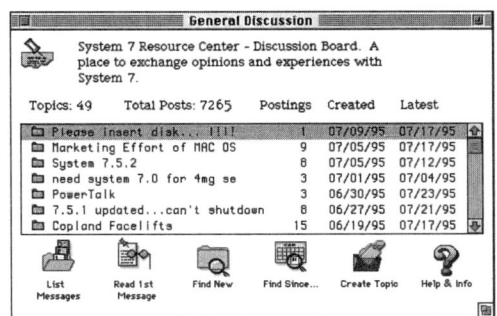

In most message boards, you have a Create Topic option that allows you to make your own folder, name it, and describe the subject matter. In the directory shown in the figure, you have a list of topics created by the forum staff and fellow AOL members. This list is your direct-entry point to a message on the topic you are interested in.

Now, about those other icons:

- **Find New.** This icon brings up a display of posted messages and the topics created since the last time you entered that forum (AOL's host computer keeps a record of your previous visit).

 **TIP** If you are visiting a forum for the first time, choosing this icon can produce literally dozens of topic folders and hundreds of messages. You may be better off using the next option.

- **Find Since.** This icon lets you set a limit for the amount of time spent searching for new messages. Its default is one day, but when you enter a forum for the first time, you might want to read all messages added in the previous 30 to 60 days, so that you can get a taste of the flavor of the forum and the kind of messages the board contains.

- **Read 1st Message.** When you open a directory of recent messages, you can highlight a folder's name and click on this icon to see the first new message in the folder.

 **TIP** After you open your first message, use the arrow keys on your keyboard to move to the next or previous message.

- **List New.** This choice brings up a directory showing the subject of each message. You can review this directory and decide which messages to read. Double-clicking on the message itself opens that message window.

- **List All.** This option displays all the messages posted in a specific topic or folder, regardless of how old they are.

How to post a message in a forum

Posting a message is like writing e-mail. You click on the Add Message icon (or Post Response in some forums), enter the subject in the first field, and insert your comment in the second field. By default, the subject of the message you were reading before you choose the Add Message button appears, preceded by the reference (Re:). You can, however, delete this subject and choose one of your own, if you are not responding to a previous message. After you write your message, click on the Post icon, and the message is added to the topic folder you were viewing. When your message is actually posted, your screen name and the time it was sent appear at the top of the message.

TIP **As with regular e-mail, it's considered good online etiquette to** sign the messages you post in a message board.

CAUTION **Posting a message more than once in a single forum is considered** bad online etiquette. Some AOL members may even get upset having to read the same message over and over again on billable time. When you have something to say, take a moment to choose the topic folder or directory that closely matches what you want to write about. In many forums, you can create your own topic to begin a discussion.

Message threading

If you are a frequent visitor to user group bulletin board systems or some of the other online services, you may be familiar with a feature called **message threading**. This technique lets you read all messages devoted to a one subject in a single group, rather than having them mixed in with other messages on other subjects.

When you post a message, you get the option to respond or reply to an individual message rather than just post a new one. Even where message threading is available, you'll want to post a message if you prefer to begin a new topic.

 Plain English, please!

> There's an important difference between responding and posting. When you **respond**, your message is added to the "thread," so other members will be able to read the original message and all the responses it brings in one group. If you **post** a message, it is simply added to the message folder or directory in chronological order, without regard to which message you're responding to. **"**

You'll find message threading available in America Online's Newsgroups area (keyword: **Newsgroups**). Since I will discuss Newsgroups in much more detail in Chapter 18, for now I'll just tell you that message threading is spreading to different message boards throughout America Online.

Chatting online

Online conferences, or **chats**, as they are more commonly called, are the most fun-filled activities you can experience online because they take place in real time.

Chats are live, interactive discussions. You and other members speak to each other by typing and sending text to a centralized display, the **chat room**. Each computing forum (and many areas in other departments) has its own chat room. People Connection also has a lot of rooms for people to chat about anything. You can even start a new room for any topic of your choosing, and have other members join you for discussion.

 **TIP**   **See Chapter 4 for more info on People Connection. Within the** chat window, you type text in the bottom part of the window and click on the Send button to send it into the upper, main portion of the chat window. (Don't choose Send until you are sure you want to send your text.)

Figure 5.16 shows a typical chat window.

Fig. 5.16
This forum chat
window shows an
online session already
in progress.

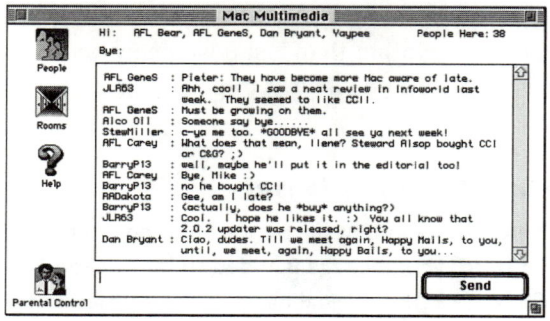

Some forums' chats are formalized, following chat protocol. This decreases the confusion that arises when you get 30 people trying to talk at once. When using **chat protocol**, if you have a question, raise your hand by sending a question mark (**?**) to the screen. The conference emcee recognizes you in order, and calls on you when it is your turn to speak. You can then send your question. Let the conference host know that you want to make a comment by sending an exclamation mark (**!**) for recognition.

To keep a text record of the chat, select Logs from the File menu. Here, you can open a chat log to record to a text file everything you see in the chat window. (I described the logging process in more detail in Chapter 2.)

The System log records all messages received by your computer while online, except instant messages and chat text. The other two logs handle those two categories.

6

From Movies to Online Games: Locating Entertainment Information on AOL

● **In this chapter:**

- **Find the latest news from the world of entertainment**

- **Become a critic right here on America Online**

- **What about online games?**

- **Visit forums devoted to sporting events**

This chapter introduces you to nifty online entertainment resources . . . .

The world of entertainment, in America Online's terms, covers everything from a television show to your daily horoscope. In this chapter, you explore such diverse topics as movies, television, music, games, sports, books, and more. You find out what America Online has to offer in those areas and how you can find it. Wherever your interests lie, America Online surely has a place where you can find the entertainment you seek.

Your first visit to the Entertainment forum

Regardless of what facet of the world of entertainment interests you—catching a movie, watching a soap opera, sitting down in front of a warm fireplace with a good book in your hands, or playing a video game—America Online can be your first and best resource for information.

Start your search for entertainment-related information in America Online's Entertainment forum. To access this area, type the keyword **Entertainment**. The directory window shows just a few of the areas you'll visit in this chapter (see figure 6.1). During your online visits, you discover many more locations that provide you not only with information but also with an opportunity to participate in discussions on a host of related subjects, and even to post your own book and movie reviews.

Fig. 6.1
The Entertainment department is America Online's gateway to the world of entertainment.

 **TIP** As explained in Chapter 2, you can save and print any text document you see on America Online by choosing Save or Print from the File menu.

Throughout this chapter, you'll learn about most of the places listed under Entertainment Features. New features are added regularly to America Online's resource roster, so you can expect this directory list to change.

 **TIP** Your quick shortcut to your favorite area is a keyword. Just press **Command+K**, enter the name of the area you want to visit (the keyword), and click OK. Then you're on your way. In this chapter, you'll find the keywords you need to find the features described.

You can survey the features of the Entertainment department in two ways. There's an alphabetical listing of the areas available on the directory at the right of the screen. On the left, there are six icons that will quickly transport you to one of your favorite areas. We'll cover some of these first.

 ## Using the What's Hot icon

This icon changes periodically to reflect the latest additions to the Entertainment department and to areas that are running special promotions or introducing new features. As this book was written, featured areas (shown in figure 6.2) included Center Stage, the area where famous entertainment figures attend online conferences; ABC Beta, from the ABC Network; the Extra TV program; Bugs Bunny; and Murder Mysteries Online.

Fig. 6.2
Just some of the forums featured in AOL's Entertainment department. This list is updated regularly.

Finding out about movies and television

For many people, the word *entertainment* produces such images as huge dinosaurs roaming the earth, spaceships racing between the stars battling evildoers of all shapes and sizes, or bold adventurers seeking fame and fortune in untamed, undiscovered lands in exotic portions of the world. Not surprisingly, these scenes describe many of the famous action movies that Hollywood has produced through the years.

 ## Using the Movies icon

At the left half of the Entertainment forum window is the Movies icon. It's your entranceway to news, views, and reviews about your favorite movies—past, present, and future. And you can learn something about your favorite stars, as well.

You also find the gateway to America Online's Critics' Choice forum, which is discussed in more detail later in this chapter. Figure 6.3 shows the TV Highlights area you can reach directly from Critics' Choice.

Q&A *How come I have to endure the download of new art work every time I visit a new online area? What's it doing to my online bill?*

America Online is a graphic-oriented online service; art work is needed to set off the special features and flavor of a particular department or forum. When you enter an online area for the first time, new art work is automatically downloaded to your computer. If the art work resources are extensive, sometimes you can opt out by not entering the area (and choosing the Cancel button instead). You'll have the option to cancel if art work resource is huge. When you revisit that area in the future, the art work update won't be repeated—unless further art work changes are needed.

If the new art work is on the opening screen you see when you log onto AOL, you'll experience the art work download when you first log on. Updates seldom take more than a few seconds to finish.

Yes, it's true that you pay a few pennies here and there for those art work updates. But this is the most economical way to provide this new art work to you (although some of it will be included in AOL's CD-ROMs, which will be distributed from time to time). If you truly want to block the art work, you can examine AOL's software libraries for a program known as Art Valve, which stops the art work download and substitutes generic AOL icons in their place. The program is not sanctioned by America Online, however, and you may find the look of the dull generic icons created when this program running is apt to become boring. You might just prefer to get those art work updates once again.

Fig. 6.3
Learn about upcoming movies and what the critics think of them in this online area.

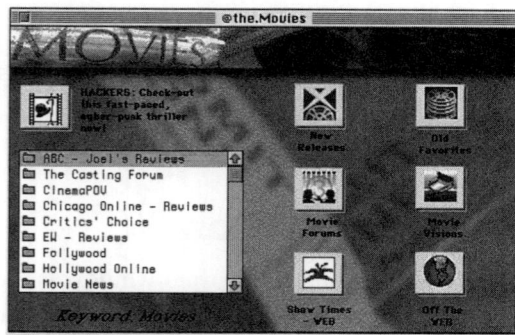

Visiting top Internet sites

Not all areas you access from America Online are actually the service's own features. America Online has an extensive selection of Internet-related services too. The places shown in the Top Internet Sites listing are part of the Internet's World Wide Web.

 Plain English, please!

The Internet is a world-wide computer network that is accessible by tens of millions of computers covering all computing platforms—from mainframe computers to Macs and PCs. America Online's Internet features and how to use them are described in Chapters 15–19.

 Plain English, please!

One of the fastest-growing Internet services is the **World Wide Web**. This Internet-based service combines text, pictures, and sounds in a fancy display you can access directly from America Online. You can travel from page to page simply by clicking on icons or underlined titles (known as **hyperlinks**).

 *What do I need to get on the World Wide Web from America Online?*

To take advantage of AOL's WWW features, you need the following:

- A color-capable Macintosh with a 68020 CPU or better with 8M or more RAM installed.

- America Online's World Wide Web browser software. This software is available from AOL's upgrade library (keyword: **Upgrade**), which you can download from an area free of online charges.

- A high-speed modem and a high-speed connection of 9600-bps speed or greater. The Web's graphical images take extra time to retrieve and display on your Mac. If you don't have high-speed access to AOL, you probably should avoid this feature for now.

The Top Internet Sites icon shown in many AOL departments and forums (see figure 6.4) is your direct link to World Wide Web features that relate to a specific online area.

Fig. 6.4
Just a sampling of the World Wide Web resources you can reach directly from AOL's Entertainment department. This list will change from time to time, so it may not look exactly as shown here.

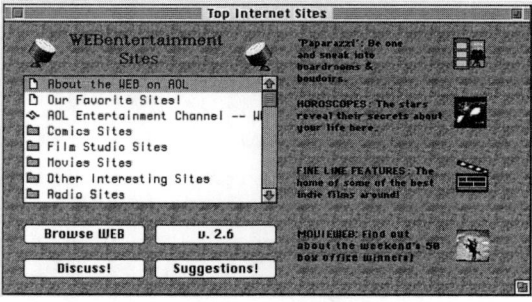

When you click one of the Web sites shown in the directory display (or the icon listing at the right of the screen), you are transported directly to the WWW resource you selected. If AOL's browser software is not running, the program launches before the site is accessed.

Let's fly through MusicSpace

The MusicSpace forum combines AOL's own music-related forums and major sites on the World Wide Web into a colorful, fun-filled, exciting area. From the beautiful art work (see figure 6.5) to the extensive list of resources, you can spend hour upon hour in this area and cover but a small portion of the features available.

Fig. 6.5
AOL's MusicSpace area is a huge repository of music-related information.

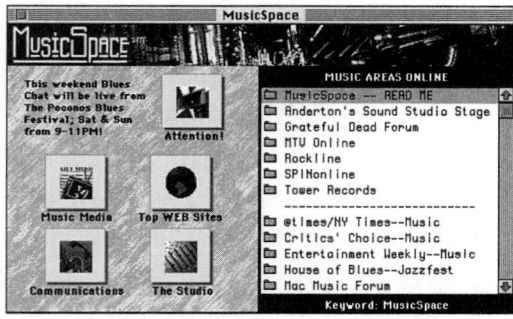

In addition to learning about new recordings from your favorite stars, you'll be able to order your favorite recordings courtesy of Tower Records, the nationwide recorded music chain. Just click the Tower Records listing in the Music Areas Online directory, and you can review a selection of the latest releases or search out older favorites.

Finding movie and television information

Whether it's your favorite flick or a popular TV network, you can access information about it in AOL's Entertainment department. Let's explore it further.

Reading ShowBiz News & Info

The popularity of entertainment news programs on broadcast and cable TV networks and newsstand magazines means we all have an insatiable hunger for news about show business. When you click the ShowBiz News & Info icon in AOL's Entertainment department (see figure 6.6), you're presented with a large resource of such information.

Fig. 6.6
From newsstand magazines to entertainment-related TV programs, you'll find the information you want on AOL.

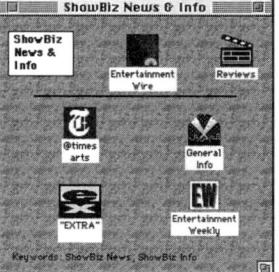

A look beneath the Television & Radio icon

The Television & Radio icon at the bottom of the Entertainment department screen provides the same sort of information about some of your favorite television shows. Before you decide what you want to watch or tape, America Online gives you a chance to preview what's coming up on the tube.

When you click this icon, you see a directory that offers you several forums devoted specifically to radio and television. Let's look into the one labeled Networks first. From the Networks icon, you can choose online forums for such diverse services as the ABC Online (see figure 6.7), the CBS Network's site on the World Wide Web, AOL's Radio forums, and additional forums related to other broadcast and cable TV networks. From the Shows icon, you can access information about popular programs. MTV Online gets a special, highly stylized, online forum (see figure 6.8).

Fig. 6.7
ABC Online offers a separate double-clickable icon as a gateway to each programming feature.

Fig. 6.8
MTV Online tells you all about the network's programming schedule and features chats with some of your favorite music stars.

And that's not all...

Still more online resources with an entertainment slant are available from the Entertainment department's directory window at the right. Some of the areas shown, such as the one devoted to the movie *Batman Forever*, appear only to support a specific movie or program and will be withdrawn when that production is out of circulation. Others, while ever-changing in appearance and organization, are more-or-less permanent fixtures on AOL. Following is an overview of some of these resources.

Accessing Hollywood Online

Keyword: **Hollywood**

At any one time, literally dozens of current motion pictures might be playing at your local theaters. New flicks are released weekly. During the summer and Christmas seasons, scores of pictures vie for your attention and your ticket dollars. What to do?

You can use America Online's Hollywood Online forum (see figure 6.9) to learn about these films before they are released.

Fig. 6.9
Hollywood Online is Tinseltown's own forum on America Online.

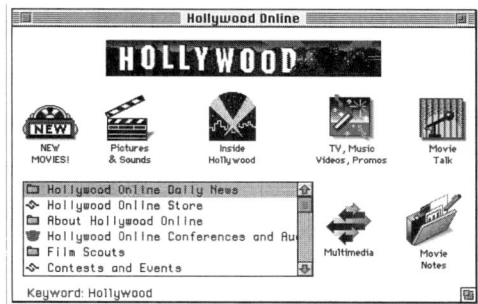

Finding music information

Keyword: **Music**

If you dig rock 'n' roll music or if you prefer country, classical, or jazz, you will appreciate America Online's music-related forums. They are your resources for information and online discussion about your favorite performers. The keyword **Music** (or the Music icon in the Entertainment department window) is just a gateway. It's a stopping-off point where you can visit the special online areas that cater to music lovers of all persuasions.

Accessing the RockNet forum

Keyword: **RockNet**

When I was a kid, it was just plain old rock 'n' roll. But this musical form represents many tastes and styles. So now you see references to Classic Rock, which emphasizes the music that was popular in the late 1960s and early 1970s (such as the Beatles and the Rolling Stones), and Alternative Rock, which represents performers at the cutting edge of musical development (such as Aphex Twin and Nine Inch Nails).

No matter what sort of rock 'n' roll music you prefer, you can read about it in the RockNet forum on America Online (see figure 6.10). You can share your feelings about your favorite bands here or just read reviews and gossip about them.

Fig. 6.10
RockNet is your source for the latest news and views on rock 'n' roll.

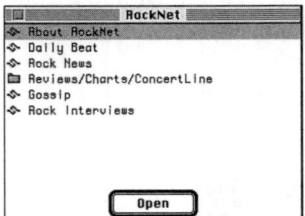

Accessing the Grateful Dead Forum

Keyword: **Grateful Dead**

Until bandleader Jerry Garcia's death at the age of 53, the Grateful Dead had the distinction of being one of the longest-surviving rock n' roll bands. Their concerts were sellouts, so they've set up their own special area on America Online for the Deadheads among you to visit, read about the band's musical legacy and influence on our pop culture, and even share messages with other fans (see figure 6.11). The Winterland: Dead Chat room is just what it says: a place where you can have online chats with other members of the online community.

Fig. 6.11
Even the Grateful Dead have their own special place on America Online.

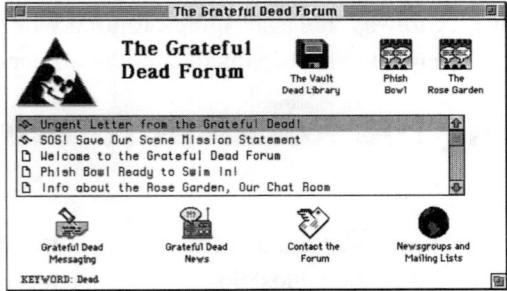

Exploring Warner/Reprise Records Online

Keyword: **Warner**

Warner/Reprise Records spans generations of music lovers. This forum covers the entire Warner/Reprise artist roster (see figure 6.12).

Fig. 6.12
This screen appears when you visit the Warner/Reprise Records forum on America Online.

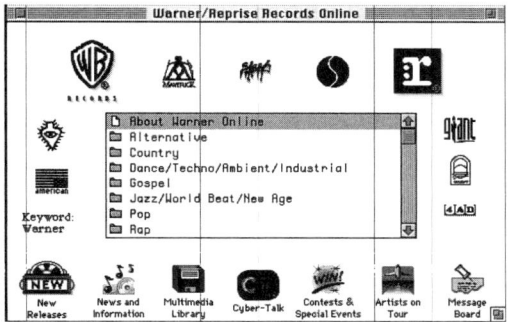

Be your own online critic

Keyword: **Critics**

Before many people buy a book, see a movie, or even rent a videotape, they want to know what the reviewers have to say about it. America Online's Critics' Choice area (see figure 6.13) is a compendium of thousands of reviews and discussions about the entire spectrum of the world of entertainment.

Fig. 6.13
The Critics' Choice area is where you can read what the critics say and where you can become one yourself (if it suits you).

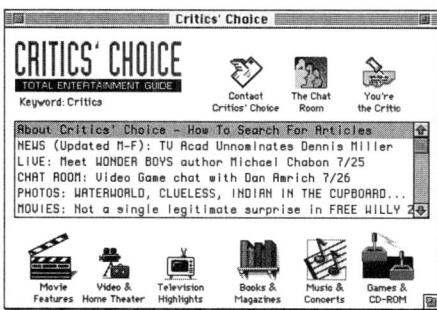

Checking out Games' online resources

Still another icon on the Entertainment department window is Games, and it represents, among other things, one of the most popular categories of software sales. A computer game enables you to turn your Mac into an outer-space battleground, a deep, dark dungeon, or even a maze. You can pit yourself against evil creatures and machines or even human players in a quest to right wrongs, locate a secret castle, or save the world from destruction.

Accessing the Macintosh Games forum

Keyword: **MGM**

The Macintosh and PC computing forums are discussed in Chapter 9, but the games forums deserve a special place here, because they are a special resource that any fan of computer games will want to visit often. Figure 6.14 shows the Games Forum screen.

Fig. 6.14
The Games Forum screen lets you find places to talk a good game.

Accessing the Online Gaming Forums

Keyword: **Gaming**

Whether you are interested in a casual game of checkers or are involved in a heavy-duty game of strategy, America Online's Online Gaming Forums area is a place you surely want to learn about and visit often.

As you can see from the forum's main directory window in figure 6.15, this forum serves as an entranceway to a number of areas that deal with gaming.

Fig. 6.15
The Online Gaming Forums screen is your first stop for information on all sorts of games.

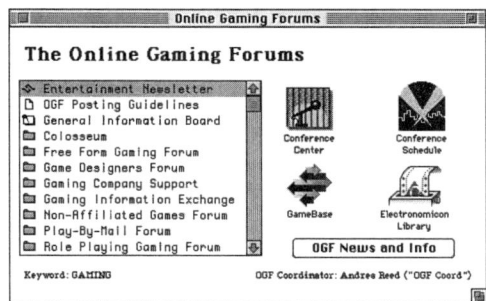

Entering the Conference Center

The Online Gaming Forum holds regular conferences. Along with online members and forum staff, you can attend these conferences to participate in chats, and attend debates and panel discussions featuring experts on the subject. To enter the conference center, click the Conference Center icon in the Online Gaming Forums main window. The screen shown in figure 6.16 appears.

Fig. 6.16
Regular conferences are held for gaming enthusiasts.

Joining the Federation

Keyword: **Federation**

In addition to learning more about your games, you can actually get in on the action with AOL's online role-playing games. These let you become a character in a far-flung fantasy you share with other members. The Federation (see figure 6.17) is an adult space fantasy where you gain points through economics and politics instead of slaying monsters or destroying enemy spacecraft.

Fig. 6.17
The Federation interactive online game lets you explore far-flung worlds in search of power and wealth. You play by entering text into a window that looks much like a chat-room window.

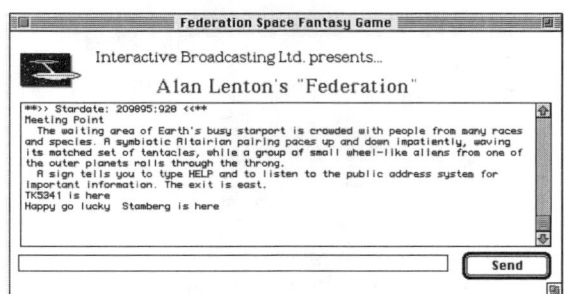

News from the world of sports

Keyword: **Sports**

If you played Little League sports when you were a child, have children interested in sporting activities, watch sports events regularly on television, or have been known to attend a game or two, you might want to visit America Online's virtual sports page frequently. To do so, choose Sports from AOL's Main Menu window to display the Sports department screen shown in figure 6.18.

Fig. 6.18
Whatever your favorite sports activity, you'll find information about it on America Online.

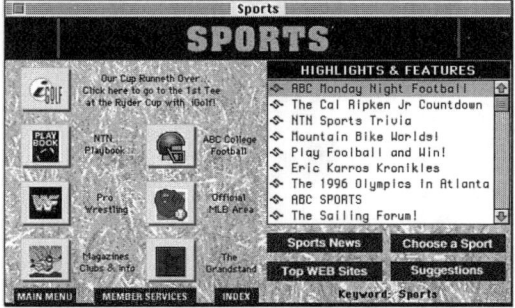

The major sports are listed in the directory window at the right of the screen. You can check the latest news from the world of sports by clicking the Sports icon. DataTimes Sports Reports, at the bottom left, is another major sports news resource. To the right of this icon is an icon that represents the most popular sport of the current season; it was football at the time this chapter was written. And then there's The Grandstand, which is shown in figure 6.19.

Fig. 6.19
Take your seat in The
Grandstand to enjoy
your favorite sport.

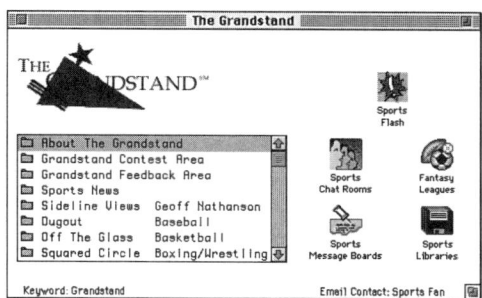

Sitting in the sports Grandstand

Keyword: **Grandstand**

The Grandstand is where all you sports lovers can find the latest news about your favorite games, learn how your favorite teams fared the night before, and participate in online conferences with other fans. It is the entrance to America Online's sports stadium.

Highlights of The Grandstand include message boards and chat rooms where you can discuss your favorite sports. The Fantasy Leagues are the best feature of all; there you can play your favorite games in cyberspace. It's all make-believe; you can have a wrestling match without breaking a sweat, and participate in an auto race without ever having to drive a car around a track.

Online book information

Keyword: **Books**

Whether you prefer fiction or nonfiction, you should check the Book Bestsellers first to see how your favorite author's works are faring in the marketplace. Choose Book Bestsellers from the main Entertainment Forum window to display the Book Bestsellers screen shown in figure 6.20. From there you can find out more about this area of America Online, check out the bestseller lists, and see what's soon to be released. Your Book Reviews is the place to post your own book reviews and read about the choices of other members of the online community.

Fig. 6.20
Book Bestsellers
provides the latest
information about
best-selling books and
upcoming works.

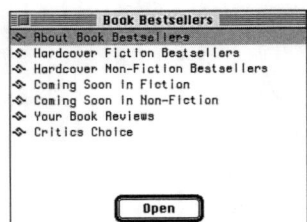

The Secrets of Safe, Online Fun for Kids of All Ages

● **In this chapter:**

- **Kids can play online games**

- **All about special conferences for young people**

- **Access the special kids-only areas of America Online**

- **Online areas devoted to parents and child care**

- **Introducing your kids to the Internet**

America Online isn't just a playground for adults. Kids can join in, too. But before your kids dive in head first, you will want to review some useful information . . . . ⊘

America Online, as you've seen so far, is basically a warm, friendly place that you might think of as your hometown in cyberspace. But, like in your hometown, there are some folks who don't always think about common sense and courtesy toward others. And when you, as a parent, allow your kids to enter the online universe, you want to be sure their visits are always friendly, fun, and educational.

Make sure your online visits are nothing but enjoyable

The online experience should be friendly and fun, and it's just that for most AOL members. As with other parts of our society, however, there are a few people who don't have the best interests of you and your child in mind. The first part of this chapter outlines the methods to help protect your child. You'll want to read them and discuss them with your children before they begin to explore AOL's online community.

Although problems seldom occur, here are a few things you and your child should watch out for during your travels on AOL:

- **Inappropriate material.** As explained later in this chapter, nude or explicit photos and related text material are not allowed on AOL. That does not stop some people from exchanging such files, however. You should instruct your child to bring information about such files directly to your attention, so that the proper authorities at America Online can be informed about it.

- **Face-to-face meetings.** You should instruct your child never to give out personal information, such as your home address or telephone number, to another AOL member (however friendly that member may seem) without your approval. Personal meetings between your child and another AOL member should be done under your supervision at a public location.

- **Online harassment.** If your child receives instant messages or e-mail that is threatening or intimidating, or if they contain objectionable content, have your child bring the material directly to your attention so that you can file a complaint against the member who sends such material.

- **Internet access.** The Internet is largely unregulated and is not subject to Parental Controls or America Online's Terms of Service. As a result, you'll want to instruct your child carefully about both the benefits and the potential downsides of Internet access before your child begins to explore that area.

In the next few pages, you'll learn how to set restrictions upon areas your child may visit and how to deal with problems if they occur.

Set Parental Controls to protect your child

Keyword: **Parental Controls**

As a concerned parent, you may want to restrict the access of your child to certain areas of America Online. That's the purpose of Parental Chat Controls. This feature permits the original account holder (the screen name created when you first established your AOL account) to block or restrict access by users of other screen names on your AOL account from certain areas and features on America Online (see fig. 7.1). Setting these limits can help protect your child against possible exposure to objectionable material and possible online harassment in some areas of the service.

Fig. 7.1
The Parental Controls center lets you set limits on your child's access to AOL forums and the Internet.

In order to activate Parental Controls, you must be logged on with your master account name (the name that's listed first among your list of available accounts in the main window of your AOL software).

CAUTION **Your account password and billing information should be** considered confidential. You'll never be asked by an AOL employee online to give out this information. If you ever receive such a request, report it to AOL's Terms of Service area immediately (keyword: **TOS**).

You can establish controls for just one or all screen names on your account. After Parental Control is set for a particular screen name, it's enforced every time that screen name logs on. The master account holder can make changes to Parental Control settings at any time.

While you're logged on with your master screen name, you can activate one or more Parental Control features. Just click on the Chat Controls button from the main window of the Parental Controls center. Here are the options you'll want to consider:

- **Block Instant Messages.** Turns off Instant Messages, which are the immediate, one-to-one communications that can only be viewed by the sender and receiver of the message.

- **Block All Rooms.** Blocks access to the People Connection. The People Connection is the live, interactive chat area of America Online; it doesn't include the chat rooms in the Computing area.

- **Block Member Rooms.** Blocks access only to the member-created rooms within the People Connection. Other People Connection rooms, such as the Lobby, Romance Connection, and so on, are still accessible when this Parental Control feature is activated.

- **Block Conference Rooms.** Blocks access to the more focused rooms found around various departments on America Online, such as the classrooms in Learning & Reference, the technical forums in Computing & Software, and the NeverWinter Nights role-playing game in Games & Entertainment. It does not affect access to rooms in the People Connection.

CAUTION **If your child commits repeated violations against AOL's Terms of** Service, your account may be closed without notice. You will have to make telephone contact with the customer service department to restore the account. You should monitor your child's activities carefully.

Protect your kids when they explore the Internet

The Internet is a huge, multifaceted, exciting, but largely unregulated place. A whole section of this book—Part V, "Getting on the Information Superhighway"—is devoted to Internet issues. This section briefly discusses common parental concerns about children making online visits.

The important thing to realize is that the Internet is not a single large online service, but a huge number of smaller networks linked by computers, modems, and telephone lines. When you visit America Online's Internet Connection (keyword: **Internet**), shown in figure 7.2, you are, in effect, leaving the service and visiting places where America Online's Terms of Service simply do not apply. Of course, this doesn't mean that you and your child can behave any differently than when you visit one of America Online's regular areas. Your conduct reflects on the service, and violating the Terms of Service during an Internet visit on AOL is the same as violating those terms in the regular areas on AOL.

Fig. 7.2
America Online's popular Internet Connection lets you explore a vast world of fascinating information.

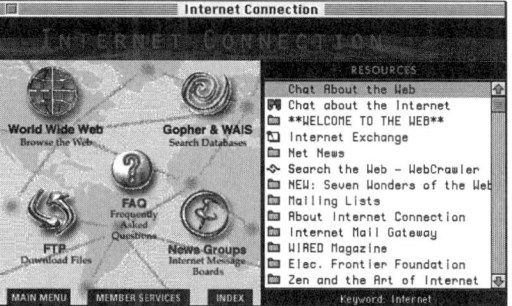

But visiting those Internet areas means that you and your child will encounter areas where the rules and regulations of this service do not necessarily apply, and where others might act in ways you don't approve of. One example is the Internet areas devoted to sexually explicit material. In addition, it is not uncommon to find material in Internet mailing lists or newsgroups that contains language you might consider offensive. What to do?

Here are a few common-sense ideas:

- Before your child enters the Internet area, set limits on the kind of material your child is allowed to see.

- Review Internet e-mail newsgroups, mailing lists, and other information before your child is allowed to participate in them.

- Although your child is entitled to some measure of privacy, stay in touch with your child's online activities. Take the time to be with your child during online sessions—not just to monitor his activities, but also to share online experiences with him or her.

Set Parental Controls for maximum safety

Despite the precautions I've just outlined, you may decide it's better for your child not to have access to certain Internet-based features. So, AOL has established a set of Parental Controls for this area too, activated in much the same way as the regular Parental Controls described earlier in this chapter.

There are two ways to activate these controls. The first is simply to click on the News Groups button when you visit AOL's Parental Controls center (shown in fig. 7.1). Or, if you've already opened AOL's Newsgroups window, click the Parental Controls button at the keyword: **Newsgroups** (see fig. 7.3).

 **TIP** **As with AOL's regular Parental Controls, you can't activate the** ones in the Newsgroups area unless you have logged on using your master AOL account.

Fig. 7.3
AOL's Newsgroups window has an option for setting Parental Controls.

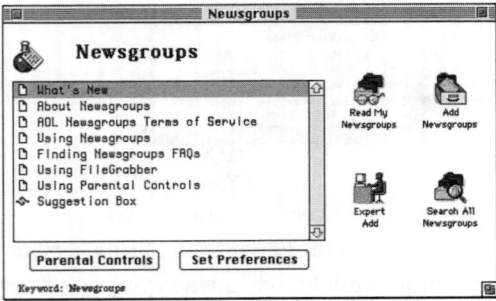

Select the person for whom you want to establish Parental Controls (by clicking the radio button next to his or her screen name), and then click the Edit button (see fig. 7.4). You'll see the dialog box shown in figure 7.5.

Fig. 7.4

Choose the account name for which you want to edit Parental Controls.

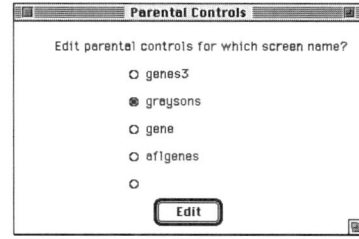

Fig. 7.5

These choices are available via Internet Parental Controls.

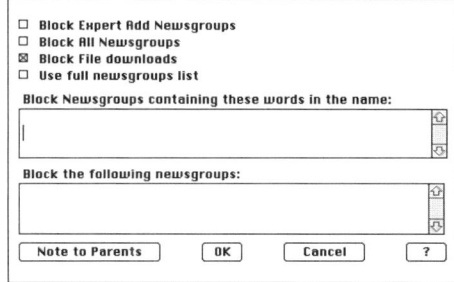

You can click the options shown in the preceding figure to control access of other members on your account to specific Internet Newsgroup features. Each option can apply to any screen name you select. Here's the run down:

- **Block Expert Add.** Use this feature to prevent someone from adding newsgroups that are not part of AOL's standard listing.

- **Block All Newsgroups.** For the ultimate level of protection, you may choose this option so your child has no access whatsoever to this feature.

- **Block File Download.** Use this feature to prevent a member from downloading encoded files in an Internet Newsgroup. Such files are a possible source of objectionable graphic files.

- **Use full newsgroups list.** Select this option for the full list of Newsgroups. This feature affords full access to all newsgroups, but you can selectively change their availability by selecting one or both of the next two items.

- **Block Newsgroups containing these words in the name.** You can use this feature to specify certain words, such as those pertaining to sex or erotica, that may represent newsgroups that offer material that's not suitable for your child.

- **Block the following newsgroups.** You can use this feature to specify the names of the newsgroups you want to block for a specific AOL screen name.

- **Note to Parents.** Click this button to get an overview of Internet Newsgroups and learn the best ways to participate in this exciting Internet feature.

By using one or more of these Parental Controls, you can allow your child limited access to the Internet within the guidelines you set, and you can help provide a safe online experience. Remember, though, that these changes can only be made when you're logged on using your master account name (the first screen name shown when you click the pop-up list of names in your AOL Mac software).

TIP   **Before you introduce your child to the online world, it might be** helpful to provide a brief instruction session on creating an America Online screen name, logging on, and maneuvering around the service. It is a good idea to go over basic computer troubleshooting tips as well, in case your computer crashes in your absence—something that's apt to happen with any personal computer. There's a detailed tutorial on using America Online's software in Chapter 2.

Q&A   *Why is my account already signed on?*

Even if you have the full slate of five screen names on your account, you can only use one of those names at a time. So if your child is using another screen name and you want to log on, you'll have to ask your child to log off first. If you want to be able to use America Online at the same time as your family members, you may want to consider setting up an extra account.

Just one more thing: If you get accidentally disconnected from America Online (perhaps because of trouble on the phone line), AOL's host computer may take a minute or two to get the hint. You'll get a message that your account is logged on, even though it's not. If that happens to you, just wait a few minutes and try again.

Find fun for kids of all ages

Keyword: **Kids**

America Online offers a variety of online activities where your kids can enjoy a number of entertaining and educational activities. You'll find discussions of some of them in the remainder of this chapter. Our first stopping point is AOL's Kids Only department, shown in figure 7.6. Not only can kids have fun, they also learn a few things and become more adept at working with a computer.

Fig. 7.6
Kids Only is a special place for children to participate in activities right on America Online.

Many of the areas discussed so far in this book have special kids-only departments as well—areas developed strictly for young people. The Kids Only department window in figure 7.9 shows just a few of the areas available, all specially designed for kids ages 5 through 14.

As with all America Online sessions, you should teach your children how to conduct themselves online. Discuss with them the basics of using America Online software, such as navigating through the network, reading and posting messages, and participating in online conferences. Your child should know how to act responsibly online and refrain from the use of vulgar language. In addition, you should establish limits as to the amount of time your children spend online because you are responsible for any charges they run up during their visits.

The next section covers some of the forums on America Online that are just for kids.

Internet sites for kids, too

Just like other areas of America Online, AOL has set aside a selection of Internet sites that cater to a particular interest. Just click the Top Internet Sites icon in the Kids Only area (see fig. 7.7), and you'll see a specially selected range of sites on the Internet's World Wide Web that will provide hours of fun and education for your child.

Fig. 7.7
Just some of the World Wide Web pages that are available through direct access via AOL's Kids Only area.

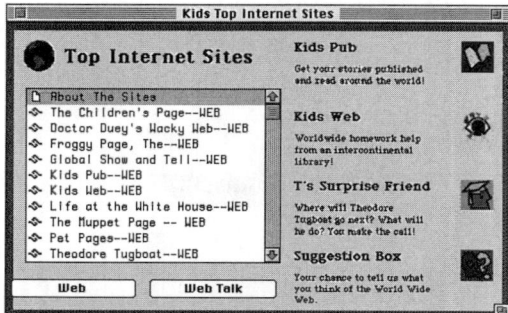

Explore *Disney Adventures* magazine

Keyword: **Disney**

Every month, *Disney Adventures* brings exciting stories to your children (see fig. 7.8). America Online is the place for your child to read about those many adventures and learn more about the world. The magazine even offers online conferences such as D.A. Live (which takes place in the forum's Odeon Auditorium), where your child can meet other kids with similar interests and enjoy an online chat.

Fig. 7.8
Disney Adventures magazine is a special resource for your child on America Online.

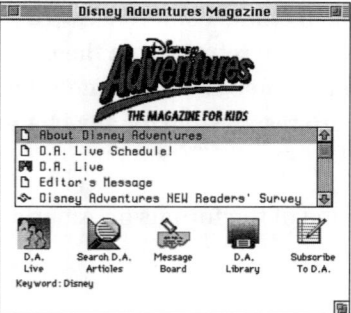

Access the Cartoon Network

Keyword: **Cartoon Network**

One of the exciting aspects of cable television is the availability of programs devoted to just one subject or one category of entertainment. Chapter 6 describes a number of the popular networks of this type that are represented on AOL. This section is devoted to the Cartoon Network forum (see fig. 7.9). Cartoon entertainment appeals to people of all ages, from children to adults. America Online has a special library of cartoon art in GIF (Graphic Interchange Format) format. See Chapters 3 and 5 for further information.

Fig. 7.9
America Online didn't forget cartoons.

Read *Tomorrow's Morning*

Keyword: **Tomorrow's Morning forum**

The folks who run the *Tomorrow's Morning* forum on AOL call it America's coolest (and only weekly home delivery) newspaper written and designed just for kids (see fig. 7.10). Your child has probably received an offer to subscribe at school. Highlights of each edition are available online, and there are additional areas worth exploring too.

Fig. 7.10
Read *Tomorrow's Morning*, the popular weekly newspaper for kids.

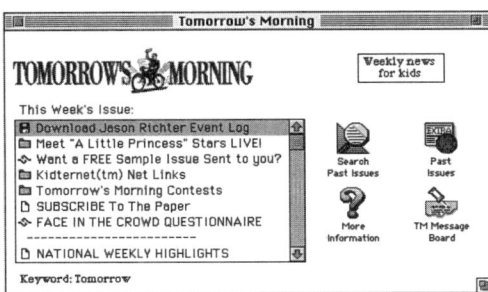

Online games

The last chapter introduced you to the various online gaming forums and told you how to search for the secrets of your favorite computer games. This chapter concentrates on games designed strictly for online visitors in the 5 to 14 age group. To reach this resource, choose Games & Computers from the Kids Only department window, and then click the Online Games icon.

You'll find a number of fascinating games. There's a choice of trivia games, puzzles, and other fun-filled activities, and sometimes prizes are awarded to those getting the top scores. The list changes frequently, so rather than list them here, I suggest that you read the ground rules before you plunge in. Then sit back and enjoy.

 *CAUTION* **Online games can run very fast, and they're exciting for young people to play, but that doesn't mean the rules of good online conduct are forsaken. If too many online participants disrupt the contest, the host may decide not to award any prizes. So please urge your child to behave properly during the contest.**

Special Kids Only conferences online

Among the most popular online activities are chatting, interacting with other AOL members, and attending an online conference (where you can sometimes meet a famous personality and ask questions). AOL's Kids Chat (see fig. 7.11) is the youthful equivalent of the popular People's Connection area and is designed strictly for members ages 5 to 14. It is carefully monitored by an enthusiastic band of online staffers, whom you'll recognize by the KO in front of their screen names.

Fig. 7.11
Participate in special youth-oriented chats on AOL.

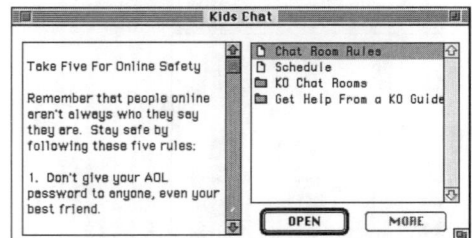

Chat Room rules

Before your youngster attends a Kids Connection event, it's a good idea to discuss the guidelines with your child. And you should attend a chat or two yourself to get a feeling for how they're conducted. As with any chat room or auditorium on AOL, the Terms of Service apply, so you'll want to review those terms (via keyword: **TOS**) that cover the common-sense guidelines for online conduct. The Chat Room Rules listing in the directory window of the Kids Connection area also summarizes some of these simple requirements.

The most important thing to consider, of course, is respect for other online members. Everyone should be treated equally and given equal opportunity to participate in an online session, free of interruptions. Someone else's misbehavior is not an invitation for others to disturb the chat as well. Each conference is monitored by a staff of online hosts who try to make sure the rules of proper online conduct are observed.

 **TIP** **If your online session is interrupted for any reason, just log on** again. Usually, you'll be able to reconnect the second time without further trouble.

Ready to chat?

There are several conference halls in the Kids Chat area: Each posts a schedule of regular chats, so consult the Calendar listings before you enter the chat room of your choice. And if you miss a really important chat, don't despair. There's also a library where you can download logs of previous chats. You'll find those logs useful when two or more interesting chats are being held at the very same time.

 **TIP** **You can make your own chat log. Simply choose Logs from the** File menu and select the appropriate option to start recording your log.

Now, some special forums for parents

It's a complex world, which makes the problem of bringing up children more and more difficult. America Online has set up several areas in which parents can learn more about coping with the problems of daily living and how to deal with the problems and concerns of their children.

Visit the Parents' Information Network

Keyword: **Parents**

America Online's Parents' Information Network is a fully integrated collection of online services dedicated to parental interests and concerns (see fig. 7.12). There are a number of special areas you'll want to consult from time to time in this forum.

Fig. 7.12
A visit to the Parents' Information Network on AOL.

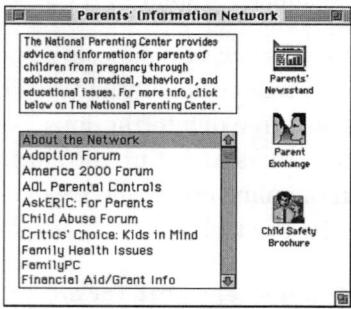

One icon deserves a special mention. Click the Child Safety Brochure icon and a colorful photo and a short, informative booklet providing helpful advice for your child's visits along the Information Superhighway appears (see fig. 7.13).

Fig. 7.13
A brochure about child safety online.

You'll want to review this material carefully; it summarizes many of the concerns parents should have about their child's participation in an online service. The entire text of this booklet can be saved or printed simply by choosing the appropriate commands from the File menu.

CAUTION **Most of the photos you see online are in full color. To view them** that way, you need a computer that not only supports color, but also a color monitor to view the photo on.

Take advantage of The National Parenting Center

Keyword: **TNPC**

AOL's National Parenting Center forum is designed to provide parents with useful information to make their jobs easier (see fig. 7.14). The center was founded in 1989, and the online area provides a large library of helpful information that deals with common problems and concerns of modern parenting.

Fig. 7.14
This forum offers comprehensive advice for parents.

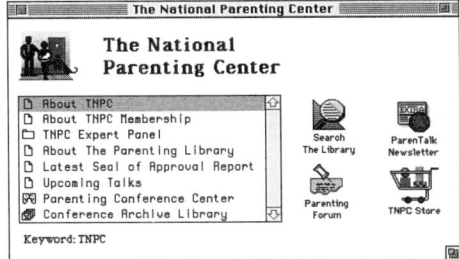

After reading about the activities of the National Parenting Center, you may want to consider becoming a member. Full membership information is provided in this online support area; AOL members are offered a special membership rate.

From Baby Boomers to Science Fiction: Online Lifestyle and Interest Forums

● In this chapter:

- **The latest information on health–care issues**

- **Find out about things to do in various areas of the country**

- **Interact with other members on hobbies ranging from cooking to science fiction**

- **Discuss the important issues of the day**

From roaming the stars to exploring new developments in health care, whatever hobbies or special interests intrigue you, America Online probably has a place for it . . . . ➤

You can explore the world-wide Internet, upgrade the sound of your stereo, research your family history, and debate with other America Online members on subjects ranging from the top news of the day to whether your Macintosh or a PC is the better computer (and I'm sure what your answer will be). It can all happen in the various lifestyle forums on America Online.

Figure 8.1 shows the Clubs & Interests main window, which you can find by typing the keyword **Clubs**. As you can see, the features you can reach from this point are numerous, diverse, and intriguing.

Fig. 8.1
The Clubs & Interests department on America Online leads you to a diverse group of features. (The artwork you see will change often as new areas are added or changed.)

When I sat down to write this chapter, I spent many, many hours exploring all the areas on America Online that cater to lifestyles, hobbies, and special interests (some of these places were also discussed in Chapter 6). You learn more in this chapter and then finish the little tour in Chapter 12.

My survey proved to be never-ending. For this reason, this chapter just touches on the highlights of America Online's Lifestyle areas, and the rest is left for you to explore at your leisure.

To make it easier to find an area that caters to a specific interest, all of the forums in this area of America Online are grouped by category, as represented by the icons at the left of the Clubs & Interests screen. Let's explore the highlights.

Top Internet Sites

As with other departments on America Online, the Clubs & Interests department has hot links to the World Wide Web, which you can begin to explore simply by clicking on the Top Internet Sites icon (see fig. 8.2).

Fig. 8.2
If a special interest area isn't on AOL, you're likely to find it surfing the World Wide Web. The list you see here will change often.

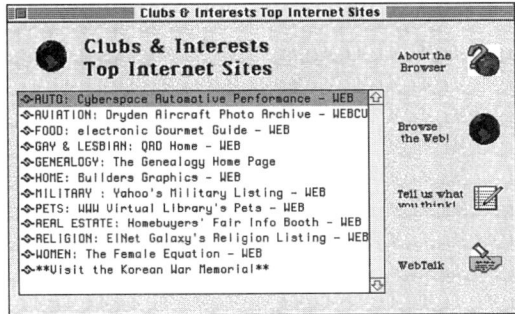

As you can see from the list in fig. 8.2, the forums you visit on America Online are but a portion of the fascinating places you can explore during your online visit. Using AOL's World Wide Web browser software, you can take off and fly across the world in search of other sources of fascinating information.

Forums devoted to special interests

You'll find many online forums that cater to special interests. Here are a few of the more popular areas.

Baby Boomers

Keyword: **Baby Boomers**

The focus on this forum is strictly interaction. You can share your experiences on a host of subjects with others who were born in the same frenetic generation.

Plain English, please!

Baby Boomer refers to the huge generation born after World War II, right up through the 1960s. People who were born during this time share a unique range of experiences, ranging from the advent of television to the Korean War, Vietnam, the Kennedy assassination, and more pleasant things such as Elvis Presley and the Beatles.

National Multiple Sclerosis Society Forum

Keyword: **NMSS**

The National Multiple Sclerosis Society has set up this forum on America Online to provide information about the disease, including updates on medical research into finding a cure. You also can find a message center, and health and medical chat rooms where you can interact with other members, including health-care professionals.

Religion & Ethics Forum

Keyword: **Religion**

The Religion & Ethics Forum doesn't favor a particular religion or belief system. It has message boards devoted to many faiths, including New Age philosophies. In the Religion & Ethics Message Center, you can debate with other online members.

SeniorNet Online

Keyword: **SeniorNet**

SeniorNet Online should demonstrate to everyone that reaching one's senior years is often when life truly begins. In a special Computer Learning Center, you can learn how to master your computer. SeniorNet Online also includes active message areas, a Community Center, where you can interact with other online members and forum staff, and a wealth of information you can read and download.

Hobbies and clubs online

Whether your interest is recreational or professional, America Online has a hobby or club forum for you. Let's visit a few of them.

Astronomy Club

Keyword: **Astronomy**

America Online's Astronomy Club is also known as Astronomy Forum (see fig. 8.3). It is hosted by a real astronomer, Mr. Astro, better known as Stuart Goldman, who is an associate editor at *Star & Telescope* magazine. If you want to learn more about the stars and planets, explore the Ask Mr. Astro message board. There, you can interact with other America Online members who share an interest in astronomy, or even ask questions of experts such as Mr. Astro.

Fig. 8.3
You can explore the stars with a little help from America Online.

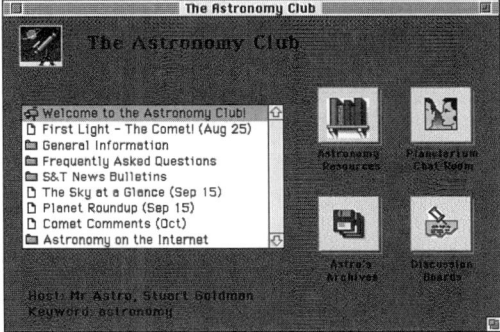

Cooking Club

Keyword: **Cooking**

Whether your efforts at cooking are limited to boiling water and warming a TV dinner, or you are a culinary expert, you can find a wealth of useful information in America Online's Cooking Club. The forum includes message boards, where you can share your favorite recipes or pick up a tip or two from other online gourmets. You can even enter a conference room, the Kitchen, where regular meetings are held on food preparation or new recipes.

The Exchange

Keyword: **The Exchange**

The Exchange is a place where you can express yourself on a wide variety of special interests. There are discussion areas related to men's and women's issues, gardening and other outdoor activities, politics, philosophy, crafts, careers, coin collecting, and other topics.

CAUTION   **As with other areas on America Online, make sure to approach** the debates in the Exchange and other message board areas carefully. Don't use vulgar language, don't insult other America Online members (even though the discussions have been known to get hot and heavy), and, most importantly, just have a good time.

Politics

Keyword: **Politics**

You can find information and debates on all sorts of issues in many places on America Online, from company support forums in the Computing & Software section, to the special places that are devoted to news and other issues that affect us the most. Politics is one of those special places (see fig. 8.4).

Fig. 8.4
You can speak your mind about the important issues of the day.

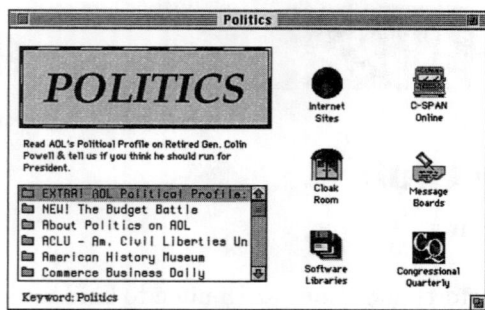

Genealogy Club

Keyword: **Roots**

This special corner of the America Online community provides advice and useful information to help you search your family tree. In active message areas, you can share information and experiences with other online members as you try to find out who your ancestors were.

The software library includes programs that help you catalog information about your family history. You can review the findings of many genealogy experts who assist you in your quest. Or you can attend the regular chats in the Ancestral Digs Conference Hall to interact with other online members.

Kodak Photography Forum

Keyword: **Kodak**

The Kodak Photography Forum, shown in figure 8.5, is conducted by Ron Baird, a photography specialist from Kodak who writes many of their technical manuals. Ron, along with fellow online members, provides you with hints and tips that can make your picture-taking experience more rewarding. If you're looking to sell that old camera and get something better, you can even check out a buy/sell section.

Science Fiction & Fantasy

Keyword: **Science Fiction**

Science fiction is the art of taking present-day science, imagining how it will develop in the future, and building an exciting story around that sort of speculation. America Online's Science Fiction & Fantasy section is an active pit stop for fans of books, comics, movies, and TV programs. You can share your views and learn about upcoming events. Figure 8.6 shows the main Science Fiction & Fantasy directory window.

Fig. 8.5
This is the place for shutterbugs of all kinds.

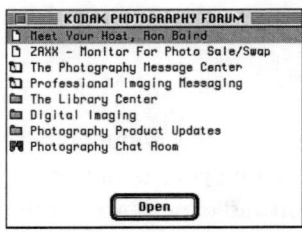

Fig. 8.6
Explore new, exciting worlds without ever leaving your computer screen.

TIP   **For information about *OMNI Magazine* Online, which features** science fiction tales, see Chapter 11.

Star Trek Club

Keyword: **Star Trek**

America Online's Star Trek Club is a meeting ground for Trekkers, where you learn about upcoming TV shows and conferences and can participate in discussions and chats with other fans. One chat I recently attended featured one of the special effects experts on the *Star Trek: Deep Space Nine* program, who let us in on how those incredible visual illusions on the show are created.

Health, home, and the environment

Here are examples of forums on these very important topics.

Better Health & Medical Forum

Keyword: **Health**

Whether you are a health-care professional or just seeking the route to better health and a longer, more productive life, the Better Health & Medical Forum is a place you might want to visit often. The Better Health & Medical Forum contains a large store of text files on all sorts of health-related issues. It's not intended to replace a regular visit to your family physician, but is designed to give you a better range of knowledge about the issues that are of most importance to you.

Environmental Forum

Keyword: **eforum**

This forum has an active message board divided into four main categories. Because the best way to deal with environmental concerns can become hotly contested at times, one board is called The Water Cooler. There, you can approach these subjects with calm and reason.

Issues in Mental Health

Keyword: **IMH**

Issues in Mental Health is a place where you can learn about how to deal with everyday problems. Active message boards enable you to interact with other online members and professionals about problems of daily living.

Network Earth Online

Keyword: **Network Earth**

Network Earth is a weekly television program broadcast on the Atlanta-based TBS super station, which is offered on cable TV systems around the country. This program features reports about the progress made in dealing with the problems of the environment.

Pet Care Forum

Keyword: **Pet**

Most of you probably think of a pet as a dog or a cat, or even a fish, but many other animals qualify for pet status. The Pet Care Forum on America Online is devoted to helping you find better ways to care for all your animal friends (see fig. 8.7).

Fig. 8.7
Learn more about caring for your pet here.

Professions and organizations

A number of professional societies have formed special areas on America Online that cater to members, as well as casual visitors who want to learn more about a specific topic. I'll discuss a few of them in the pages that follow.

Aviation Forum

Keyword: **Fly**

Whether your interest in aviation is limited to reading about it in your living room, building a model plane, or piloting a craft yourself, the place where you can find others who share your interest is America Online's Aviation Club (see fig. 8.8).

Fig. 8.8
The Aviation Forum is a fascinating place for both armchair and active aviators.

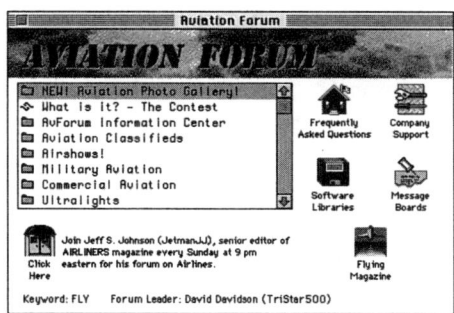

 **TIP** **If you can't find the specific forum that interests you on America** Online, try locating it with a **keyword**. Most keywords either contain the name of an area or its subject. So if you don't know which keyword is correct, don't hesitate to try a few out for size. Suppose, for example, that you want to learn more about Dolby Surround sound. Type the keyword **Dolby** and guess what? It takes you directly to the Dolby Audio/Video Forum on America Online.

Military & Vets Club

Keyword: **Military**

America Online's Military & Vets Club is dedicated to those of you who have served the country in the armed forces, whether in war or peace. You can find message areas for veterans and for those still serving in the military.

National Space Society

Keyword: **NSS**

The National Space Society is devoted to promoting research and exploration of space (see fig. 8.9). Its Board of Governors features such luminaries as Hugh Downs, Arthur C. Clarke, Jacques Cousteau, John Glenn, Nichelle Nichols (the communications officer from the original *Star Trek* TV show and movies), and Alan Shepard.

Fig. 8.9
America Online's
center for space-
related research.

Leisure and entertainment

Here are some examples that provide a more entertaining outlook on life.

Car and Driver

Keywords: **Car and Driver**

Before you buy a new car, you'll want to be up-to-date on the new models
and how they perform on the road. *Car and Driver* is one of the oldest
magazines that caters to automobile enthusiasts. Its online forum, shown in
figure 8.10, includes feature articles from the magazine itself, complete test
reports of the hot new models, and an active message area where you can
learn about the experiences other AOL members have had with these models.
By the way, *Car and Driver's* sister magazine, *Road and Track*, has its own
AOL forum, too. Keyword is **Cars**.

Fig. 8.10
*Read Car and Driver
before you take that
test drive.*

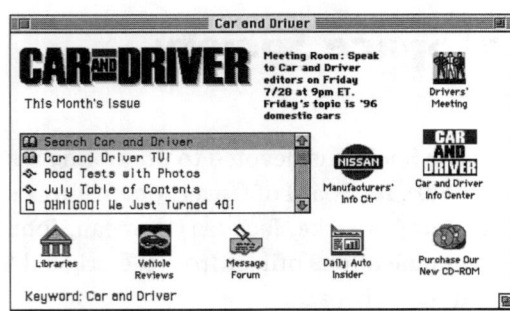

Dolby Audio/Video Forum

Keyword: **Dolby**

The name Dolby was originally synonymous with techniques to provide better-quality sound with reduced background noise (or hiss) on audio compact cassettes and professional studio recordings. It also describes a technology, Dolby Surround, that provides uncanny realism in your favorite motion pictures.

The Dolby Audio/Video Forum on America Online (see fig. 8.11) features experts from the audio and video industries, and active fans who interact on a whole range of issues, ranging from where to hear the best movie sound to how to set up a Surround sound installation in your home.

How can I get those pretty pictures?

Many of the forums described in this chapter (and throughout the book) contain beautiful artwork that you can download and view on your Mac, or print (a color printer is nice if you want to see a hard-copy representation in all its glory). The forums devoted to photography and space travel are examples of places where artwork will be located. These files are usually offered in **GIF** and **JPEG** formats, which are graphic image formats that are used to provide the highest possible quality and keep the file sizes small (and shorten download times).

The neat thing is that your AOL Macintosh software can read these files in the same way you can read simple text files. You'll see the graphic images appear on your computer when you download them; to see a file you've already downloaded, choose Open from the File menu, and select the file. It's that simple.

Some images, such as AOL's weather maps, are available in a special format called **ART**, a very compact file-conversion technique developed by Johnson-Grace Company, which produces a picture file you can download in just a few seconds. To see whether it's an ART file, click the file icon (or double-click the file name) instead of choosing a download option. This starts the file download, which is very, very fast.

Fig. 8.11
The world of Dolby
Surround sound is
brought to your home.

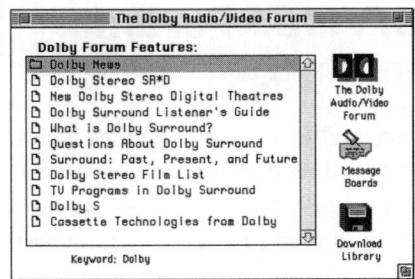

Consumer Electronics

Keyword: **CE**

Consumer Electronics (see fig. 8.12) is a comprehensive forum that covers
everything from household gadgets to home theater. Whether you want to
buy a new telephone pager or a satellite receiving dish for your TV, you'll find
information and fascinating discussions in this forum.

Fig. 8.12
Home electronics of all
sorts are at the
forefront in this
fascinating AOL forum.

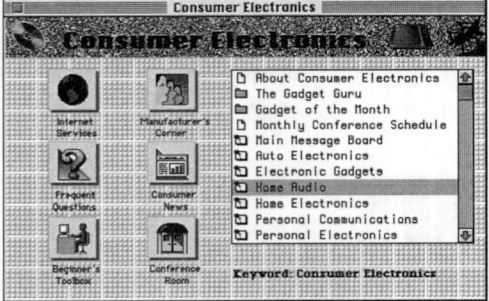

Towns and cities online

Some of your favorite cultural centers are now participating in forums on
America Online. You can travel to Chicago, New York, the San Francisco Bay
area, or even the nation's capital simply by clicking an icon or entering the
appropriate keyword. For the rest of this chapter, I'll cover a few of the
forums devoted to these areas.

Chicago Online

Keyword: **Chicago**

Much like the city for which it's named, this forum is a huge, sprawling place with many areas to visit. This section just covers the highlights and leaves you to explore the rest at your leisure.

When first visiting Chicago Online, click on the Chicagoland Calendar listing in the main forum directory (see fig. 8.13) for the latest news and event information. If you're traveling to Chicago for business or pleasure, you'll probably want to read the Chicago Tribune News & Features area for the latest forecasts and important information.

Fig. 8.13
Chicago Online is the gateway to information about happenings in the Windy City.

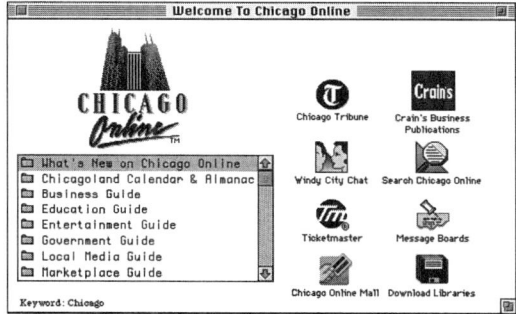

Chicago Tribune

Keyword: **Chicago Tribune**

One of the biggest challenges for the large daily newspapers has been to decide just how to deal with the Information Superhighway. The Chicago Tribune Forum (see fig. 8.14) is the way one publisher is meeting the challenge.

Fig. 8.14
You can read an entire daily newspaper online.

The Chicago Tribune Forum (run by the sponsors of Chicago Online) delivers the same news, sports, and features that you find in the printed editions. One section is even devoted to classified ads. You can view, save, or print text files that you select. And you can search the contents of each daily edition for specific news items.

Just part of the picture

New Clubs & Interests forums are being added regularly to America Online, so if you don't find an area that caters to your special interest, check back often. A number of the special forums mentioned briefly in this chapter, and other information pertinent to your lifestyles and interests needs are also discussed in more detail throughout this book.

Get Advice, Help, and Software from AOL's Computing Forums

● In this chapter:

- Where to learn how to master your computer

- Find computing advice and software

- Get free support from computer manufacturers

- Ask for help with a computer-related problem

Because you interact with America Online by computer, the online service is a natural place to learn how to make your computer work better for you . . . . ▸

Whether you want to download a fancy new shareware program, solve a specific problem, or if you just need some advice on how to upgrade your computer for better performance, America Online can help you find the answers.

Suppose, for example, that you try to run a new program and your computer crashes every time. It's Friday evening; the manufacturer's technical support people have gone home for the weekend. You need that new software to finish a special project. What to do?

Or suppose you're looking for a program that can help remind you of special events. Relief is just a download away in America Online's vast software libraries. You have a software selection numbering in the tens of thousands, and more is being added daily.

Just log onto America Online, where you can find both members and manufacturer's support people ready and willing to help you out of your jam.

Preview your favorite computer books and magazines

When you want to learn more about how your computer works, find out how to use a specific piece of software, or just sneak a preview of upcoming products, you are likely to venture into your local bookstore and purchase a book such as this one.

America Online gives you a chance to preview some of those publications before you buy them. You can even search through back issues of many of your favorite computing magazines for a specific article of interest, all during your online session. Here are a few choice publications you'll want to check out:

Work at home? Look here

Keyword: **Home Office**

If you work from an office located in your own home, you might want to read *Home Office Computing*. This magazine caters to small-business folk, offers advice on buying new hardware and software, and provides helpful tips on making your office run more productively (see figure 9.1).

Fig. 9.1
Home Office Computing's forum on America Online is a valuable resource for small businesses.

Your computer is almost a member of the family

Keyword: **HomePC**

The personal computer has taken over almost every area of our lives. Our children work with computers at school; low-priced computers are now available at specialty stores, discount stores, and consumer-electronics chains. *HomePC* magazine (see figure 9.2) is for users of both the Apple Macintosh and IBM PCs and compatibles, emphasizing the home rather than business user.

Fig. 9.2
HomePC magazine takes a personal approach to the world of personal computing.

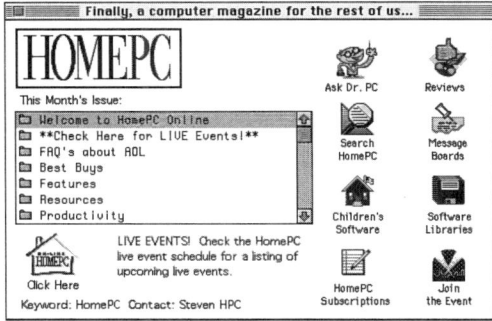

Reading *MacHome Journal*

Keyword: **MacHome Journal**

If you are new to the world of desktop computers and find such jargon as CPUs, RAM, hard drive access speeds, and other phrases to be a foreign language, you need to read *MacHome Journal*. This publication is designed for those who want to learn how to use a computer more effectively without wading through confusing paragraphs of technical material (see figure 9.3).

Fig. 9.3
You don't have to be a technological wizard to find valuable information in *MacHome Journal*.

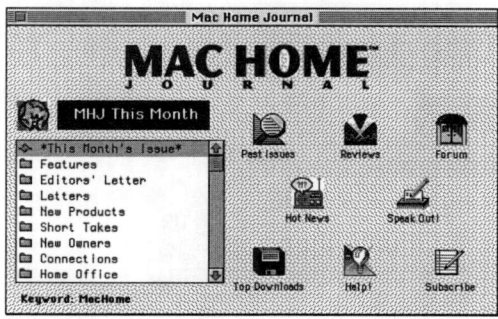

Exploring *MacTech* magazine

Keyword: **MacTech**

If you want to write software for the Macintosh, you'll want to check out *MacTech* magazine. This publication caters strictly to the interests of developers and programmers. Each issue is filled with helpful information to help you learn programming, advice on how to debug your software, and even suggestions on finding a solution to a sticky coding problem.

Exploring *Macworld*

Keyword: **Macworld**

When you buy a new Apple Macintosh, you get a free trial subscription to *Macworld*. But even if you haven't made a new computer purchase lately, you might want to keep up-to-date on all the new hardware and software products. In *Macworld's* special sections, Macworld News and New Products, you can learn just what Apple has up its corporate sleeve for the newest generation of Macintosh computers. Figure 9.4 shows the *Macworld* screen.

Fig. 9.4
Macworld magazine is highlighted on America Online.

On the road with *Mobile Office Online*

Keyword: **Mobile**, **Portable**

The proliferation of laptop computers has made it possible for you to do your work almost anywhere in the world, even in the middle of a desert, so long as you have a spare set of batteries or an available source for AC power. *Mobile Office Online*, as shown in figure 9.5, is the AOL counterpart of the popular newsstand magazine that caters to this new generation of traveling workers.

Fig. 9.5
Mobile Office magazine keeps tabs on the growing world of laptop computing.

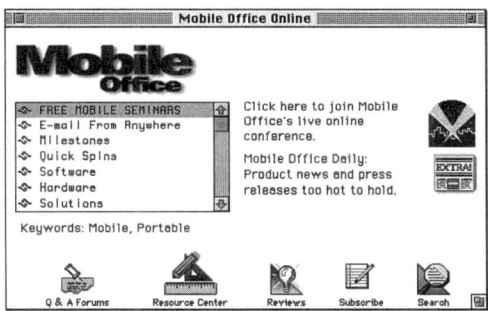

AOL is for both Mac and PC users!

Crossing platforms? It's very common these days for folks to have to work on both Macs and PCs in an office or home setup. America Online's software is designed to look very similar on both platforms (although the available features are somewhat different), so you can interact with the service in a similar manner. You'll find all the differences spelled out in full detail in my other AOL book, *Using America Online with Windows 95.*

You'll also find that the computing forums for the other platform and magazines that cater to the other platform are easily accessed from both sides of the fence. So you don't have to worry about not being able to get to the Mac forums while using your PC, and vice versa. The Computing department, keyword *Computing*, offers a cross-platform gateway. Or you can reach a specific area by its keyword, which is usually the same whether you're logged on with a Mac or PC.

Exploring the Computing Forums

Keyword: **Computing**

Your computer is crashing whenever you try to open a new document. If you want to learn to use your computer more effectively, or just talk computers with fellow online members, visit America Online's computing forums.

The following paragraphs briefly highlight many of the forums. Because a picture is truly worth a thousand words, look closely at the figures throughout this chapter for a list of many of the services that the forums offer.

As you can see in figure 9.6, the Computing department screen provides an entrance to America Online's computing forums and other valuable information resources. You can find special areas devoted to specific aspects of computing, updated computing news, company support forums, and schedules for upcoming chats that you don't want to miss.

Fig. 9.6
The Macintosh Computing & Software screen is your gateway to the Mac software forums on America Online.

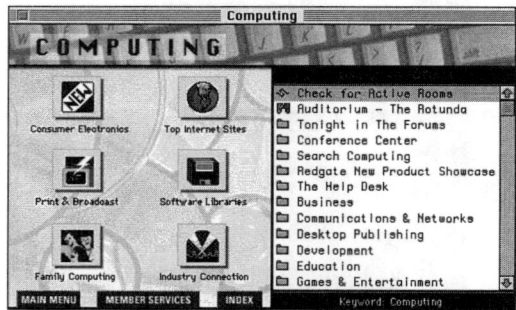

Accessing computing Internet sites

Many of the major computing manufacturers and publishers have created home pages on the World Wide Web. By clicking on the Top Internet Sites icon (see figure 9.7), you'll have a direct passage to many of these information resources. The listing of available sites changes so often that I am not giving you a lineup, except to tell you that you'll always find such companies such as Apple Computer, Motorola, and even Power Computing (the manufacturer of Mac-compatible computers) among the list.

Fig. 9.7
A number of World Wide Web sites are directly accessible from this convenient area of AOL's Computing department.

66 *Plain English, please!*

On the World Wide Web, a **home page** is the first or main screen at a Web site. The home page will often present introductory material about the site and offer hot links to access additional information (and sometimes software files) from this location. In some cases, you'll even see a list of other sites containing related information. Chapters 16 through 20 cover AOL's various Internet-related services. 99

Get answers from the Macintosh Help Desk

Keyword: **Help Desk**

Every Mac computing forum on America Online has a little icon with a shaded question mark. It's labeled Help & Information, and it's your entry to the Mac Help Desk (see figure 9.8).

Fig. 9.8
When you need a helping hand, the Mac Help Desk on America Online is there for you.

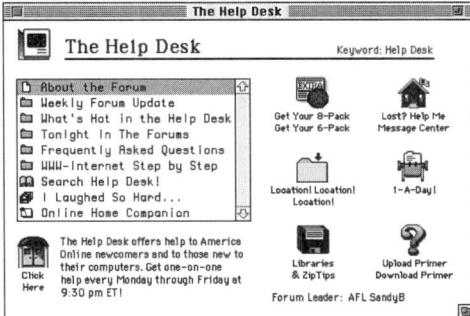

TIP   **Before you post a question, read older messages in the same** message folder or in other message areas dealing with a similar topic. You might find a response and a solution to a question much like yours.

The Macintosh Business Forum helps empower you at the office

Keyword: **MBS**

You might be seeking a better spreadsheet program to display those all-important numbers. Or perhaps you're looking for software that can help you build a mailing list or prepare invoices for your clients.

The Mac Business Forum is your center for information and advice on how best to select and use the software on which your business depends (see figure 9.9).

Fig. 9.9
From spreadsheets to financial planners, your source for business-related programs is the Mac Business Forum.

Learn about modems and networks from the Mac Communications Forum

Keyword: **MCM**

If you're thinking of buying one of those newer, high-speed modems, or finding a better way to network your computer with a printer or another computer, pay a visit to the Mac Communications forums on America Online. Figure 9.10 shows the Communications Forum screen.

Fig. 9.10
The Communications Forum is your America Online headquarters for Macintosh modem and networking issues.

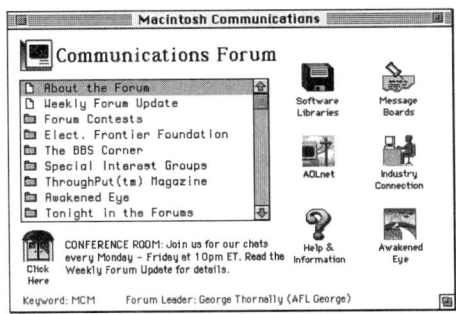

The world of DTP is the focus of the Macintosh Desktop Publishing Forum

Keyword: **MDP**

Desktop publishing owes its lineage to traditional typesetting. But instead of using machines that melt down hot sticks of lead, or expensive minicomputers that generate characters on photosensitive paper with flashing lights and lenses, you now can create professional publications—like this book, for example—on a desktop computer. Whether you're a beginner or seasoned pro, you'll want to visit AOL's forum dedicated to this field, the Macintosh Desktop Publishing Forum, whose main screen is shown in figure 9.11.

Fig. 9.11
Desktop publishing is the descendant of traditional typesetting, and a whole forum covers it on America Online.

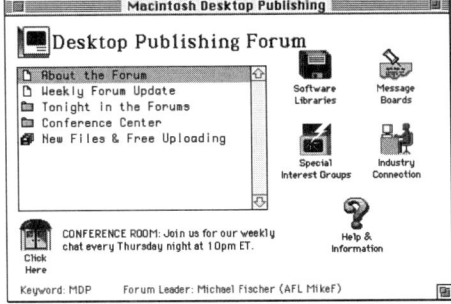

Learn programming from the Mac Developers Forum

Keyword: **MDV**

If you want to write your own software or if you're a professional looking for advice on dealing with a specific problem in writing code, America Online's developers' forums are resources you can use again and again. Figure 9.12 shows the Developers Forum screen.

Fig. 9.12

When you want to write your own Mac software, the Developers Forum is a place you want to visit.

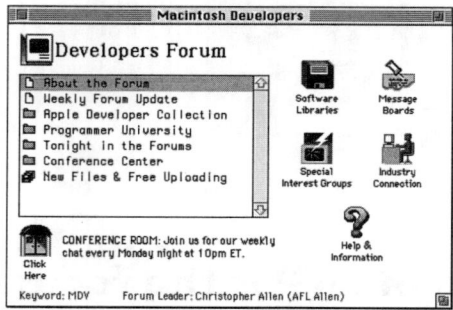

Learn from the Macintosh Education Forum

Keyword: **MED**

More and more young people are using computers in the classrooms. Even those in kindergarten and first grade often find a small desktop computer on a teacher's desk. And as your children grow older, they might find a computer lab available in their school as well.

The Macintosh Education Forum is a resource for students, educators, and parents to help our youth learn more about how to use their computers and learn from them (see figure 9.13).

Fig. 9.13

When you use your computer for education, visit the Macintosh Education Forum.

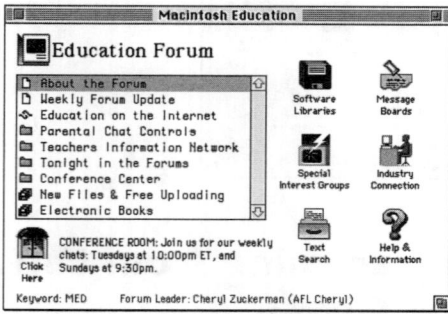

Play the Games Forum

Keyword: **MGM**

In Chapter 6, you were introduced to many of the ways you can have pure, simple fun on America Online. The Games forums contain shareware games, add-ons, demos of many popular commercial games, and, just as important, helpful advice on how to make playtime (for adults and children) more rewarding. Figure 9.14 shows the Games Forum screen. (For more information, refer to Chapter 7.)

Fig. 9.14
You have time for a little fun with a game downloaded from the Macintosh Games Forum.

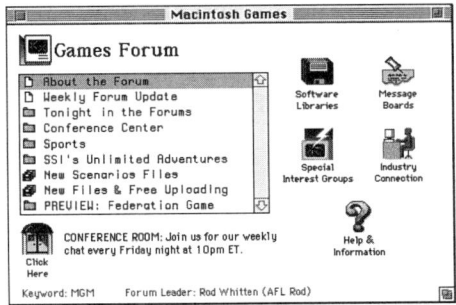

Illustrating the Graphics Forum

Keyword: **MGM**

If you are a computer artist or want to become one, you need to drop in to visit the Mac Graphics forum on America Online. This forum contains huge resources of information to help you learn your craft and produce better work (see figure 9.15).

Fig. 9.15
The Macintosh Graphics Forum is America Online's resource for graphics professionals.

Getting an advance look at the newest Mac hardware

Keyword: **MHW**

New computers are coming out so often that keeping a scorecard is difficult. Before you buy a new model only to learn that it will be outdated the next day, check out America Online's Mac Hardware forum, shown in figure 9.16. You'll also want to attend the forum's regular chats, where you can meet the designers of your favorite products and ask them whatever is on your mind.

Fig. 9.16
If you're buying a new Macintosh computer, you need to visit the Mac Hardware Forum first.

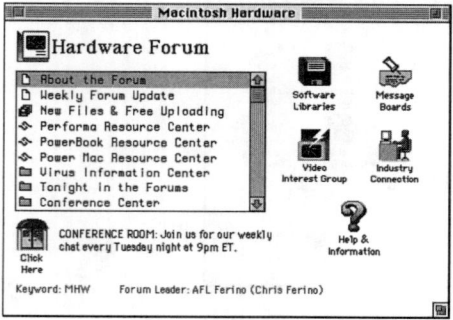

Learn basic programming from the Macintosh HyperCard Forum

Keyword: **MHC**

HyperCard is a personal, easy-to-use programming language that you can use to build your own programs based on the metaphor of a stack. A **stack** is like a Rolodex card, containing useful information that you can read or print, or that enables you to perform a particular function. Unlike the often arcane, difficult-to-master programming language used in commercial software, HyperCard programming often requires only a little practice.

The HyperCard Forum on America Online is the place where you can learn how to develop your own HyperCard stacks or just download ones from other enterprising programmers (see figure 9.17).

Fig. 9.17
The HyperCard Forum gives you help with HyperCard, your personal programming language.

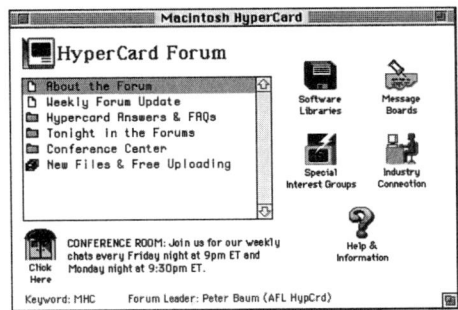

Using the Mac Multimedia Forum

Keyword: **MMM**

The word **multimedia** has been bandied about the computer world for a number of years. Multimedia refers to the marriage of audio and video (still or moving) on your desktop computer. As computers have become more and more powerful, the tools to manipulate the sometimes huge audio and video files have become cheaper and easier to use.

Even more interesting, it's no secret that many of the major movie production houses have been using desktop computers for their work. America Online's Mac Multimedia Forum (see figure 9.18) is a meeting ground for both amateurs and professionals to share experiences and learn more about this growing art.

Fig. 9.18
Video and sound combine to produce multimedia, and this forum is where you can keep up to date with the emerging technologies.

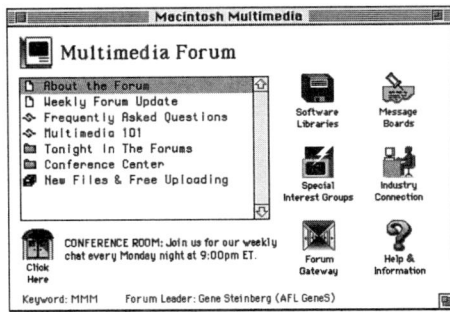

Exploring the Mac Music and Sound Forum

Keyword: **MMS**

In the 1980s, music came into its own on a desktop computer. More and more recording artists (some whose names are household words) have begun to use personal computers to create and store sounds. With a few inexpensive add-ons, you can even make your computer into a miniature, multitrack recording studio and produce digital-quality audio.

Interested? Then pay a visit to the Mac Music & Sound Forum on America Online (see figure 9.19).

Fig. 9.19
The Macintosh Music &
Sound Forum is for
professional musicians
and amateurs alike.

Getting the lowdown on the latest Mac operating system

Keyword: **MOS**

The operating system is usually the most invisible part of your computer's software. But every function, from turning it on and booting your computer to moving and copying files, is managed by the operating system. The software you use to do your work uses tools provided by the operating system for many of its functions.

For help and a preview of what's to come, you'll want to visit the Macintosh Operating Systems Forum. It's your information center for System 6, all flavors of System 7, and Apple's UNIX front end, A/UX (see figure 9.20).

Fig. 9.20
Your computer can't start without its operating system, the subject of this forum on America Online.

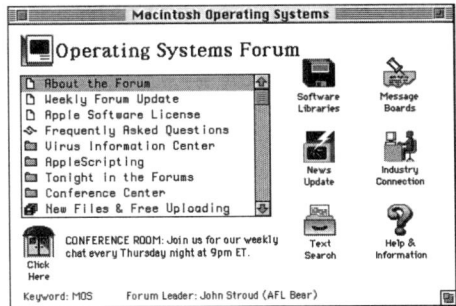

Exploring the Personal Digital Assistants Forum

Keyword: **PDA**

PDA is an abbreviation for Personal Digital Assistants, and it refers to a computer that you can hold in the palm of your hand, such as a Sharp Wizard or an Apple Newton. Whether you have just bought one of these neat examples of electronic wizardry or you are wondering whether it's something other than a high-priced toy, you can visit this forum to learn more (see figure 9.21).

Fig. 9.21
Learn about hand-held computers in this America Online forum.

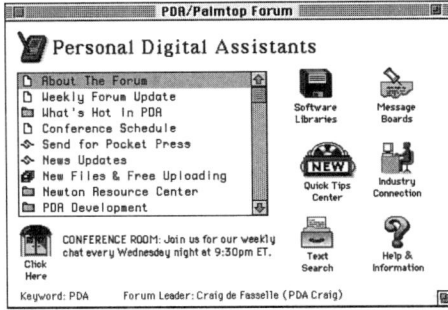

Using the Macintosh Utilities Forum

Keyword: **MUT**

A **utility** can be a program that enhances your computer's operating system—such as a screen saver, an address book, or a reminder program—or software that diagnoses the condition of your computer's hard drive and fixes minor problems.

The Macintosh Utilities Forum, shown in figure 9.22, is your gathering place for information and advice about those little programs that you might often take for granted but that can make a huge change in the way your computer works.

Fig. 9.22
One of America Online's most popular Mac computing forums is the Utilities Forum.

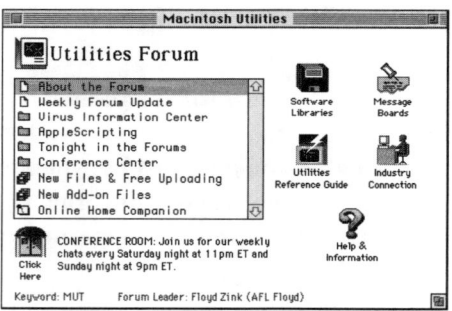

Visiting the User Groups Forum

Keyword: **UGF**

When you first buy a personal computer, you're no doubt anxious to meet other computer owners to receive advice, and share tips and tricks to make your computer run more effectively. A **user group** is a club, pure and simple. It's an organization consisting of computer owners who usually devoted to one specific platform, such as Macintosh or PC. If you're a member of a user group or just want to learn about joining one, pay a visit to America Online's User Groups Forum (see fig. 9.23).

Fig. 9.23
Meet with fellow computer owners right here on America Online.

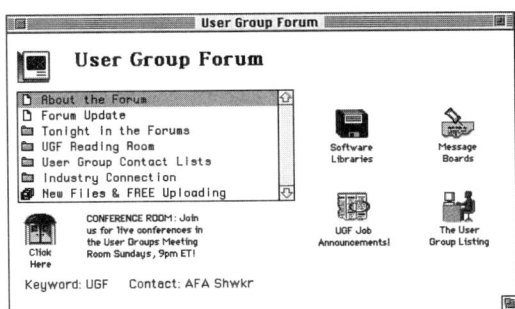

Accessing the Software Center

Keyword: **Software**

You have several ways to locate software on America Online. One is by doing a file search, which is described in more detail in Chapter 10. Another method is to visit a forum that caters to that software category. Still a third is the Software Center, which is a repository for popular software from across the entire America Online community. Figure 9.24 shows the Software Center screen.

Fig. 9.24
You can find your favorite Macintosh software all in one place.

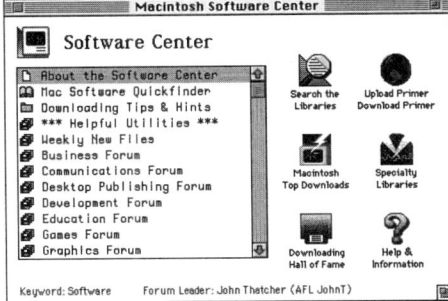

Seeking company support

Keyword: **Industry Connection**

If you've ever waited long minutes listening to voice mail when you try to telephone a hardware or software manufacturer for some help, you'll appreciate America Online's solution. More than 200 firms, ranging from small utility software publishers to the major manufacturers of computer hardware, are represented in America Online's Industry Connection areas, as shown in figure 9.25. What's more, additional firms are being added almost daily, so it's likely that most of the publishers you want to contact are online now, or will be shortly.

Fig. 9.25
Get help right from the source using America Online's Industry Connection.

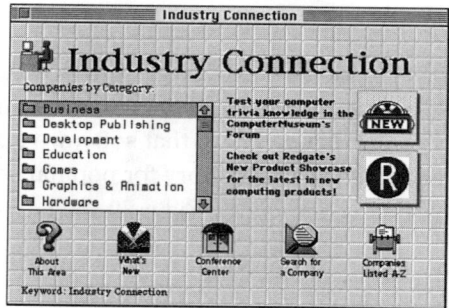

These support forums are places where you can get advice on how to use a company's product more effectively and how to solve problems when they arise. The company's own support personnel usually staff the forums, and they are often ably assisted by knowledgeable America Online members.

Software publishers often give you free maintenance updates to their products in their support areas, so you don't have to wait for that product update to be mailed to you. You'll also want to check the software libraries often, in case they contain an update that you need.

Finding a company

You can also find computing industry support areas in the computing and software forums that cater to the kind of product the companies support. Suppose, for example, that you want to access a modem manufacturer in the Hardware and Communications forums. Click on the Industry Connection icon to see whether the firm is represented.

But the fastest route might simply be to use a keyword to go directly to the firm you want. If you want to find Claris, Apple Computer's cross-platform software subsidiary, for example, type the keyword **Claris**. In just a few seconds, you are transported directly to the front door of the company's America Online support forum (see figure 9.26).

Fig. 9.26
Apple's Claris software division publishes software for both the Mac and Windows platforms.

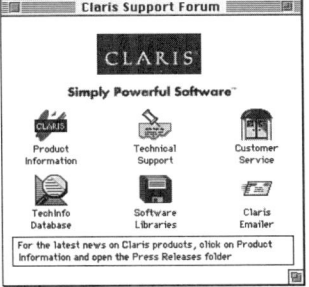

Posting—once is enough!

Don't **cross-post.** In other words, don't post your message in more than one message folder in a single forum. America Online members don't always take kindly to reading the same message over and over again. Before you issue your plea for help, take a few moments to find the right place to post it. Look for a computing forum or a company support area that's appropriate (the Hardware Forum, for example, for a malfunctioning printer), and leave your message there.

Using industry connection help

A technical support person can't help you solve your problem if you don't give enough information about your setup and the difficulties you're having with the product. This typical letter is often found in the message boards:

```
Help! My computer is crashing all the time. I can't get any
work done when I use your software. I need help.
Signed: Harried Harry
```

This sort of letter is only going to postpone the helping process because the letter lacks any information to enable a technical support person to diagnose and, if necessary, try to reproduce your problem. Remember that the only information a manufacturer rep has to go on is what you provide in your letter.

The following list gives you some helpful hints on how to ask a company support person for help:

1 Describe the kind of computer you have, including the model number.

2 Briefly describe your setup, including the operating system version and the amount of installed RAM, and list the accessories attached to it, such as a video card or an additional hard drive.

3 Identify the manufacturer's product by model or version number. Quite often a problem might affect only a single version of a program or piece of hardware.

4 Describe the kind of problem you're having. If your computer is crashing, report whether an error message appears on your computer's screen. That kind of message might be crucial for finding out what went wrong.

5 If the problem can be reproduced, describe the steps you've taken to reproduce it. That way, if the problem is unique to your setup, the steps can give a clue for the support person to attempt to reproduce the problem.

6 If the problem started after you made a change in your setup, such as a new hardware addition or a software installation, mention that, too. That new installation might have caused your troubles.

7 Finally, don't expect miracles. These products are manufactured by human beings and they have the same shortcomings as the rest of us. No hardware or software product is ever perfect, but you want to get it to work as efficiently as possible in your home or office.

Sometimes a problem is just too complex to deal with by e-mail or a message board. In that case, the company invites you to contact its technical support people directly for further assistance.

10

How to Find the Software You Want

● In this chapter:

● **Find software in America Online's libraries quickly and easily**

● **Transfer that software directly to your computer**

● **Take a look at the Download Manager window**

● **What kinds of software can you find on America Online?**

● **Upload your own files to America Online's huge software libraries**

America Online is like a software playground, with tens of thousands of files available for you to download . . . . ➤

A s you continue to explore America Online, you'll discover that there are thousands upon thousands of Macintosh software for you to download. If you cross computing platforms on occasion, you'll find large numbers of DOS, OS/2, and Windows software as well. Whether it's an arcade game, a program that lets you create a to-do list, or an update to commercial software you own, America Online is the place to find it.

Get the hang of AOL's software libraries

When I first joined America Online in 1989, I was the owner of a brand new computer, and I wanted to stock up on software. As an inveterate software junkie, I was a frequent visitor to the service's vast software libraries. It took me a while to discover the rich array of information services available elsewhere online.

Before we go on, let's define a couple of computer terms you'll see often in this chapter.

- **Downloading** a file is simply the act of transferring a file from an online service's host computer (or another modem) through the telephone lines and to your computer by way of your modem.

- **Uploading** a file is the process of sending a file from your computer directly to an online service or another modem.

A fast primer on virus protection

Because there is always the danger that a file can be contaminated by a computer virus, America Online's forum staff checks all uploaded files with an up-to-date virus-detection program before posting them online. You should, however, always install and use the latest virus-detection software so that all your files are safe and sound.

Not all software that you can retrieve during your AOL session comes from AOL's own software libraries. Through AOL's Internet feature, you can access worldwide software repositories. Since the quality of managing such libraries may not be as stringent as on America Online, you should use virus detection software to analyze those files before you try to use them. You can check out the latest information on computer viruses in AOL's Virus Information Center (keyword: **Virus**).

The easy way to search for files

The fastest way to locate software you want is to let America Online's host computer do the searching for you. So let's bring up America Online's File Search window:

1 Press Command+K and type the keyword **File Search** (see fig. 10.1). Or choose Search Software Libraries from the Go To menu of your AOL software.

Fig. 10.1

Your gateway to America Online's convenient software database.

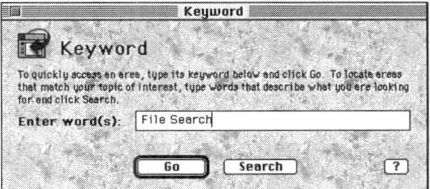

2 In seconds, you see a large window on your computer that gives you a number of search options (see fig. 10.2).

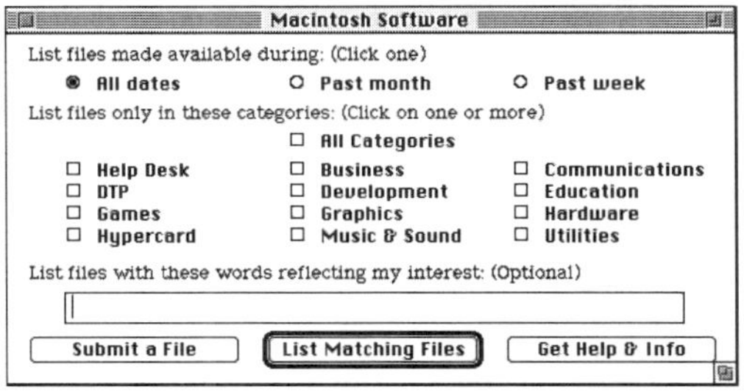

Fig. 10.2

You can find the software you want from a specific forum or over a specific time frame (so you can see all the newest files listed at once).

3 You can search for software in many ways. You can limit your search to a specific category, such as Games or Graphics. You can even restrict the search to a specific time frame; for instance, perhaps you only want to find a file that was posted in the past month.

4 If you want to locate a file by name or subject, enter the information in the List files field. If you want to find a screen saver, for example, you'll enter **screen saver** as the subject of your search.

In this example, we'll try to locate a copy of the popular Macintosh shareware arcade game *Maelstrom*, written by programmer Andrew Welch. I looked for the file by its name, *Maelstrom*, for this search routine. I could also have used *Games* as the search term, and come up with the same result. But with thousands of games to look for, I would have been presented with an unwieldy list of files to pick from. The best thing to do is be as specific as you can.

5 If files matching your description cannot be found, you'll see a message window that notifies you that a match to your search request is not available.

6 If files meeting your description are located, you'll see a File List window on-screen (see fig. 10.3). A file may be listed more than once if it is in more than one library on America Online. Because only 20 files are loaded to the File List at one time, you might need to click on the List More Files button to see additional entries.

Fig. 10.3
Success! AOL found 117 files that contained the search word Maelstrom; you'll have to scroll through and check some file descriptions to find the one you want.

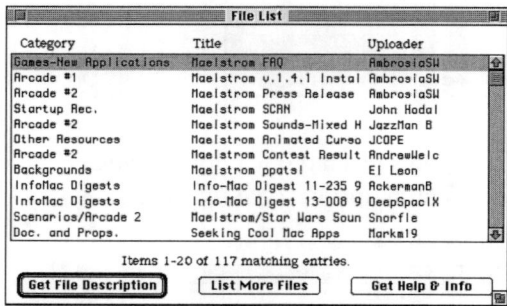

7 To learn more about the file that interests you, either highlight the file name and double-click on it, or select the Get File Description button, either by clicking on it or by pressing Return or Enter. You'll see a window very much like the one shown in figure 10.4.

Fig. 10.4
To learn more about the file (including the kind of Mac and operating system it needs), review the file description first.

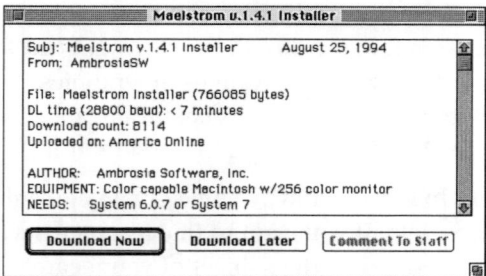

Downloading files from A to Z

Now that you've found a file you'd like to download to your computer, the next step is to start the download process. Your first option is to create a file **queue**, which is a list of files to download. That list or directory will be stored in America Online's Download Manager (which I'll describe in more detail a bit later in this chapter). Your second option is to download the file immediately.

 **TIP** Before downloading a file, check the File Description (shown in fig. 10.4). This description not only tells you more about the file but contains information about what kind of computer it works on.

Now that you've found the file you want, the next step is to transfer that file to your Mac. Here are the steps you'll follow:

1 The default selection in the software list, at the bottom of the file description window, is Download Now, which brings up a standard Save dialog box that allows you to indicate where you want to store the file that's being transferred to your computer (see fig. 10.5).

Fig. 10.5
Select the place where you want the file sent.

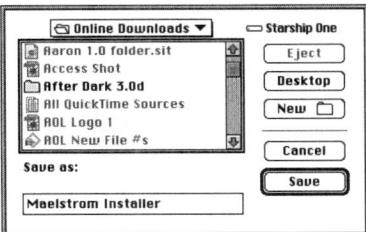

2 You have the option to rename the file (enter the new name at the bottom of the Save dialog box).

3 Click on the Save button or hit the Return or Enter key to begin the download process (see fig. 10.6).

Fig. 10.6
The download in process.

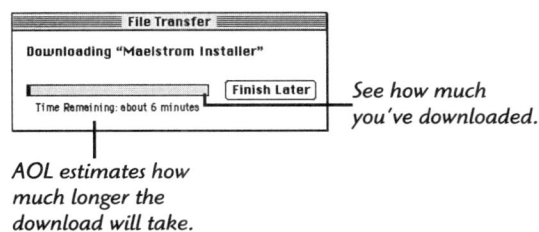

See how much you've downloaded.

AOL estimates how much longer the download will take.

TIP **To speed up file transfer times, you may want to log on to** America Online at a non-peak hour, perhaps early in the morning, when network traffic is less busy.

4 When your file download begins, you see a progress bar showing approximately how much of the file has been sent, and an estimate of how long it will take to transfer that file to your computer.

TIP **Macintosh users of System 7 or MultiFinder under System 6 can** click on the desktop and resume other work while the download is in progress. Avoid CPU-intensive tasks, such as calculating a spreadsheet, while downloading. Doing so could slow down or even interrupt the download process.

5 When the file has been transferred, America Online's friendly narrator will (if the sounds are enabled) announce, "File Done."

Q&A *Help! Performance is really slow on AOL right now and the download is taking forever. Can I stop the download and start it again later?*

If you decide you don't want to download the file after all, hit the Finish Later button. In a minute or two, the download will stop. If you intend to resume the download at a later time, *don't* delete the partial file that has been transferred to your computer; if you do, the Download Manager cannot resume downloading at the point where it left off.

There's another advantage in choosing to finish your download at a later time. If AOL's network traffic is high, you can run a FlashSession at another hour, when performance is better, thus reducing the time it takes to retrieve the files you want.

The Download Manager

You can build a download queue or list by using the Download Manager, and you can start the download any time during your online session or when the session ends. When you add a file to the list, you see an acknowledgment message.

To use the Download Manager, choose the second option available to you when downloading a file—Download Later. You find that button in the file description window (refer to fig. 10.4).

Check the Download Manager anytime after adding files to the queue to see if you want to make changes in the listing before downloading begins. The files will be shown in the order in which they'll be downloaded (this isn't something you can change except by removing a file from the list).

CAUTION **If you log onto America Online as a guest, using another** member's software, the Download Later function will not work nor will you be able to use AOL's FlashSession feature.

Q&A *Some of the files I find in a forum don't show up with AOL's file search feature. Why?*

As this book was going to press, some areas of AOL weren't a part of the file search capability. These included specialty forums in departments other than the Computing area, and company-support forums. By the time you read this book, though, you may find that these libraries are also part of the file search feature.

Also, it can take 12 to 24 hours for the file search database at AOL's host computer to update its directory. So newly posted files may not always show up.

America Online's Download Manager lets you manage the entire download process from a single window. You can open the Download Manager window when notified that a file has been added to the download queue by selecting the Download Manager button, or you can use America Online's File menu. The Download Manager displays all files you've selected for downloading. There is also help available (see fig. 10.7).

Fig. 10.7
AOL's Help menu offers advice on how to get the most efficient use from your online visits.

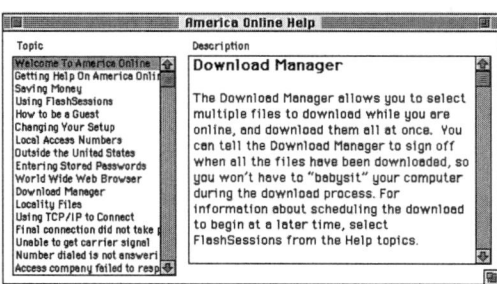

The Download Manager window

The Download Manager window lists the total size of the files you've selected for transfer to your computer and gives an estimated transfer time at your modem connection speed. Downloads can take a little longer than the estimate during the evening prime-time period or when there is noise on your phone line. At other times, you may find your downloads moving more swiftly than estimated. Here are the different parts of the Download Manager window:

View Description
Your first option, in the bottom left of the window, gives you the chance to check whether you really want to download the file.

Help
As with many other areas on America Online, Help produces America Online's comprehensive Help menu, with plenty of instructions and quick tips.

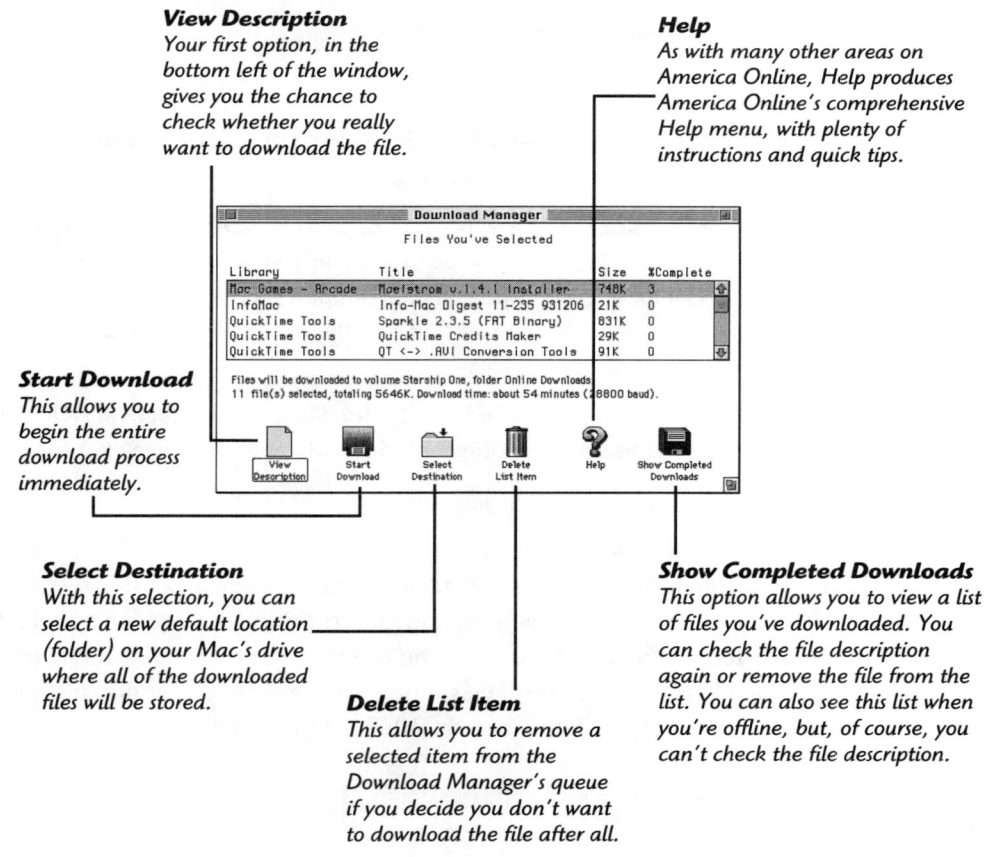

Start Download
This allows you to begin the entire download process immediately.

Select Destination
With this selection, you can select a new default location (folder) on your Mac's drive where all of the downloaded files will be stored.

Delete List Item
This allows you to remove a selected item from the Download Manager's queue if you decide you don't want to download the file after all.

Show Completed Downloads
This option allows you to view a list of files you've downloaded. You can check the file description again or remove the file from the list. You can also see this list when you're offline, but, of course, you can't check the file description.

How do I use the files I've downloaded?

Most larger files in America Online's software libraries are compressed to save disk space and to reduce transfer time, thereby reducing online charges.

America Online's software can be set to automatically expand files that you've downloaded as soon as you log off. Because some files may be compressed in a format that isn't supported by the software, those files will have to be expanded before you use them.

Before you pick a file to download, read the file description carefully to make sure that your computer, operating system, and software setup are compatible with those of the file. If you make a mistake and download a file you can't use, type the keyword **Credit** to request a rebate to your account for the time you wasted online.

If you get a message that the file has been damaged after download, you need to remove the file from your computer and download the file again. You also can request account credit at any time for a bad file. Although files are not damaged often, sometimes a file may not arrive in perfect condition due to noise on the telephone lines or to a network-related problem.

 *CAUTION* **If your download is interrupted for any reason (perhaps your** connection was terminated because of poor phone-line conditions), a fragment or partial file is left on your computer's drive. If you want to resume the download when you log on again, *don't* delete or move the partial file. Otherwise, you won't be able to resume your download where it left off.

How to help your computer view a file

If you get a message on your Macintosh that the application that created your downloaded file can't be found, log on and check the file description, or view it offline in the Download Manager's list of Completed Downloads. You may need other software to use the downloaded file, either to decompress it or to run it after it's decompressed.

If the file description doesn't offer the information you need, e-mail the staff who manages the forum from which you downloaded the file for further help. The easiest way to do this is to open the file description window for that particular file, click on the Ask the Staff button, and write and send your message.

The AOL forum staff who receives these messages will often work at various hours of the day, so don't expect a response for several hours at the very least.

Q&A *I downloaded some files. Now I can't find them. Where are they?*

When you install your AOL software, the Download Manager sets a default location for downloaded files. It's the Online Downloads folder inside your AOL program folder. You can change this destination by activating the Download Manager (from the File menu) if you prefer, of course.

Another point: Sometimes the file that you download has a different name from the title it's shown under in a forum's software library. You can click on the Show Completed Downloads icon of AOL's Download Manager to recheck the actual file name (or while online, return to the forum from which you downloaded the file, to check the actual file name as shown in the file description).

If you still cannot locate the file, use the Find File feature of your Mac operating system to determine where it is.

What kind of software is available?

Before you begin to fill your software library, let's discuss the kinds of software that are available and the types of software you are apt to find on America Online.

Commercial software

Commercial software are retail products that you can find at your local computer dealer, software reseller, or through one of the mail order firms that cater to this type of merchandise. You can even order commercial software on America Online through a publisher's company support area or through forums devoted to shopping (see Chapters 9 and 14).

You will not usually find commercial software in America Online's software libraries, but you can, from time to time, locate a free update program. The author or publisher of a software product can make an update program available so that you can revise your copy of the software to a newer version, usually to fix some bugs.

Like most software, commercial software is covered by a license agreement. Though licenses vary from product to product, in most cases, the license states that you are not buying the software itself, but the right to use it. The agreement spells out what those rights are. For most of you, those rights include being allowed to use the software on one single computer at a time, and to make backup copies in case the master disks are damaged.

Because many of us use laptop computers for travel, some software licenses allow you to install the software on both your home or office computer and a portable, assuming that not more than one person will use the software at the same time. If you're going to install the software on multiple computers, you need to buy a site license from the author or publisher.

Demoware

Demonstration software is designed to let you try out all or most of the features of a software product before you buy it. **Demoware**, as it's known, may be either a commercial or a shareware program. In most cases, you can use the software for a limited period of time, ranging from a few days to a week or two; it then expires and you cannot use it again until you buy a copy. Some demoware may simply lock out some program features (such as the capability to save and print a document), which become available in the version you buy. When you purchase the program, you will often receive a special password that allows you to turn the demo program into the full-featured version.

Shareware

Shareware exemplifies the original try-before-you-buy concept. The author or publisher of a software product gives you a fully functional version (though a feature or two may be restricted). You can try it out on your computer for a period of up to a month. When that period expires, you are asked to pay the author or publisher a small fee for a license to continue to run the program.

Shareware is one of the last vestiges in our society of an honor system. The publisher has no way of knowing whether you are continuing to use the software. If you decide to continue to run it, consider the time and energy the author put into writing and testing that software. Also consider how you would feel if you were not paid for your work.

Shareware is often less expensive than commercial software because it lacks fancy packaging, manuals, and a fully staffed technical support department. Some shareware, however, has become commercial, such as the compression software America Online uses for its Macintosh version StuffIt. StuffIt was first written by a 15-year-old high school student. It's now published in shareware form, as StuffIt Lite, and as a more fully-featured commercial product, StuffIt Deluxe (published by Aladdin Systems).

Freeware

This category covers a wide range of products. **Freeware** is available to you without cost, but the author retains all rights to the program, including how it is to be distributed. Freeware may include a fully functioning program or an update to an existing product. Don't attribute cost to value. You can often find a wealth of very useful programs in this category.

Public domain software

Public domain software can be used and distributed freely. The author has given up all rights to this program.

Uploading files from A to Z

America Online's computing forums have a special department labeled New Files and Free Uploading. This department allows you to upload software to America Online's software libraries without being charged.

CAUTION **Demoware and shareware can contain restrictions on whether** they can be uploaded by anyone other than the author, so read the instructions that come with the software before you decide to upload it to America Online. In general, commercial updates, such as system–related software from Apple Computer, may be uploaded to America Online only by the publisher.

Where to upload

You must do a little research to find out the appropriate place to upload the file and to verify that you have the right to send it. Each computing forum has a description file that tells you its purpose and the kind of software wanted. Rather than waste your time and the forum's by uploading to an inappropriate location, read the description files to be sure that you are uploading your software to the most suitable forum. A screen saver, for example, will likely go in a Utilities forum.

Before uploading the file—especially if you are not the author—use America Online's File Search feature to make sure that the file you want to send isn't already posted somewhere on America Online.

How to upload

When you visit a computing software library (see Chapter 9), you'll see a button at the bottom of the software directory labeled Upload File. When you want to send your file, click on the button, which opens the window shown in figure 10.8.

Fig. 10.8
Enter information about the file you're sending here. This material will become part of the file description when your file is released by a forum staff (though they may edit it).

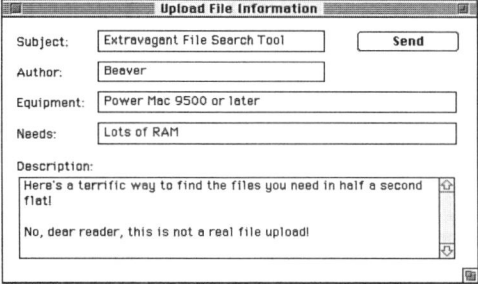

The Upload File Information window has several fields:

- Subject: Extravagant File Search Tool
- Author: Beaver
- Equipment: Power Mac 9500 or later
- Needs: Lots of RAM
- Description: Here's a terrific way to find the files you need in half a second flat!

No, dear reader, this is not a real file upload!

 **TIP**   **Before filling out the Upload File Information window, review** the descriptions of other software to become familiar with the way the descriptions are written and the kind of information required.

The Upload File Information window has several fields that you need to fill out. Enter the title of the file in the Subject field, then the name of the author of the file, and the kind of equipment needed to use it. Next, give a brief description of the file you're sending. You can enter a list of suggested keywords so that others can locate the file easily. (You don't have to include keywords, though. The forum staff will do that if this field is left blank.)

When you upload the file, you'll see a File Transfer window that's very much like the one displayed when you download a file (refer to fig. 10.6). After the file is received, it is reviewed by forum staff who decide whether it's suitable for their forum. The file description you give may be edited.

Because many of the staff members who review these files are volunteers, expect several days to pass before you hear of the forum's decision. If posted, your file will turn up in their New Files and Free Uploading library.

11

Learning and Reference Sources Online

● **In this chapter:**

- **Seek help for your child's homework**

- **Tap the resources of huge libraries**

- **Take diploma- and degree-granting courses without ever attending a classroom**

You can learn something about almost anything on America Online . . . .

C ombine the vast resources of a major encyclopedia, home study schools, libraries, museums, and dozens of other information centers, and you'll find nearly all the information you need during your visits to America Online. In the previous century, your resources for learning were confined to written material, such as books, newspapers, and magazines; or verbal descriptions. The twentieth century brought into play the audio and visual mediums as well. But interactive learning capabilities have come into their own with the advent of online services such as America Online.

Because of the extent and scope of the educational resources available on America Online, a separate chapter would be needed for each of the Learning & Reference forums just to contain the full scope of their services. So just consider this chapter a get-acquainted visit.

A visit to the Reference Desk

Keyword: **Reference**

The Reference Desk is your gateway to many resources on America Online. Many of the services listed in figure 11.1 are no doubt familiar to you. Some of the magazines, such as *Consumer Reports* and *Disney Adventures*, are discussed in more detail in other chapters. Other services offer huge databases of information that you'll want to explore. For now, stay with me if you want to begin a search for knowledge.

Fig. 11.1
The Reference Desk on America Online offers you a wide variety of information resources.

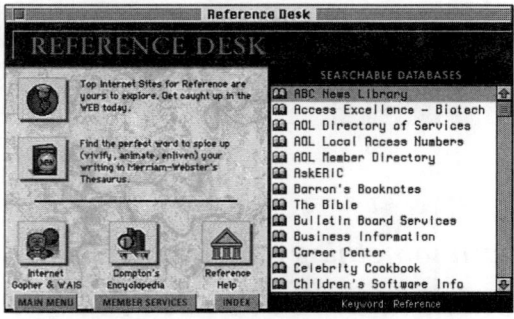

Internet sites for reference

There is a huge store of reference information available to you on the world-wide Internet, with an emphasis on the World Wide Web. By clicking on the Top Internet Sites for Reference icon, you'll see a large list of specially selected World Wide Web and other Internet-based resources (see fig. 11.2).

Fig. 11.2
AOL's Reference Web opens the door to a huge range of information resources.

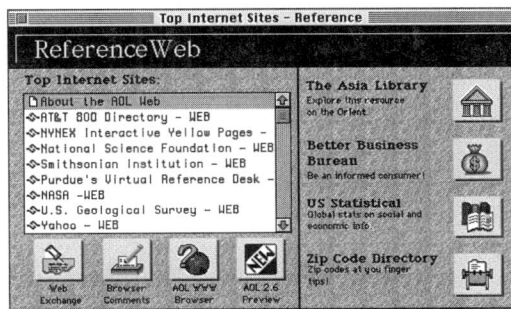

And the word you want is...

Keyword: **Thesaurus**

You can easily find the right word to make your written words more exciting by accessing Merriam-Webster's Thesaurus. Just enter the word for which you seek an alternative in the list field (see fig. 11.3), click on the Look Up button, and you'll soon see a list of available alternatives (see fig. 11.4).

Fig. 11.3
Merriam-Webster's online Thesaurus helps you find the right word.

Fig. 11.4
And here's the result.

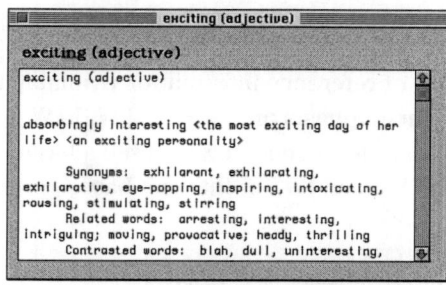

One more thing: if you need to check the spelling of a word, the folks at Merriam-Webster can help you there, too. The keyword: **Dictionary** will bring up Merriam-Webster's Collegiate dictionary.

AskERIC

Keyword: **AskERIC**

ERIC is not a person. It's short for Educational Resources Information Center and it's an Internet-based information center—an electronic library containing thousands of pieces of information for educators (as shown in fig. 11.5). There's also a resource to have your education-oriented questions researched and answered by the ERIC staff.

Fig. 11.5
AskERIC is a question-answering service and information library for parents and educators.

Barron's Booknotes helps you with your studies

Keyword: **Barrons**

As you might already know, Barron's guides are useful abstracts about the great literary works. You can search the vast library of Barron's Booknotes on America Online (see fig. 11.6).

Fig. 11.6
Barron's Booknotes is your source for abstracts on great literature.

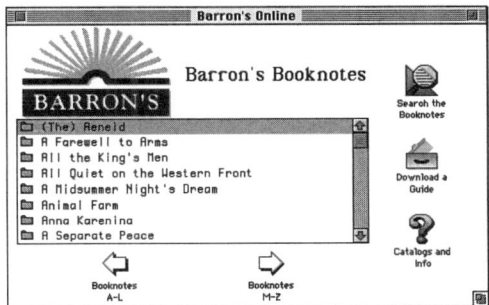

Visit Compton's NewMedia Forum

Keyword: **Comptons**

Not so long ago, looking up something in an encyclopedia meant a trip to the public library or purchasing a huge set of books for your home. Although you might not want to replace those voluminous, color-filled works on your bookshelves, consider America Online your second reference resource.

The folks at Compton's NewMedia have created a complete multimedia learning center on America Online (see fig. 11.7). All you have to do to tap that huge resource is click on one of the colorful icons.

Fig. 11.7
You can tap the resources of a huge encyclopedia, download multimedia learning materials, join chats, and more at the Compton's NewMedia forum.

If you've finished your studies for the day, or you just need a moment or two to recharge, click the Study Break icon for a fun-filled time. You'll find a Rap Room there, where you can have pleasant chats with other AOL members, or you can download a challenging puzzle or strategy game or two that you can play at your leisure.

The Career Center helps you reach a job decision

Keyword: **career**

One of the hardest tasks many young adults have to face is deciding what line of work to enter. Although some of you might have chosen your career during your early childhood, others work hard and long to find the line of work for which they are suited. And with cutbacks rampant in many industries, sometimes one has to make a mid-life career change.

America Online's Career Center is an electronic career and employment guidance forum (see fig. 11.8). The forum features an extensive lineup of services that can help you find the right career or even tap a huge database of available jobs.

Fig. 11.8
America Online offers a center for career counseling and employment opportunities. If you're job-hunting, you'll find a library of resume templates you can alter to your personal needs.

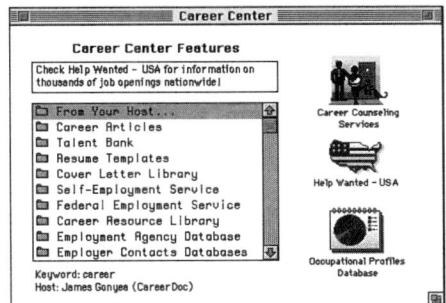

Court TV shows how courts really work

Keyword: **Court TV**

For most of us, knowledge about the workings of the court system is limited to such TV programs as *Matlock* or *Perry Mason*. In real life, trials are not resolved in 55 or so minutes plus commercials. The legal process is complex and convoluted and often difficult for the layman to understand.

The intense national attention over the O.J. Simpson murder case has placed such Cable TV sources as *Court TV* (shown in fig. 11.9) into the spotlight. *Court TV* is a 24-hour network devoted solely to the legal process and how it works.

Fig. 11.9
Court TV is the popular cable TV network devoted to the legal system.

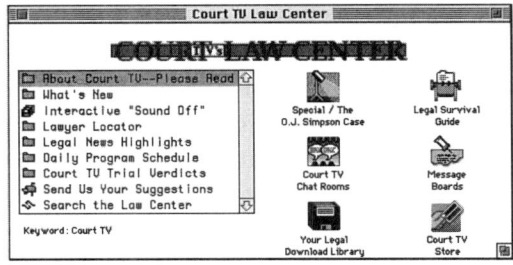

Access *C-SPAN* to see Congress in action

Keyword: **CSPAN**

Whenever an important hearing is being held in Congress, or a major address by the President or another important government figure is being given, *C-SPAN* (short for Cable-Satellite Public Affairs Network) is often there with gavel-to-gavel coverage. Figure 11.10 shows the *C-SPAN* Online welcome screen.

Fig. 11.10
You can find out all about *C-SPAN* from your computer.

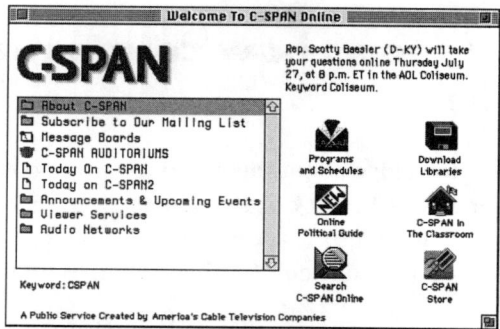

Smithsonian Online—your interactive museum

Keyword: **Smithsonian**

Most of you probably never hear much about the Smithsonian Institution except when reading news about a particular exhibit that's on display. When visiting the Smithsonian museums in person isn't possible, a visit to the Smithsonian Online Forum on America Online provides a useful substitute (see fig. 11.11). You can even download GIF photos of some of these exhibits.

Fig. 11.11
You can visit the
world's largest museum
on America Online.

>
>
> **GIF files are discussed in more detail in Chapter 4. To recap**
> briefly, the current versions of America Online's Macintosh software can
> open and view GIF files, plus graphics created in other popular formats, such
> as PICT and JPEG. If you download files created in these formats (and they
> are not compressed), you will see them display on your screen, gradually, as
> the download is in progress. If you want to look at a file already down-
> loaded in one of these image formats, simply choose Open from the File
> menu, and select the file you wish to see.

Let's explore the Education Center

Keyword: **Education**

America Online's Education department, shown in figure 11.12, complements
the Reference Desk, providing a wide range of information and tools to
advance your education. Some of the resources are identified with colorful
icons on the right side of the Education department's main screen. The full
roster of available facilities is listed in the directory at the right side of the
department window.

Fig. 11.12
You can consider the Education department an online educational institution. Some of these facilities are also shared with the Reference Desk.

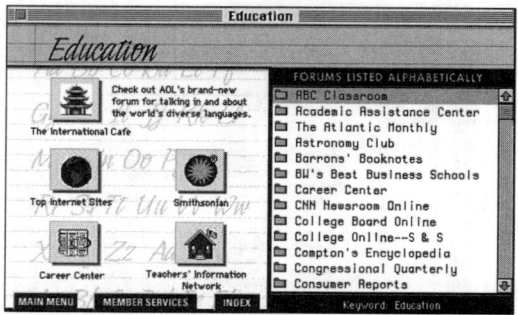

Visit top education Web sites

You can explore museums and educational institutions and view pictures of dinosaurs and planets using AOL's direct access to the World Wide Web. Just click on the Top Internet Sites icon in AOL's Education department to bring up a list of sites you'll want to explore further (see fig. 11.13).

Fig. 11.13
Explore museums and read the works of Shakespeare courtesy of the World Wide Web and AOL.

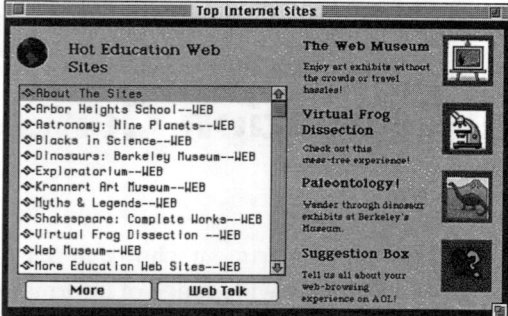

Visit the Academic Assistance Center

Keyword: **homework, aac**

Whether you are pursuing higher education, preparing for the College Board exams, or just trying to figure out how to do a homework assignment, consider the Academic Assistance Center as one of your resources for help (see fig. 11.14).

Fig. 11.14
America Online's
Academic Assistance
Center offers help to
the harried student.

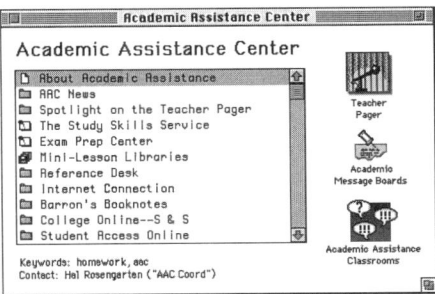

Paging a teacher on AOL

Suppose that term paper or homework assignment is due tomorrow. You, or a student in your family, have worked for hours trying to put it into shape, and you still have questions you need solved. There's a real life teacher available on AOL to help you resolve the problem.

First use the keyword **Teacher Pager** to enter this special area, click on the Teacher Pager folder, then click on the Make a page listing, which brings up a message window where you or your child can make your request for help.

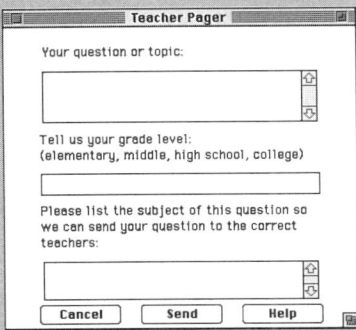

Here's how it works: your child, a grade school student, asks this question:

"How do you add and subtract numbers with more than a single column?" You ask your question, and then click on the button that reflects the grade level. Also indicate the time you want to meet with your online teacher. When you or your child asks the question, stay online for at least five minutes because, more often than not, your answer will be there in a jiffy in your mailbox. If not, you have the chance to meet with the instructor at the appointed time. In some cases, the student is invited into the Homework Help conference room for a one-on-one tutorial session.

A look at the *CNN* Newsroom

Keyword: **CNN**

CNN Newsroom is a daily 15-minute news program that is offered to schools by Ted Turner's Cable News Network. The online *CNN* Newsroom focuses on that program and related issues (see fig. 11.15). The forum has message areas where you can communicate with other America Online members or with *CNN* staff.

Fig. 11.15
Visit the *CNN*
Newsroom online,
where you also can
participate in the
regularly scheduled
conferences that
feature *CNN* represen-
tatives.

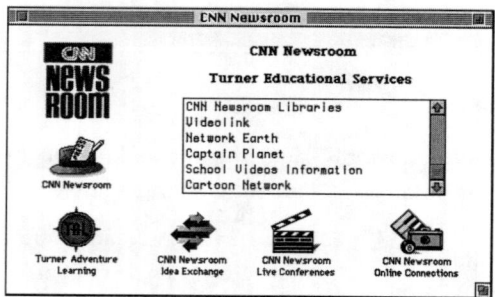

Using College Board Online

Keyword: **College Board**

The College Board is a national organization devoted to the interests of secondary and higher education. You can use the online forum to order books and other materials to help prepare you or your child for college entrance exams, and to deal with some of the tougher academic subjects (see fig. 11.16).

Fig. 11.16
College Board Online is a source of advice and assistance to students.

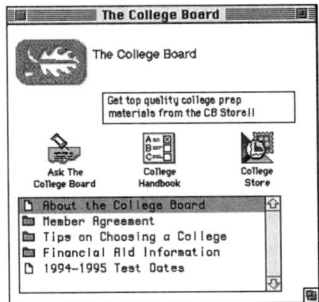

Explore the Electronic University Network

Keyword: **eun**

Although attending college is often viewed as an exciting time for most students, sometimes traveling to classes just isn't possible. Work and family commitments might be preventing you from attending class for an advanced degree, new career studies, or a much-needed remedial course. If so, the Electronic University Network might be able to help you. It's a group of educational institutions that offer interactive learning programs on a variety of subjects (see fig. 11.17).

Fig. 11.17
AOL's Electronic University Network lets you attend college and stay home at the same time.

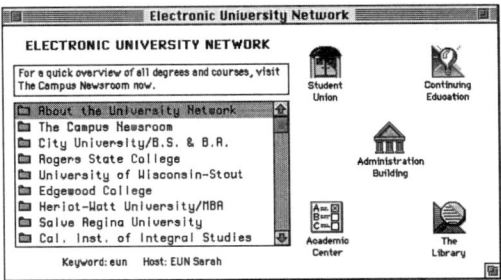

Attend Kim Komando's Komputer Klinic

Keyword: **Komando**

Kim Komando is a newspaper columnist and radio talk show host who has developed a line of tutorial videos designed to make the sometimes obscure world of personal computing understandable by using simple words instead of complex technospeak. You may have even seen the TV commercials about these tapes, entitled "Komputer Tutor." The Komando Forum is a resource of tips and secrets to help you use your computer more effectively (see fig. 11.18).

Fig. 11.18
The Komputer Klinic is a place to get help with your computer-related troubles.

A trip to the Library of Congress Online

Keyword: **Library**

One of the largest information centers in the world is owned by the U.S. government. It's the Library of Congress, and if you are ever in Washington, D.C., you can visit its teeming information archives in person. You also can explore this huge resource from right in front of your computer using America Online (see fig. 11.19).

Fig. 11.19
You can tap the huge information resources of the Library of Congress online.

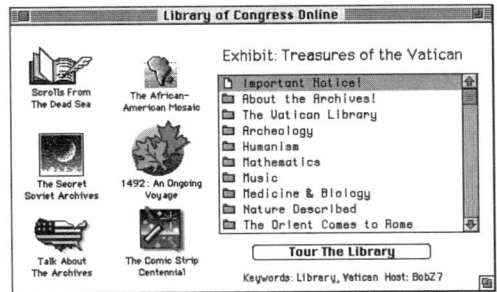

One popular Library of Congress area is devoted to the Dead Sea Scrolls. Since their discovery in the Judean Desert in 1947, scholars have spent countless hours researching their scope and meaning. You can access this area by clicking the Scrolls from the Dead Sea icon on the main forum window, which enables you to review the scholars' findings as well as learn the exciting background of this extraordinary archaeological find.

Join the *National Geographic* Society

Keywords: **geographic, ngs**

No doubt you've seen the elaborate, colorful *National Geographic* magazine. The magazine represents just a portion of the *National Geographic* Society's work, which is represented in its online forum, *National Geographic* Online (see fig. 11.20).

Fig. 11.20
Unique online resources are provided by the *National Geographic* Society.

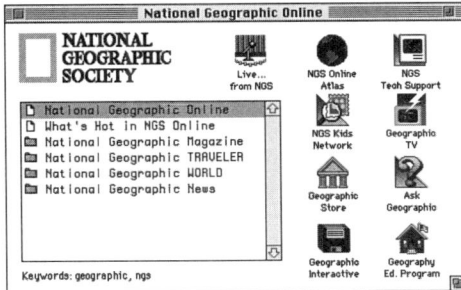

Access *National Public Radio* Outreach

Keywords: **NPR, radio**

When you tire of silly disk jockey chatter, the same repetitive music over and over again, or endless confrontational and sometimes exploitive talk shows, and you want something a little more stimulating, *National Public Radio* is the way to go. It's not available in every town—but it should be.

The *National Public Radio* Outreach forum on America Online is your way to interact with this public broadcasting network (see fig. 11.21).

Fig. 11.21
National Public Radio runs a popular AOL forum where you can stay in touch with the network's activities.

A visit to the Scholastic Forum

Keyword: **Scholastic**

The Scholastic Network Sampler is an online resource for teachers and students (see fig. 11.22). Professional educators can interact with their peers, and if you are a teacher, you can even join the network online.

Fig. 11.22
From your child's classroom to America Online, the Scholastic Forum is the place for educators.

Relax at the Afterwards Cafe

Keyword: **Afterwards**

Having spent these many hours deeply immersed in your studies on one subject or another, the time has come when you want to relax and perhaps meet with other students for a chat.

America Online's Afterwards Coffeehouse and Cafe is a pleasant, relaxing environment for serious discussions about all sorts of topics, from current events to literature and the arts (see fig. 11.23).

Fig. 11.23
When your studies are done, you can relax at the Afterwards Cafe, a place to get a virtual cup of coffee or soft drink after completing a day's hard work.

12

Your Online Newsstand

● **In this chapter:**

- ● **The news of the day**

- ● **Current weather maps**

- ● **Late-breaking news from Hollywood**

- ● **Information resources**

- ● **News and opinion journals**

- ● **Advice and information about business, stocks, and bonds**

A visit to America Online is like having many magazines and newspapers at your beck and call without having to travel to the corner newsstand . . . . ⊘

You can find a summary of the top news of the day, commentaries from your favorite columnists, or updates on how your stock portfolio is doing. And you don't have to travel to a newsstand or bookstore to locate any of this material. You can read it all in one place on America Online.

In this chapter, let's open up the pages of some of the magazines and newspapers AOL offers online. I have space to cover only a select portion of the publications that maintain online forums; many more are available for you to examine during your online visits.

A look at Today's News

Keyword: **News**

When you first sign onto America Online, you're greeted with the friendly, familiar In The Spotlight Welcome window and voice message (if you've got your computer's sound turned on, of course). The top news story of the day is always featured (and it may change from hour to hour, depending on new developments). You can see the major headlines by clicking on the Top News icon (see fig. 12.1). What you have here is organized very much like the sections of your daily newspaper. We'll read through each section and give you an idea of what information you can find.

Fig. 12.1
America Online's Today's News department (referred to as Top News on the In The Spotlight screen) is organized in much the same way as a typical daily newspaper.

When you bring up the Today's News screen, you'll see the major stories of the day in a directory window, which you can scroll through for additional information. By double-clicking on a story listing, you'll be able to read the text of that news item. As with other America Online text windows, you can save the story or print it for later reference. Just like your daily newspaper, some of these stories include photos, too (see fig. 12.2).

Fig. 12.2
Some of the stories you'll read online include color pictures, and they'll download to your computer in just seconds.

U.S. & World News

Keyword: **US News**

Now that you've read the front page, let's examine the table of contents of your daily newspaper and check out some of the other features (see fig. 12.3). During your online travels, you can set aside pages for reading later. You may also read the news of the world by category, simply by clicking on the pop-up menu labeled Click Here for Categories. There are separate folders for National News, Washington News, Europe, and other categories. If you are seeking information about a particular topic, you'll want to click on the Search News icon.

Fig. 12.3
This is your online newspaper's table of contents; you can read any of these stories simply by double-clicking on the title.

Business News

Keyword: **Business News**

Let's turn now to the business section (see fig. 12.4). All the information is divided into convenient categories, so you can easily locate material on a particular topic. The Search News icon at the right allows you to quickly access all the articles on a single topic. The Market News icon is useful for checking the goings-on in the world's various stock markets. Additional icons are used to access publications or forums with related interests, which you can access with a single click. These will change from time to time as AOL's forums are updated.

Fig. 12.4
Your online financial section covers the major business stories, plus related feature articles with a business orientation.

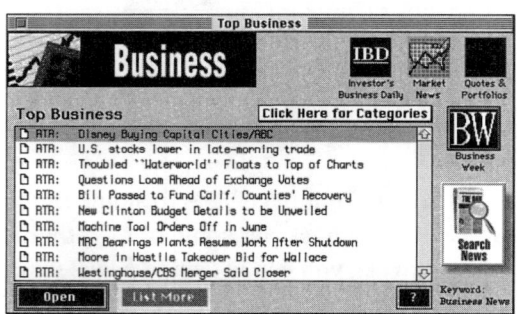

Finding the news that interests you

Reading news on America Online can be done two ways. You can browse through the contents of each section simply by reviewing the directory of stories (consider it the online equivalent of turning the pages in your daily paper). Or you can use the Search News feature to locate specific articles you want to read right away.

As with other searchable databases on America Online, looking for a news item is a simple process. Just click the Search News icon to bring up the search window, enter the topic of your search, and you'll see a display of the available

articles on that subject—as long as there are articles available, of course. AOL will often display related articles containing material covering similar subjects.

You'll also note that many of the news-related forums on America Online are interrelated. So if you open one screen, there will be icons that will allow you to switch to another area that has related information. An example is the Politics Forum icon at the right side of the U.S. & World news screen.

As an example of the sort of information one finds in the business news area, we selected the High Technology pages, where headlines separate current developments (see fig. 12.5). You can access these articles from the pop-up menu labeled Click Here for Categories. You can select an article, double-click on the title, or click on the Open button. The entire article can be saved as a text file for printing later or for offline reading. Just choose either the Save or Print command from the File menu.

Fig. 12.5
News with a techno-logical bent.

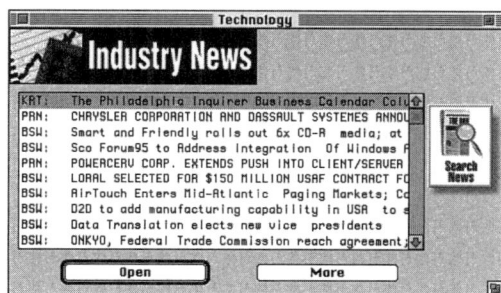

Weather News

Keyword: **Weather**

Since we already read the sports and entertainment pages in Chapter 6 (yes, I read them first, too!), let's skip the Entertainment and Sports icons in the Today's News screen and move on to the final category.

Although we can't do much to change the weather, we can at least be fully informed about it. By turning to the weather section in our virtual newspaper, you can review both articles and special forecasts countrywide (see fig. 12.6).

Fig. 12.6
When severe weather has a major impact, AOL has the latest information.

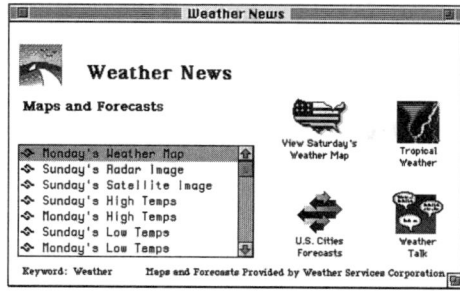

You can also see maps of weather trends right on your own computer, simply by selecting and downloading them. The forum updates the weather maps daily. You can see them in full color if you have a color screen. Choose from a satellite view or radar displays, and view charts of maximum and minimum temperatures not only for today, but for tomorrow and the next day as well (see fig. 12.7).

The forum offers these maps in the cross-platform **GIF** format (short for **Graphic Interchange Format**). Once you download the file to your computer, you can use the latest versions of AOL's Macintosh software to open and view the file.

During the summer and fall seasons, there is a special area devoted to tropical storms and hurricanes. Check this section to see if any severe weather is expected in your area, and what the trends are for the very near future (within the limits of the science of weather forecasting, of course).

Fig. 12.7
Within seconds, you'll see the latest weather maps displayed on your computer.

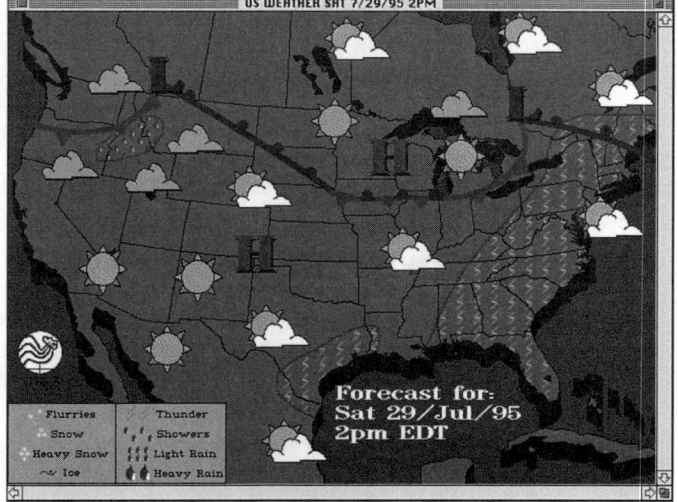

Q&A *Every time I want to view one of those fancy online maps, it takes so long for them to display on my computer. Why?*

Whenever you access new artwork from America Online, it has to be transferred to your computer. AOL uses a special artwork format for such features as weather maps to reduce file size, so you can retrieve them faster. But if you have an older modem that only works at 2,400 bps, you may wait several minutes for the artwork to reach you.

The best solution is a fast modem. Since even 14,400 bps modems these days cost less than $100, it's a great investment toward making your online visits more productive (and it also helps reduce your online bills, too, which will cover the cost of a high-speed modem in just a short time. And, for just a few bucks more, you can get a V.34 modem, providing up to 28,800 bps connections to America Online. Now that's really fast!

U.S. cities forecasts

Whether you are a regular traveler or a vicarious sojourner, you're no doubt curious as to the weather in other parts of the country. No problem— America Online's weather page has information about that, too, grouped by country or continent and updated regularly. If you're planning a trip abroad, consult this area before you pack your bags.

Top Internet sites

Not only can you explore AOL's own virtual newsstand, but you have quick access to the huge information resources available through AOL's World Wide Web feature. Just click on the Top Internet Sites button to see a selection of current offerings (see fig. 12.8).

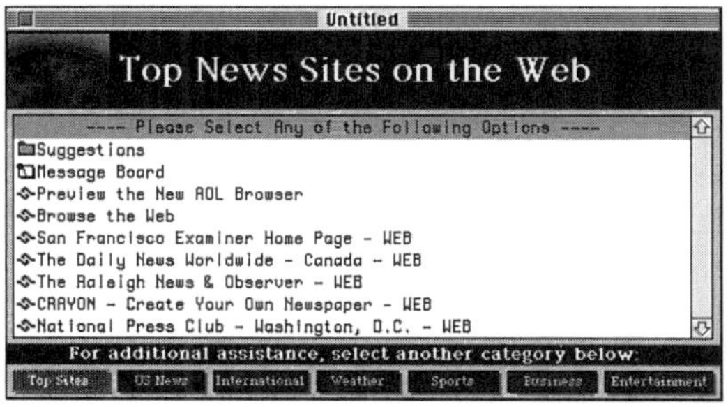

Fig. 12.8
The major newspapers and information resources are quickly adding World Wide Web access.

The listing you see in fig. 12.8 is subject to rapid changes, so you may expect to see a more diverse and larger offering when you begin to explore this area.

Browsing the online Newsstand

Keyword: **Newsstand**

Having read the latest news of the day, let's now pay a visit to America Online's huge newsstand. You can get there from anywhere on AOL with that single keyword—**Newsstand**. I described three of the major daily newspapers, the *Chicago Tribune*, the *San Jose Mercury*, and *The New York Times* in Chapter 8. There, I focused on the features you find in daily newspapers. Double-clicking on the appropriate directory listing under Publications, as shown in figure 12.9, will return you to those newspapers. The following are some other titles available from our virtual news dealer. Some of these publications, by the way, exist solely in cyberspace. You won't find them at your corner newsstand.

Fig. 12.9
The list of available magazines on AOL's newsstand is increasing rapidly.

- *The Atlantic Monthly*

  Keyword: **Atlantic**

  Several important magazines regularly appear online at the same time they appear in your favorite bookstore. One of these is *The Atlantic Monthly* (see fig. 12.10). You'll find the entire content of the latest issue of this popular literary magazine on AOL, plus an active message board and live chats.

Fig. 12.10
Read *The Atlantic Monthly* on AOL.

- Columnists & Features Online

Keyword: **Columnists**

You were exposed to the latest news and business reports in the Today's News department earlier in this chapter. Now let's pause for a few moments to review some commentary and opinion on the feature pages. Rather than poring through a pile of newspapers to find your favorite columnists, look in Columnists & Features Online (see fig. 12.11). This forum is sponsored by the Newspaper Enterprise Association (NEA), featuring many of the popular columnists such as Hodding Carter, Nat Hentoff, William Rusher, and Bruce Williams.

Fig. 12.11
Your online feature's page on AOL.

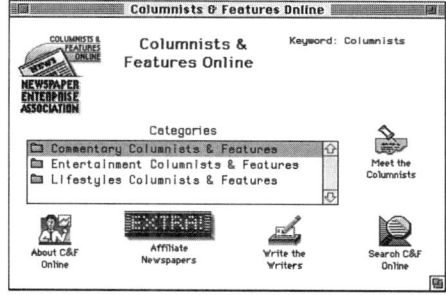

- *Consumer Reports*

Keywords: **Consumers**, **Consumer Reports**

Before you make a single purchasing decision, read *Consumer Reports*. This magazine offers comprehensive reviews on major new products of all types, from dishwasher detergents to new cars (see fig. 12.12).

Fig. 12.12
Learn all about new cars, how often that new VCR might need repair, and much more in this major resource for the product information.

TIP **Many of the regular articles and columns of your favorite magazines** are available on AOL. You can save or print the text windows for reading at your leisure, as you can with other text files on America Online.

- Cowles/SIMBA Media Information Network

  Keyword: **CowlesSIMBA**

  The word **media** connotes a variety of industries, from advertising agencies to broadcasting and publishing businesses. The Cowles/SIMBA Media Information Network is a major resource for information about this challenging and ever-changing business field.

- *The New Republic*

  Keyword: **New Republic**

  The New Republic is a magazine of opinion that takes an unabashedly liberal viewpoint of the nation and the world. It covers politics, literature, and the arts with its own unique slant. The magazine is interesting, controversial, and always entertaining, whatever your political leanings (see fig. 12.13).

Fig. 12.13
Whether you agree or disagree with the views offered, *The New Republic* is a magazine many opinion-makers read.

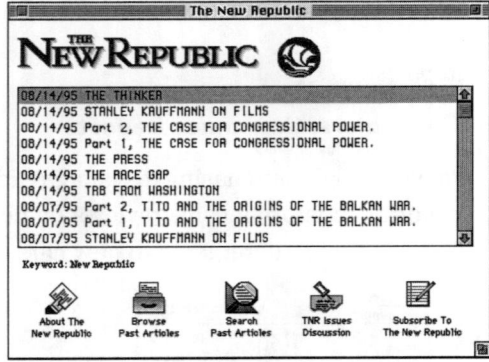

- *OMNI* Magazine Online

  Keyword: **OMNI**

  Whether you're interested in space exploration or in UFOs, you can explore scientific interests by visiting the OMNI Magazine forum on AOL (see fig. 12.14). In addition to reading many of the features from the latest issue of OMNI, you can attend a number of regular chats. One

exciting and controversial section of OMNI is the Antimatter department, which explores the frontiers of science and features reports
about psychic phenomena and strange things seen in the skies
(generally referred to as UFOs).

Fig. 12.14
Science fact and
science fiction are
combined in *OMNI*
magazine.

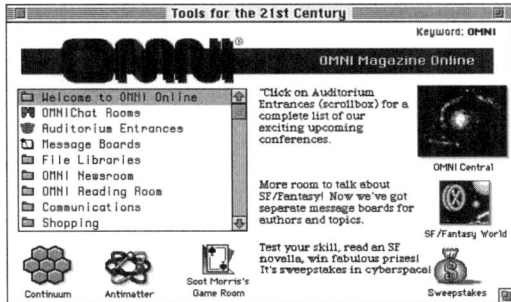

- *Saturday Review* Online

  Keyword: **Saturday Review**

  Many of you probably remember *The Saturday Review* as a magazine
  of arts and culture that existed for many years and folded in 1986.
  During its over half a century of existence, this journal covered such
  subjects as politics, science, business, literature, and even the world of
  entertainment.

  So what is a magazine that no longer exists doing on America Online?
  Well, unlike the other online magazines we've discussed so far in this
  chapter, *Saturday Review* Online doesn't exist as a printed publication—it's strictly an electronic magazine brought to you by the publishers of OMNI and I-Wire (another magazine that only exists online) (see
  fig. 12.15).

Fig. 12.15
The *Saturday Review*
reborn as an electronic
magazine on America
Online.

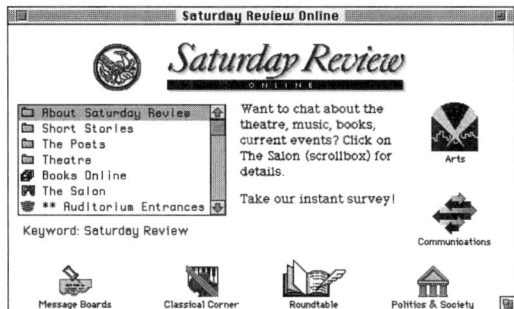

- *Stereo Review* Online

  Keyword: **Stereo Review**

  It started out years ago as *Hi-Fi Review,* and then it was *Hi-Fi/Stereo Review* when stereophonic audio became popular in the early 1960s. Now it's just *Stereo Review* (shown in fig. 12.16), and it remains one of the most popular consumer audio magazines in the USA. If you are looking to buy a new stereo system, exploring the frontiers of home theater (Surround Sound), or you just want to read reviews about the latest recordings, you'll want to visit *Stereo Review* Online.

Fig. 12.16
Learn all about home audio in *Stereo Review* magazine on AOL.

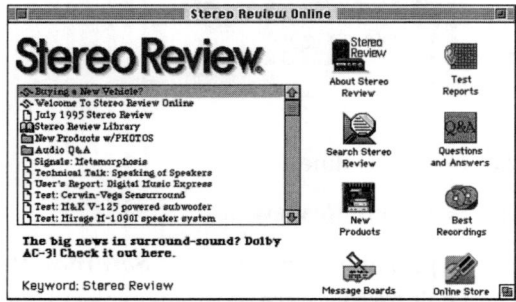

- *TIME* Magazine Online

  Keyword: **TIME**

  When you want to find out how long you've spent on America Online, you might be inclined to type the keyword **Time** (rather than **Clock,** which is the correct choice). Instead of seeing time spent, you'll see the very latest issue of *TIME* magazine. The full content of the current issue is posted on America Online before the printed magazine hits the newsstands (see fig. 12.17).

Fig. 12.17
An issue of *TIME* on AOL.

• *WIRED*

Keyword: **Wired**

The rise of the Information Superhighway means that we are all truly connected by telephone line, by satellite, or by our computers talking to one another. *WIRED* explores what it calls the "Digital Generation," which has grown up and experienced the joining of computers, telecommunications, and the media (see fig. 12.18).

Fig. 12.18
The voice of the Digital Generation on AOL.

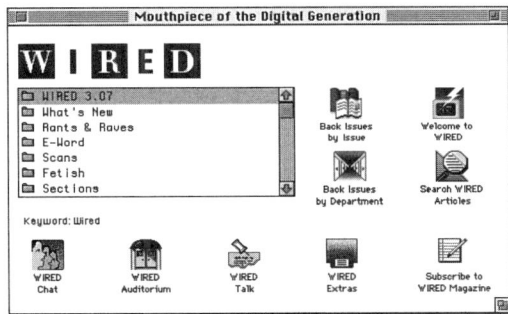

• *Woman's Day* Online

Keyword: **Woman's Day**

From the recipe of the month to advice on health and special interests, *Woman's Day* has long provided an informative, optimistic outlook with pages and pages of solid information (see fig. 12.19). The contents of each regularly scheduled issue are posted in the magazine's colorful online forum at the same time they appear at your local newsstand.

Fig. 12.19
A quick look at the contents of *Woman's Day* magazine on AOL will show recipes (one of the magazine's most popular features) and useful information about new developments in health care.

- *Worth* Online

  Keyword: **Worth**

  Here's a different approach to presenting financial information. Instead of dealing with business news in a cold, dry, analytical fashion, *Worth* magazine attempts to take into account what it considers one's personal needs in providing financial information (see fig. 12.20).

Fig. 12.20
Worth magazine helps you decide how best to manage your finances with clearly explained information. It's a different slant on dealing with your finances.

13

Make that X-Large, Please: Secrets of Online Shopping

● **In this chapter:**

- Search for products you want to buy

- Buy the items you want while online

- Join a service that will help you save money on your next car

- Place your own classified ad, free!

- Have groceries and pharmaceutical items delivered right to your door

- Tap a huge database of employment opportunities

Shopping should be fun, yet it seems to become harder. You have to fight traffic, search for a parking space, wait in a checkout line. America Online offers an easier way . . . . . ⊙

Do you want to save a few dollars on your next purchase? Perhaps you just want to get the most up-to-date information about a particular product or service before you decide whether to buy. America Online is the place to do both.

Up until now, this book told you how to locate information resources on America Online. In this chapter, you'll go on an enjoyable shopping tour by way of the Information Highway. You'll make several brief stops at different shops in an online mall, and you'll even buy a few items along the way.

Your virtual Marketplace

Keywords: **Marketplace**, **Shopping**

America Online's Marketplace department, shown in figure 13.1, is a gateway to AOL's huge shopping mall. Since my next chapter is devoted to using America Online for your travel plans, this little excursion is limited to the items that strictly concern shopping. Of course, the merchandise you buy during this journey may well be suited for that trip you're planning to take.

Fig. 13.1
When you first enter the Marketplace, you may see a window labeled Spotlight, where you see a list of features you want to check further. Just click the Go to Marketplace button to return to the department itself.

Before you go on, you should realize that the Marketplace, as with other online areas, is definitely a work in progress. Artwork is always being updated, and new shopping features are regularly being added to the mix. So the Marketplace you visit when you take your next online shopping tour might look a little different from the one described here. (Some of the icons shown in fig. 13.1, for example, represent nationally known chain stores who have established an online presence.)

Top Internet Sites

Through AOL's convenient World Wide Web feature, you not only have access to shopping areas on AOL, but to other shopping areas across the globe. Just click on the Top Internet Sites icon in AOL's Marketplace (see fig. 13.2) to take a gander at some of the available shopping resources you can easily access with AOL's Web browser software. (I'll explain what that's all about in Chapter 18.)

Fig. 13.2
Double-click your way to World Wide Web shopping on AOL.

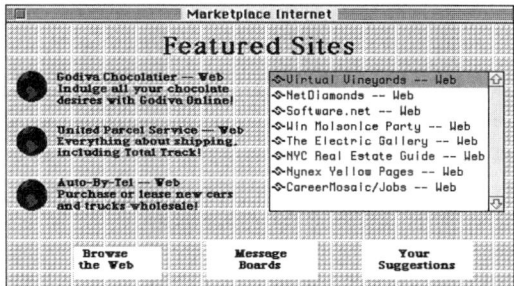

CAUTION In order to access sites on the World Wide Web (or WWW, for short), you need to have AOL's version 2.6 software, plus the WWW browser software. You can get both by accessing the Upgrade area (*keyword*: **Upgrade**) and downloading both software packages. If you already have AOL 2.6, you just need to download the browser software. To learn more about WWW access, read Chapters 18 and 19.

Place an order with the AOL product center

Keyword: **AOL Store**

America Online has its own custom line of merchandise, which you can wear, send as a gift, or just keep as a souvenir. Since I collect fancy T-shirts myself, let's order one. The steps you're going to take here are similar to those you'll follow for most online ordering on America Online.

First, click the America Online Shop the Store icon in the main store directory (which comes up via the **AOL Store** keyword), then click the A to Z Product Listing icon, and you will see the screen shown in fig. 13.3.

Fig. 13.3
Choose the product
that interests you from
the directory listing.

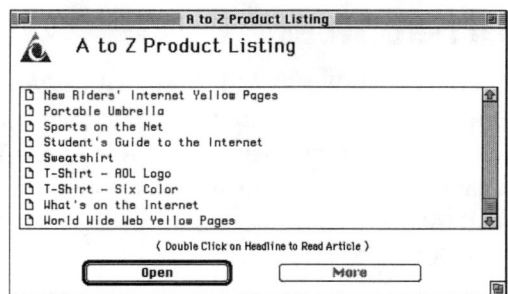

From the list of products, choose the Logo T-shirt. To see a product description and a full color photo of the product (see fig. 13.4), just double-click the product's name in the directory. To order one of these shirts, select the Click Here To Order button (see fig. 13.5).

Fig. 13.4
AOL's graphical
interface lets you see
the product before you
buy. The descriptive
window gives you the
very same sort of
information you'd find
in a mail-order catalog.

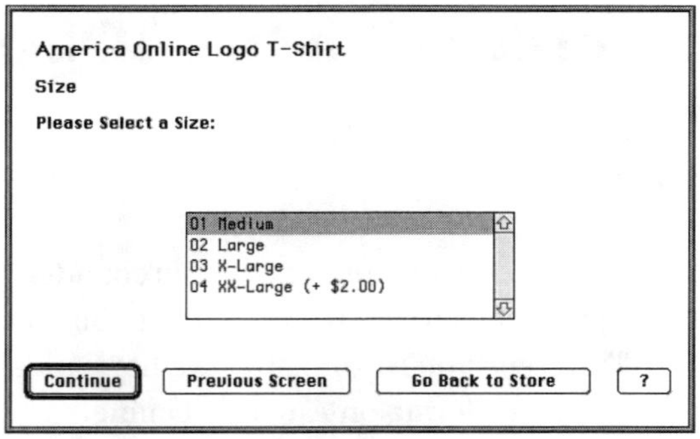

Fig. 13.5
Ready to order?

Choose the shirt size you want by double-clicking the entry in the directory window. After you've selected the merchandise you want to order, you will probably want to double-check the shopping cart to make sure that you've selected the correct item. When you choose an item, AOL's software will display a confirmation that the product you want has been added to your shopping cart (see fig. 13.6).

Fig. 13.6
Your selection is confirmed.

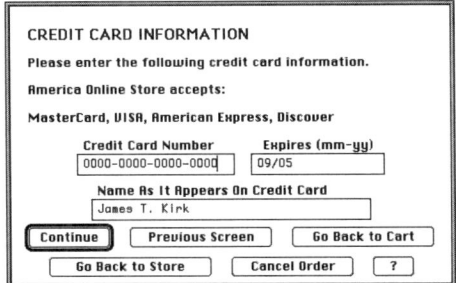

If the information listed in your shopping cart is correct and you're done shopping, click the Checkout button, which brings up the window shown in figure 13.7.

Fig. 13.7
Enter your billing information here.

✓ **TIP** **Before visiting your online shopping center, have your credit card** handy so that you can enter your billing information without delay.

After you've entered your billing information, click the Continue button to enter your correct shipping address. By default, the address recorded for your online account is listed as the billing address (see fig. 13.8). You can have the same address automatically entered for shipping or enter a different shipping location.

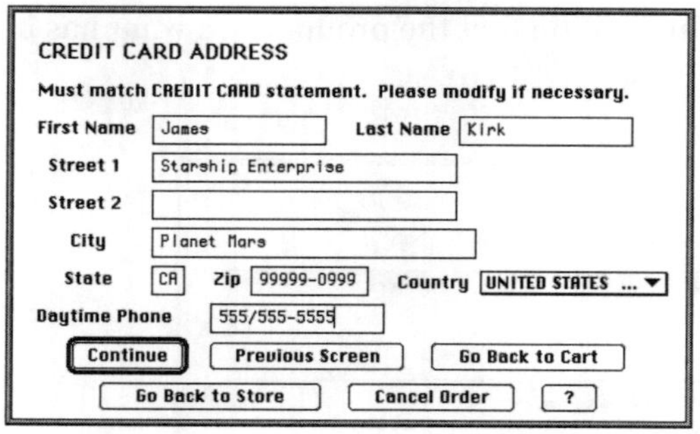

Fig. 13.8
Completing the order.

CREDIT CARD ADDRESS

Must match CREDIT CARD statement. Please modify if necessary.

First Name [Janes]   Last Name [Kirk]

Street 1 [Starship Enterprise]

Street 2 [ ]

City [Planet Mars]

State [CA]   Zip [99999-0999]   Country [UNITED STATES ... ▼]

Daytime Phone [555/555-5555]

[Continue]   [Previous Screen]   [Go Back to Cart]

[Go Back to Store]   [Cancel Order]   [?]

How to get an AOL software upgrade

From time to time, America Online upgrades its software to add new features and offer better performance. Whether you use a Mac or Windows, you can choose the software version you want and download either (or both, if you have computers from both platforms) from this download center.

Before you download the new version, you might want to refer to the file description for the new version to see what's being offered.

TIP   **You can download the newest AOL software releases for free by** using the keyword **Upgrade**, selecting the upgrade you want, and choosing the Download Now option. If you choose Download Later, you will leave the free area and end up paying for the download time.

Buying a car

Keyword: **AutoVantage**

AutoVantage is an online database of new and used car information, and a center where you can arrange to service your car, buy accessories, and even order your new vehicle at a discount price (see fig. 13.9).

Fig. 13.9
AutoVantage is your
online resource for
automobile informa-
tion.

AutoVantage®

Get $20 of FREE gasoline when you join AutoVantage!

Plus, get $1,000 in car maintenance coupons at over 16,000 locations nationwide, prenegotiated discounts on new cars, savings on car leasing, new and used car information, and complete family coverage. Join today for only $1!

What's New   About AutoVantage

Access For Members   Access For Non-Members   Join AutoVantage   Free Gasoline Offer

Keyword: AutoVantage, Auto

AutoVantage provides an interface that's very different from other areas on America Online, so this section discusses it in detail. If you have experience with a command-line (text) interface in DOS, you no doubt will find this setup familiar. This interface may seem a bit strange to Mac users, but AutoVantage makes it really easy to navigate. You are prompted every step of the way, and your answers govern the information that's presented.

To take advantage of AutoVantage's services, you have to join, but there's almost always a low-cost introductory membership available. To join, follow these steps:

1 Click the Access AutoVantage (Access for Non-Members) icon (refer to fig. 13.9).

2 In the first window, specify how long your row of text should be. A good size is 60 or 80 characters, which will work effectively on the average 13- and 14-inch computer screen. The narrower the screen, the longer it takes to scroll through the section. If you don't make the correct selection, just close the window, open it again, and start over.

3 The Main Directory lists the services available to non-members (see fig. 13.10). Because this is a text-based interface, you cannot just double-click the item you want to select. You have to let the descriptions in the text window guide you to what to do next. In this case, you have 13 items from which to choose. Simply enter the number of the item you want to learn more about, and either click the Send button or press the Enter or Return key.

Fig. 13.10
The AutoVantage main directory window is used to take you to different areas of the service.

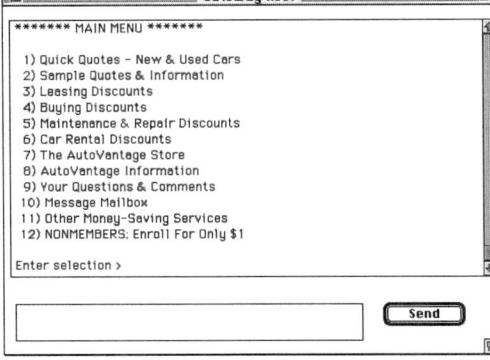

4 For each selection, you are asked to enter a number or further information. If you want to join, you'll be presented with a brief questionnaire that asks for your name, mailing address, and billing information. Pressing Enter or Return when you are finished entering the requested data sends it to AutoVantage's gateway, and you are then prompted for further information.

5 After you have completed your visit to AutoVantage, you can close the window to leave the text-based service behind, and return to your familiar America Online icons and windows.

If you opt to join AutoVantage, you'll receive a letter and other material in a few weeks to confirm your membership along with helpful hints on how to use the service.

Sending flowers

Keyword: **Flowers**

Your next stop along the Information Superhighway shopping mall is the cute little flower shop shown in figure 13.11. Maybe a friend or relative is celebrating a special occasion, or you want to give a bouquet of roses to your significant other. You can place your order at 800-FLOWERS. That order is then transmitted to a local florist near the home of the person who will be receiving the flowers. That florist will deliver your order.

Fig. 13.11
Say it with flowers or other choice gifts, such as the Valentine Day's candy collection shown here.

> **TIP** **The quality of the image you see on your computer screen**
> depends on the size and quality of the monitor, and the capabilities of your
> computer to display an image at a specific resolution. The image is sent in
> full color, but whether it appears in black and white or clear, crisp, full
> color varies from installation to installation.

If you want to know more about the product being displayed, simply click the
Featured Product Info button. You'll see a capsule description of the product,
and have a chance to place your order through very much the same technique
that was described earlier. You'll have an opportunity to select your billing
option and review your order before it's sent.

Buying books online

Keyword: **Bookstore**

America Online's Bookstore is stocked with shelves and shelves of the latest
titles, both fiction and nonfiction, in all of the major categories (see fig.
13.12). There's a special database that allows you to search for a specific title;
select the Search for Books icon in the upper right corner of the Online
Bookstore forum window. The Special Requests and Questions icon takes
you to a message area where you can post your request for a book that might
not be in stock, or simply ask for additional information about available
volumes.

Fig. 13.12
Use the bookstore's
database to look for
that best-seller. Once
you find it, you can
place your order in just
a minute or two.

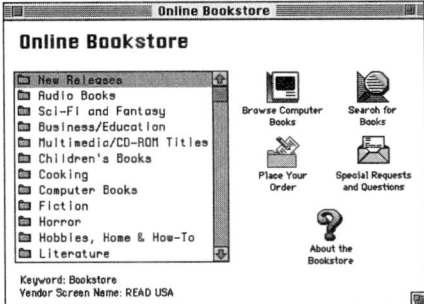

You can get large discounts on many computer products on AOL. You can
even order a brand new system, and benefit from a big selection and good
prices. Here are some online resources for these products.

Computer Express

Keyword: **Computer Express**

Maybe you want to buy a neat new computer game, you need some hard drive utility software, or it's time to replace that old modem with one of those new high-speed models (and take advantage of America Online's 14,400 and 28,800 bps service). Computer Express (see fig. 14.13) is your resource for discount prices on all sorts of computer-related merchandise.

Fig. 13.13
Computer Express lets you search for a specific product or check out the newest software titles and special Hot Deals.

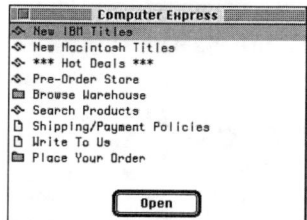

As with all stores in America Online's shopping mall, entering your order is simple. You list the items you want to buy (sometimes you have to also identify them by a part number), enter your billing information, recheck your order, and send it. The shopping service will usually have information about how long it takes to process orders.

The online gift shop

Keyword: **2Market**

America Online's 2Market department is quite literally an online gift shop. You can order special gifts for any occasion. (Figure 13.14 shows the promotions in effect just before Mother's Day, for example.) You can also take advantage of special deals on a variety of products.

The most attractive way to order is with the help of 2Market's CD. You can place your order for the CD during your online visit. It'll arrive in just a short time, and it provides entertaining, interactive demonstrations from many of the major manufacturers of the products offered through 2Market.

Fig. 13.14
2Market is also available in CD-ROM form, so you can view colorful, interactive demonstrations on new products.

Even if you don't have the CD handy, you can still see a full-color picture of the product and a complete description showing the important features. Just click the Product Spotlight heading once, and then choose a product from the directory listing (see fig. 13.15).

Fig. 13.15
AOL's 2Market service offers a high quality photo and full product description.

 **TIP** **The popularity of CD-ROMs is not lost on the folks who run** America Online. Over time, you'll begin to see more CD-ROM-based offerings on America Online. Some of the art content for the service itself might also be offered on a CD. The advantage of this is that it allows the service to provide more detailed artwork and sound in a form that contains too much data to download to your computer efficiently.

Using Shoppers Advantage Online

Keyword: **Shoppers Advantage**

Shoppers Advantage is a discount buying service that lets you purchase up to 250,000 different items right from the comfort of your personal computer (see fig. 13.16). Like AutoVantage, the interface for Shoppers Advantage is text-based. That is, you navigate through the service by entering simple commands in the text field. By choosing numbers or typing simple words, you are able to view the vast catalog, read product descriptions, and place your order for prompt shipment to your home or office.

Fig. 13.16

The drab text-based interface doesn't really tell the tale. Shoppers Advantage Online is your interactive discount mail order catalog, offering over 250,000 items.

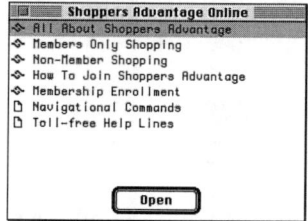

When you look over a product's description, you'll see two prices. One is for members; the other somewhat higher price is for non-members. When you find a product you want to order, you'll discover quickly enough whether the low membership fee covers the purchase of a single item (and quite often it does). Members also get a two-year warranty on the products they buy. A typical online shopping trip for a new computer can bring a huge list of choice products from Apple Computer, IBM, and other manufacturers.

Using the Classifieds Online

Keyword: **Classifieds**

The Classifieds Online forum is the place to post your own ads or check out advertisements from fellow members and commercial outfits. You aren't limited to just the computer-related merchandise shown in figure 13.17; you also can place ads for home appliances, electronics, and other types of merchandise.

There are thousands of ads in the Classifieds message area. Most of them are placed by well-meaning firms and individuals; in most cases, you will receive the exact merchandise you order. But, as with all mail order transactions, approach the deal with some healthy skepticism. It's a good idea, for example, to use a credit card when you make your purchase. That way, if you are not satisfied with the product or service, the credit card issuer will usually investigate the transaction on your behalf and even credit your account, if necessary.

Fig. 13.17
America Online's buy/sell/trade center is a place where you can check out ads for all sorts of merchandise, not just computers.

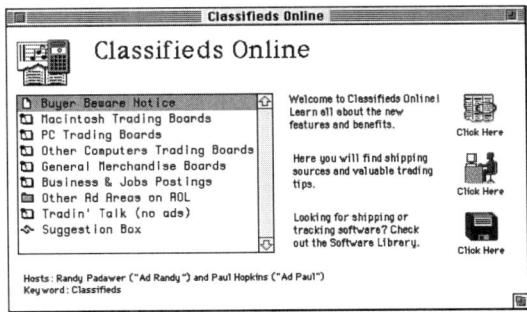

Still more online shopping resources

Whenever you want to buy something new, you are faced with a bewildering array of choices. This section discusses one resource where you might find a little help in sorting through these choices to make the one that's right for you. You'll also find coverage about a nationwide buying service, a bill-paying service, and an online resources for another kind of shopping—job hunting.

Home delivery from AOL

Keyword: **Shoppers Express**

Normally, when you have a prescription filled, you go to your local pharmacy; when you buy groceries, you go to a supermarket or convenience store. With Shoppers Express on America Online (see fig. 13.18), you can order the merchandise you want from home and let the skilled buyers at Shoppers Express fill your order and bring it right to your home or office.

Shoppers Express works with merchants in your area to provide fast, home delivery of the products you want. Before deciding to try the service, click the Service In Your Area icon to see if Shoppers Express is represented by a store in your community.

Fig. 13.18
Order food, pharma-
ceutical items, and
general merchandise,
and have them
delivered right to your
home. Click the
Request a Catalog icon
to receive a catalog at
your home or office.

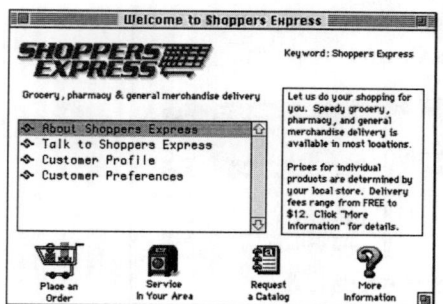

Common-sense tips for online shopping

Consider your online shopping tour a modern day equivalent of browsing
through a mail order catalog. Although you can learn a lot about a product or
service from the descriptions, there are occasions when the product you buy
just won't meet your requirements, or the merchandise you've received just
doesn't work as it should.

Before you order

There are some steps you should take before making an order:

- Read the product description thoroughly. If you have further questions,
  contact the staff of that particular shopping area.

- Read any posted Terms and Conditions carefully, in case you need to
  return the product for an exchange or refund for any reason.

- Merchandise sent via mail will usually include a shipping charge of
  some sort. If you're comparison shopping, be sure to include the
  shipping charge as part of the total price.

- Check the product description for estimated shipping times. Remember
  that shipments can be delayed as a result of conditions beyond the
  vendor's control, such as late delivery of merchandise from the manufacturer or delays on the part of the shipping agency.

- If you're ordering a product for a special occasion or as a gift, allow
  extra time for it to reach its destination.

- Make a copy of your order, so you can refer to it later in case you have a
  further question about the merchandise you've ordered.

- Bear in mind that you are ordering the merchandise directly from the vendor, not from America Online, which simply makes the vendor's service available. Complaints about products or services are best addressed directly to the vendor.

- If you plan to buy merchandise from an AOL classified ad, don't be hesitant about asking the seller for some references. Remember, it's your money and you have a right to spend it carefully.

TIP **Some online order forms consist of multiple text fields, and** choosing the Save option in the File menu might not save the complete text of your order. If this is the case, enter the full details of your order in a text document using AOL's memo feature, or use a screen image capture program to record the actual order screen itself.

After the package arrives

There are also some things to keep in mind after you receive your order:

- When you receive your package, examine the box for signs of damage. If the box seems ruined beyond repair, contact the online vendor immediately about getting a replacement.

- If you have a problem with the merchandise you've received, follow the instructions that came with the package or are posted in the vendor area about whom to contact for customer service.

- If the product you ordered needs to be repaired, review the warranty information supplied with the package. Quite often, service must be done through a manufacturer's own authorized service center and not the vendor.

- If you use a credit card to make your purchase (and, in most cases, you will), you might also contact the card issuer to assist you if you run into problems dealing with a particular vendor. Remember, too, that some credit cards provide extended warranties and other benefits when you use them to purchase large-ticket items.

14

The Travel Chapter

● In this chapter:

- **Check flight schedules and fares**

- **Make your airline, car, and hotel reservations**

- **Try a bed-and-breakfast establishment for a change**

- **Find out about attractions in your destination city**

- **Protect yourself by checking for travel advisories**

Want to go to some exotic place for your honeymoon or a weekend getaway? From flight to hotel to rental car reservations—let AOL help you plan your trip . . . . ▸

I n this chapter, we'll explore AOL's Travel department. Instead of visiting the neighborhood travel agency when you're planning a trip, let's go to an agency located in cyberspace, available through the friendly interface of America Online. Following a few simple steps, you can pick a spot for a family vacation and gather information about the place you're going to visit without ever leaving your own home or office. You can select a hotel, make airline reservations, and even rent a car.

A visit to the Travel department

Keyword: **Travel**

Your first step in preparing for this vacation is to pay a visit to AOL's Travel department. To access this area, click the Travel icon in the Main Menu or use the keyword **Travel** (see fig. 14.1). Some of the online areas available in this department are described in the next few pages.

Fig. 14.1
The Travel department on AOL provides the resources you need before making a business or vacation trip.

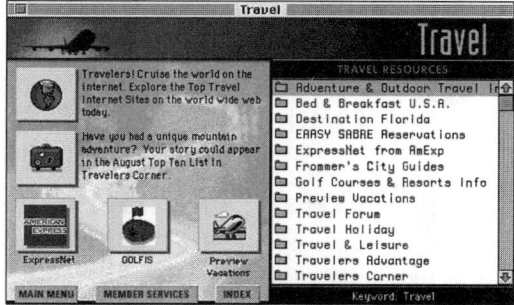

Cruise the world on the Internet

When you click on the little globe at the upper left of the Travel department window shown in fig. 14.1, you see a directory of easily accessible travel resources on the World Wide Web (see fig. 14.2). You'll travel across the USA and around the world, and locate fascinating, far-flung travel spots and valuable information that will serve you well on your next trip.

Fig. 14.2
WWW travel resources are easily accessed during your AOL visits.

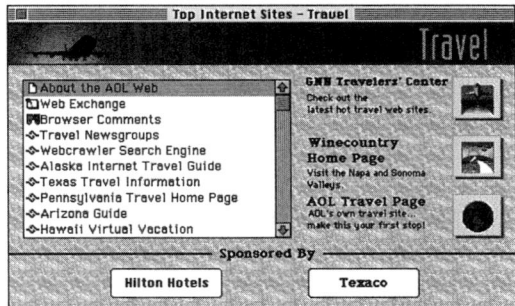

One resource you'll want to check out, shown at the lower-right side of the screen shown in fig. 14.2, is **Webcrawler**, an easy-to-use gateway that will help you locate WWW information of all sorts (not just related to travel, but to most any subject under the sun). Once you locate a specific place to visit, you can easily travel to that site by double-clicking on the entry. I'll tell you more about that in Chapter 19.

Using the EAAsy Sabre System

Keyword: **EAAsy Sabre**

EAAsy Sabre is an online travel agency, where you can make your airline, car rental, and hotel reservations (see figure 14.3). It's sponsored by American Airlines, but covers all the airlines in its lists.

Fig. 14.3
America Online's EAAsy Sabre gateway is your entrance to full-featured travel reservation service.

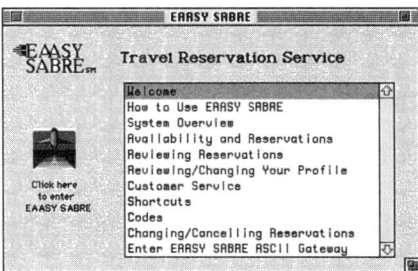

If this is your first visit to this area, you'll want to briefly review the information texts in the forum directory window before you click the icon at the left of the screen, which takes you to the EAAsy Sabre main menu. This way, all of the new commands and procedures will be easy to get used to.

When you've located all the information you want, you can make your reservations, confirm those reservations, and bill the charges directly to your credit card. Your plane tickets and confirmation information will be mailed to your home or office.

TIP **If you have a special preference, such as a nonsmoking seat,** window view, or a vegetarian meal, you need to list those preferences in your application. Getting correct reservations is much easier that way.

First, you can view weather reports

If you're about to leave on that trip, you'll probably want to see a weather report for the city you're going to visit. Just double-click on Weather in the directory listing of the EAAsy Sabre main menu. Once you've selected this option, you are asked to name the city for which you want to check the weather. You receive information about the current forecast and the expected weather for the following day (see fig. 14.4).

Fig. 14.4
EAAsy Sabre provides the latest weather information on the places you want to visit.

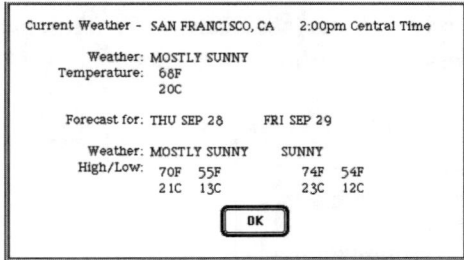

Finding the best fares or flights

The ongoing airline price wars have made just about everyone (your cheerful author included) confused about airline fares. Each airline has its own schedule, with specific rules to obtain those highly touted discount fares. And the prices seem to change almost daily, in response to another airline's announcement about still lower and sometimes more confusing price schedules.

Before making your reservation, you'll want to find out just what the prices really are. First, click the Flights and Fares icon at the top left of the EAAsy Sabre main menu. In response to the message prompts, enter information about your planned flight. You are then asked the name of the city from which you're leaving, the final destination of your flight, the dates you plan to travel, and the time you want to leave. Armed with that information, you'll be able to save money and get the flight that meets your needs. Using EAAsy Sabre, you can also locate the latest discounts on car rentals and hotels.

 **If you want to bring your laptop computer with you, ask the hotel** if they provide a data port or other easy access to their phone lines, so you can easily get online to do your America Online sessions and other online transactions.

 **The national daily newspaper *USA Today* is a great source for** up-to-date news for travelers. Just select the USA Today Travel News folder from the main menu of the Travel window (you probably have to scroll down to see the folder). You then see a list of travel articles. Don't forget, you can read, save, and print the latest news before planning your trip.

How to use ExpressNet from American Express

Keyword: **ExpressNet**

In setting up ExpressNet forum (see fig. 14.5), American Express has teamed up with the folks at America Online to provide a fully-equipped interactive customer service center for you. If you're already an American Express card holder, you can use this forum to check your account status, and take advantage of some of the special shopping-service offers. But even if you're not a card holder, you'll find valuable travel information that you'll want to know before you make your reservations. There's also a list of the company's own travel agencies throughout the world.

Fig. 14.5
Before you leave home, be sure you have your credit card ready.

A Trip to Travelers' Corner

Keyword: **Travelers Corner**

The next stopping point in this tour is the Travelers' Corner. This forum is hosted by the editors of Weissman Travel Reports. The Corner's main focus is comprehensive profiles of major U.S. and international destinations. You get a brief overview of the high points of a specific city and a list of its main attractions. The report not only describes these attractions, but also suggests the kinds of people who would most like to visit them. This information is especially important if you're taking your children with you.

To visit the Travelers' Corner, choose the Travelers' Corner icon from the Travel department window. The Travelers' Corner screen appears (see fig. 14.6).

Fig. 14.6
The Travelers' Corner profiles some favorite travel spots and provides tips about local culture and etiquette.

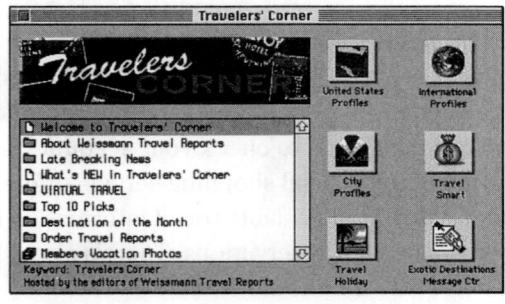

If you want to read more travel-related material at your leisure, click the Travel Holiday icon to access the current issue of *Travel Holiday* magazine. Order Travel Reports gives you a special offer to purchase comprehensive professional profiles of the places you want to visit. These profiles are the same ones that are available through your local travel agency.

How to preview vacations online

Keyword: **Vacations**

They say a picture is worth a thousand words, and while it's really nice to read text documents about travel locations online, wouldn't it be great to actually see what these far-off locales look like before you plan your trip?

That's what Preview Vacations Online is all about (see fig. 14.7). This forum lets you view full color photos of popular travel spots, and even participate in a real auction where you can bid on the vacation of your choice.

Fig. 14.7
Preview Vacations on AOL is a lot more than just a collection of travel photos.

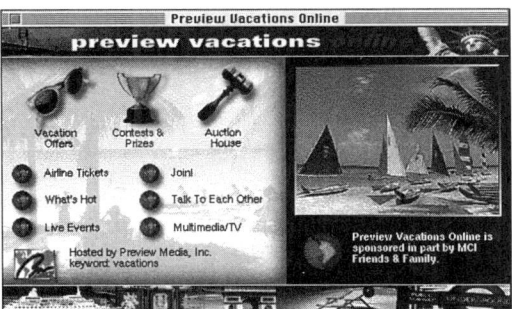

A trip to the Travel Forum

Keyword: **Travel Forum**

The Travel Forum consists of a wealth of resources that contains much of the information you need to know before planning your trip (see fig. 14.8). The main window of this forum contains useful articles on many travel-related subjects. If you're going to travel by air, you receive up-to-date reports on the lowest fares. When you travel abroad, you need to know specific things about the country you are going to visit.

Fig. 14.8
America Online's Travel Forum is your first resource for information about the places you want to visit.

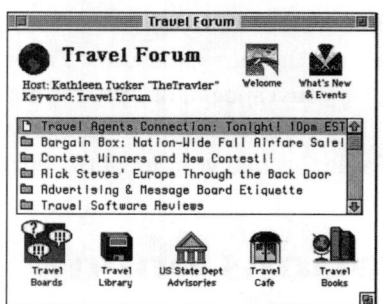

> **TIP** As with all America Online text windows, you can save the window by using the Save command, or you can print the text window by using the Print command.

Key resources of the Travel Forum, identified by colorful icons, include a What's New & Events department, where you learn the latest tips and information. The Travel Cafe is a chat room where you can have online meetings with other members in a traveling frame of mind. You can exchange messages with other members in the Traveler's Boards area. The Travel Library includes downloadable text articles, and Travel Books provide news and views of books available at your neighborhood store.

Taking a hike online

Keyword: **Backpacker**

Not all travel plans involve cars, boats, or planes. Some involve traveling the old fashioned way, on foot. That takes us to *Backpacker* magazine on America Online (see fig. 14.9). This magazine caters to those who enjoy walking through the forests, trails, and deserts around the world in search of adventure.

Fig. 14.9
Backpacker magazine is a popular hiker's resource.

Experiencing Bed & Breakfast U.S.A.

Keyword: **Bed & Breakfast**

Bed and breakfast refers to private homes that rent out rooms to travelers, or inns that provide extra-special personal service. Sometimes they're referred to as guest houses or tourist homes. The Bed & Breakfast U.S.A. forum provides an up-to-date listing from across the country of this unique kind of accommodation (see fig. 14.10).

Fig. 14.10
Bed & Breakfast U.S.A. offers an alternative to conventional hotel/ motel lodging.

Using the DineBase Restaurant Listing

Whenever I travel to a new, unfamiliar part of the country, the first thing I seek out is a list of the best local restaurants. Goldwyn's DineBase makes this task easy (see fig. 14.11). This forum is a huge database that lists thousands of highly rated restaurants. You can search the listings by state, city, or even by cuisine.

Fig. 14.11
DineBase is an easy way to find the best restaurants.

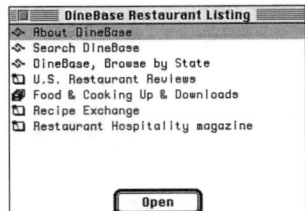

In search of an Outdoor Adventure Online

Keywords: **Adventure, OAO, Outdoor**

Some travelers are content to vacation in a hotel, or visit popular restaurants and shows. But if you want to take your travels to the great outdoors, you'll want to visit Outdoor Adventure Online (see fig. 14.12). It doesn't matter whether you're interested in hiking, skiing, scuba diving, or a host of other outdoor-related pursuits.

Fig. 14.12
Satisfy your quest for adventure with Outdoor Adventure Online. This forum helps you tap a huge database of exciting outdoor excursions of all types.

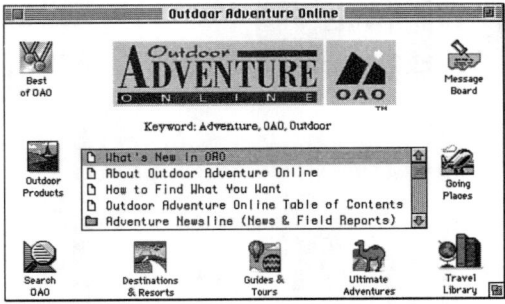

While planning your trip, you'll want to make sure you have just the right wardrobe and gear; for example, you might need a set of waterproof binoculars, or a set of skis. The Outdoor Products area offers hundreds of product reviews on field-tested equipment, and an active message board where you can read about the hands-on experience of other members who've tried these products.

Consulting the U.S. State Department Travel Advisories

Keyword: **Travel Advisories**

Because the world situation is apt to change at any moment, you'll want to view the official U.S. State Department travel advisories, shown in figure 14.13. You can tap into a huge database of information that covers the entire world, and learn if there are any special considerations for traveling to a specific country.

Fig. 14.13
The State Department's travel advisories can be searched on AOL.

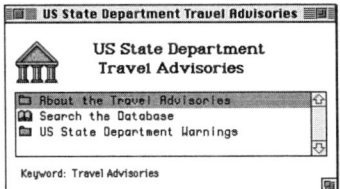

The U.S. State Department Warnings folder contains the latest alerts about problems and limitations of traveling to specific parts of the world. You'll want to review these text files before you plan your travel itinerary.

15

The Internet Connection

- ## In this chapter:

  - **What the Internet is**

  - **AOL's Internet services**

  - **How to learn more about the Internet**

*The word **Internet** is plastered across our newspapers and TV screens. Here's what America Online is doing about this incredible, global computer network.* . . . . ⊘

Take a look at a typical business card or an ad from any large company—or even from your local doctor, lawyer, or bagel baker. You'll see a phone number, an address, and something more: something about the "Internet" or "World Wide Web." Now what's that all about?

Yes—what *is* this Internet stuff all about?

The Internet is one of the hottest topics in the news media these days. Here's one recent example: Congress engaged in hot debate, not about the budget or about Social Security, but about censorship on the Internet. And all the online services are quickly jumping on the Internet bandwagon, led by America Online.

66 *Plain English, please!*

The word **Internet** means, literally, between networks. So the Internet isn't just a single amorphous entity, but a bunch of computer networks linked together worldwide, consisting of millions of computers. Not just the Mac and Windows operating systems are used, but UNIX and other computer operating systems participate on the **Net** (as it's sometimes called). 99

What you get from the Internet

The Internet provides a whole range of features that go beyond those on America Online, and it lets you get in touch with members of other networks and online services. Here are some of the Internet services offered through your AOL membership:

- You can send and receive e-mail across the world, even with users of other online services.

- You can search huge databases located at remote computer sites for files and information.

- You can join mailing lists and receive information on thousands of topics.

- You can engage in freewheeling, spirited discussions on newsgroup message boards.

- You can tap sources for hundreds of thousands of software files.

- You can access the colorful World Wide Web, the fastest growing Internet service.

CAUTION **The Internet is still very much like the wild west of the 19th** century. It's an open, largely unregulated frontier where you may encounter subject matter and language that goes against America Online's Terms of Service. So it's a good idea to carefully monitor your child's access to AOL's Internet areas. (See Chapter 7 for information about controlling your child's access to the Internet.)

And while it's true that most Internet veterans are only too happy to show new users (known as **newbies**) the ropes, a few prefer to jealously guard their Net access and aren't so friendly to those unfamiliar with its procedures and traditions. Therefore, before you access America Online's Internet Connection, read this chapter and perhaps the next four, and maybe explore some of the information texts that America Online has provided to introduce you to the Internet.

Let's explore AOL's Internet features

Keyword: **Internet**

America Online's Internet Connection is the focal point of its Net services (see fig. 15.1). All of AOL's Internet features are easily accessible simply by clicking the icons.

Fig. 15.1
America Online has a special department that is designed to welcome you to the Internet and tap its resources.

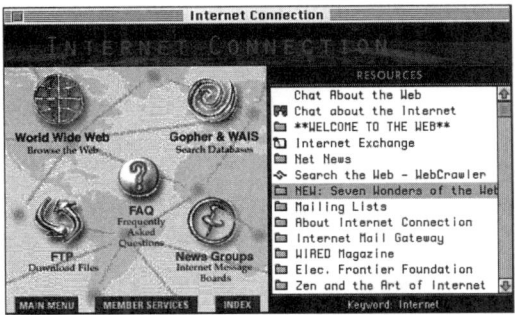

The Internet and e-mail

The fledgling Internet became a useful way for engineers and scientists to communicate with one other by sending messages across the network. This process became known as **electronic mail**, or **e-mail** for short. In addition to sending messages, files were also placed on some of the computers so that they could be shared among users of the network.

Over time, e-mail exchanges were shared among larger groups of users. In addition to simple messages, articles and reports were also included, and this became the beginning of the Internet mailing lists that are common today.

Preparing for the future

The really neat thing about the Internet is that you don't have to live in a specific country to use it. And you don't have to own a particular type of computer. You can access the Internet from anywhere in the world, as long as you're near a phone line or a computer network of some sort.

It doesn't matter whether you're using a Power Macintosh running System 7.5.2, a mainframe computer, or a Compaq Pentium 90 running OS/2. It's like a country with no borders—the Internet is available to almost anyone with access to a computer.

Accessing the Internet

Not too long ago, it wasn't so easy to get Internet access. You could only connect to the Internet from a scientific facility or educational institution, or you had to pay a huge sum to set up your own computer to tap these resources.

But this isn't the case anymore. A number of Internet access services offer simple ways for users to get into the Net. And America Online has

been working feverishly to integrate the Internet with its own local content to provide seamless access for all its users. Because of its wide reach, the Internet has become the place to be!

So now, get ready to travel across the Internet from the comfort of your own home or work area and your own personal computer.

In addition, all of the major departments of America Online have their own direct Internet access. Throughout this book, I've described the little icons, usually labeled Top Internet Sites, which adorn many AOL areas. These icons put you a click away from some of the most popular sites on the Internet.

Throughout the rest of this chapter, I'll briefly cover AOL's Internet services, and in the next four chapters I'll cover them in more detail. Over time, AOL will add still more Internet features, so stay tuned. The best is yet to come.

AOL's Mail Gateway is your Internet e-mail center

Keyword: **Mail Gateway**

America Online lets you send e-mail to your friends and business associates even if they aren't members of the service. AOL's Mail Gateway (see fig. 15.2) provides useful information on sending e-mail to members of other online services and to businesses, universities, and more. Because the ground rules for setting up Internet e-mail are somewhat different from addressing mail to fellow AOL members, I've devoted Chapter 16 to the subject.

Fig. 15.2
Learn more about sending your messages beyond AOL's borders from AOL's Internet e-mail center.

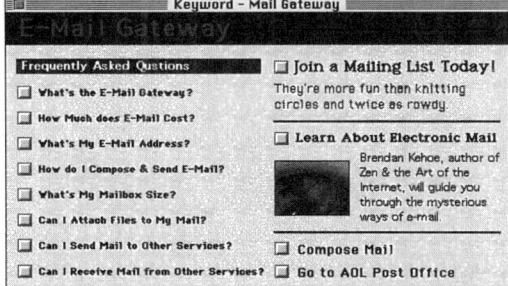

 **You don't have to be in AOL's Mail Gateway or Internet** Connection to compose Internet e-mail. All you have to do is open a blank mail form, address it, compose the message, and send it. You can even write your message while offline and send it via a FlashSession.

The wild world of USENET newsgroups

Keyword: **Newsgroups**

The closest thing to a message board on the Internet is **USENET** (see fig. 15.3), usually known as **newsgroups**. But the superficial resemblance to a message board doesn't extend to the content of the messages. Because it's largely uncontrolled, you'll find the discussions are often unfettered by any consideration of language or good taste, and America Online's Terms of Service are usually unknown in these discussion groups.

You'll find thousands of newsgroups to choose from, and they cover most every topic under the sun and a few (such as psychic phenomena and UFOs) that take you beyond the sun. Before getting involved, though, I suggest you read Chapter 17, which covers the ground rules you'll want to check before you plunge in.

❝ *Plain English, please!*

USENET is short for *user network,* and it's one way of referring to the popular message boards that dot the Internet landscape. They're also known as **newsgroups,** which is the way I'll refer to them throughout this book. **❞**

Fig. 15.3
Choose from thousands of Internet newsgroups and engage in free-wheeling discussions on many, many subjects.

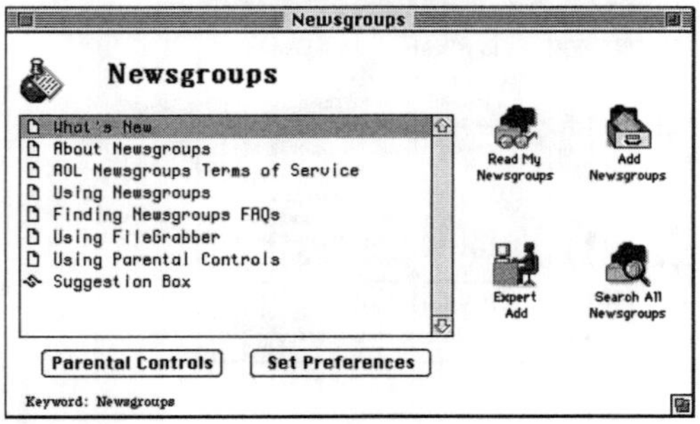

```
┌─────────────────── Newsgroups ───────────────────┐
│  📓  Newsgroups                                    │
│  ┌──────────────────────────────┐                 │
│  │ D  What's New                 │   🖥️      📥    │
│  │ D  About Newsgroups           │  Read My    Add  │
│  │ D  AOL Newsgroups Terms of Service │ Newsgroups Newsgroups │
│  │ D  Using Newsgroups           │                 │
│  │ D  Finding Newsgroups FAQs    │                 │
│  │ D  Using FileGrabber          │   🧑‍💻      🔍    │
│  │ D  Using Parental Controls    │  Expert   Search All │
│  │ ◇  Suggestion Box             │   Add   Newsgroups │
│  └──────────────────────────────┘                 │
│    [ Parental Controls ]  [ Set Preferences ]     │
│  Keyword: Newsgroups                               │
└───────────────────────────────────────────────────┘
```

The Internet provides huge resources of information

Keyword: **Gopher**

There's so much information to be found on the Internet, it's hard to know where to begin. Well, America Online makes it easy to find this information with its Gopher and WAIS feature (see fig. 15.4). And you can use the same search capabilities I've described throughout this book: just enter the topic you want to know about, and in seconds you see a directory of the information that matches your search string.

Fig. 15.4
You can tap into a huge range of information on thousands of topics via AOL's Internet database search tools.

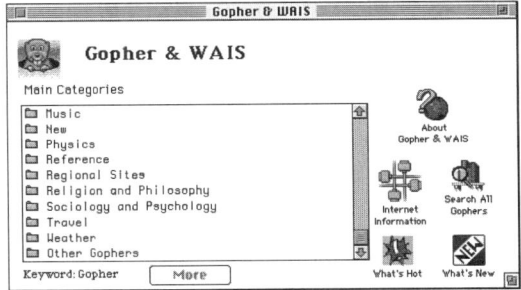

You can join an Internet mailing list

Keyword: **Mailing Lists**

An Internet mailing list is like a traveling discussion group. When you subscribe to such a list, you'll receive regular e-mail messages containing information on topics ranging from wineries to UFOs (with lots of stuff in between). It's easy to locate a mailing list—just access AOL's Mailing Lists area (see fig. 15.5) and use the search capability you'll find there. Once you locate a list that interests you, and you subscribe to it, your AOL e-mail box will be filled with lots of fascinating information.

Fig. 15.5
Joining a mailing list from AOL is no more difficult than sending e-mail to the folks running the list.

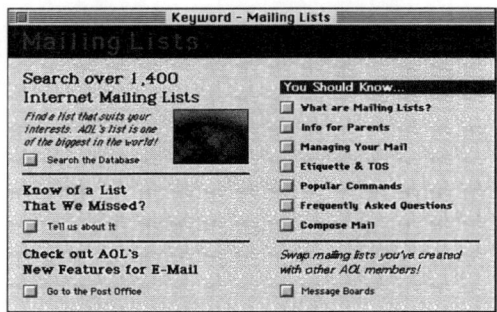

 **CAUTION** When you first discover mailing lists that interest you, you might be tempted to go overboard and subscribe to lots of them. My advice: be careful. Any single list can fill your mailbox with dozens of new messages each day. If you become overwhelmed with new messages, consider canceling your subscriptions to lists that produce messages you don't intend to read right away.

Transferring files on the Internet

Keyword: **FTP**

America Online's own software libraries have tens of thousands of software files. And there are hundreds of thousands more to choose from on the Internet. You'll be able to get files from commercial sources such as Apple, Microsoft, and Novell, and from private software libraries.

Internet files are transferred using a technique called **File Transfer Protocol (FTP)**, and AOL offers a gateway that lets you access the sources (see fig. 15.6). Getting those files involves many of the same steps you use to download software direct from AOL's own libraries, which makes the entire process easy to learn.

Fig. 15.6
Tap huge software repositories on the Internet via AOL's FTP gateway.

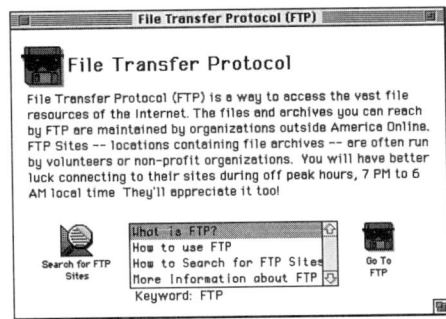

❝❞ *Plain English, please!*

File Transfer Protocol, usually known as **FTP,** describes the technique used to transfer files across the Internet. While the file transfer process on AOL doesn't seem much different, the underlying technology used in FTP transfers is much more complex because allowances must be made for different computing platforms and operating systems. ❞❞

Experience graphics and sound on the World Wide Web

Keyword: **WWW**

The World Wide Web is the Internet's multimedia center. While other Internet services are text-based, the WWW combines text, graphics, and sometimes sound to provide a dazzling experience. The sample you see in figure 15.7 is from my publisher's home page, and it's just an example of the sort of fancy stuff you'll find on the Web. It's a place you'll want to visit often, as new sites are going up almost every day. There will be more about the subject in Chapter 18 and Chapter 19.

 **TIP**   **If you want to access the World Wide Web from America Online,** you need version 2.6 of AOL's Mac software plus AOL's browser application (which is a program used to access the Web pages themselves). You can download both from an area free of online charges (if you use the Download Now feature). Just use the keyword *Upgrade* to get the software you need, if you don't already have it installed on your Mac.

Fig. 15.7
The **home page** (starting point) of Macmillan Publishing's World Wide Web facility, as seen from AOL's Web browser.

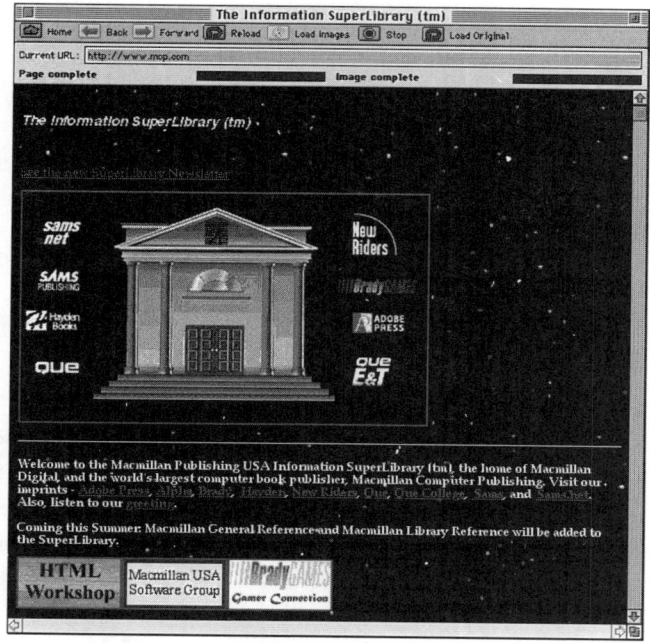

Q&A *Can I connect to AOL from the Internet?*

Yes you can, if you have direct Net access. Computers that hook up to the Internet speak a language called **TCP/IP** (Transmission Control Protocol/Internet Protocol).

If your computer network has such a connection (ask your network administrator about it), it's very easy to call up America Online through it. All you have to do is change your modem setup (see Chapter 2). Just choose TCPack as your AOL Connection File (in your modem Setup box) as I've done in figure 15.8.

Fig. 15.8
It's easy to log on to
AOL via a TCP/IP
hookup.

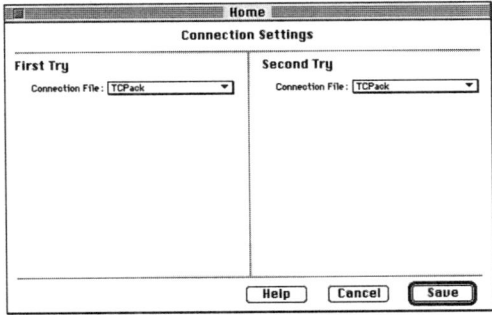

When I visited AOL's headquarters recently, I logged on to the service via their direct TCP/IP connection. The speed was just incredible—much faster even than a regular 28,800 bps modem—so if you do have access to a high speed TCP/IP line, you'll definitely want to use it to log on to AOL.

You can also sign up with a local Internet provider to get such a connection, but usually it's not worth the bother. First, remember that you would be paying for both the local provider's regular fee and AOL's hourly charges. Also, AOL offers direct 28,800 bps connections now, and you won't get any faster speed from an Internet service unless you invest in a high-speed network setup (which is much too costly to benefit a single user).

If you want to use AOL's TCP/IP capabilities on your Mac, you need a copy of Apple's MacTCP software. You can get MacTCP with System 7.5 and separately from your software dealer or by calling Apple Customer Assistance at 800-SOS-APPL.

If you have a Macintosh that uses Apple's Open Transport networking software, you'll find the required settings in the TCP/IP Control Panel.

Direct Internet hookups to AOL may not be as secure as using your regular modem and AOL's huge network of local access numbers. Information that passes back and forth between AOL and your computer via the Internet may be intercepted and read by computer hackers. This could include your account name and password, so if you connect to AOL via TCP/IP, it's a good idea to change your password on a regular basis. This will reduce the chances of someone finding out what your password is.

16

Internet E-Mail Made Easy

● In this chapter:

● Want to send e-mail on the Internet?

● How to send files in the body of your Internet e-mail

● How to use Internet mailing lists

Sending e-mail to those who don't subscribe to AOL is as easy as sending it to those who do. . . . . **⊳**

When you use America Online's highly flexible and speedy electronic mail features, you are not restricted to sending your messages to other AOL members. Through AOL's Internet Connection, you can send e-mail to members of other online services and, in fact, to anyone with Internet access. In addition, you can subscribe to any of thousands of mailing lists and place discussions and information on all sorts of topics in your AOL mailbox.

How to send and receive Internet e-mail

It's no surprise that e-mail is one of the most popular services offered, not only by America Online, but through the Internet as well. Right now, you can send electronic mail to, and receive it from, anyone connected to the Internet. It makes no difference whether they use America Online. If you have friends who use one of the other online networks, such as Prodigy, eWorld, CompuServe, MCI Mail, AT&TMail, AppleLink, and others, you can send them e-mail by using America Online's regular e-mail feature. America Online handles millions of Internet-based transactions each day.

America Online's Mail Gateway is a full center that provides information and support on using Internet e-mail (see fig. 16.1). There, you'll see updated listings that cover addressing and receiving e-mail, plus you'll have access to AOL's Internet search tools (such as Gopher and WAIS).

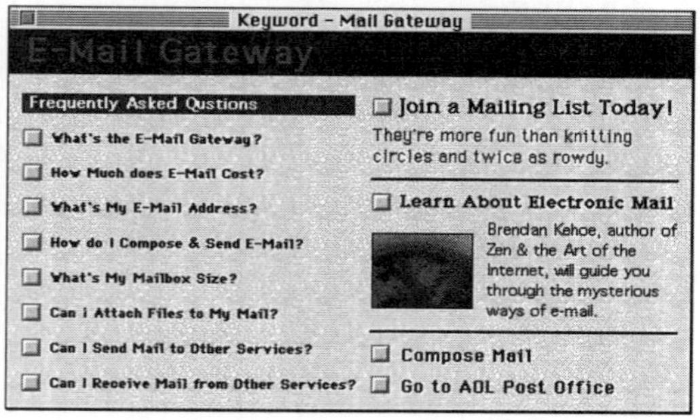

Fig. 16.1
AOL's Mail Gateway can be used to send e-mail throughout the world via the Internet.

You can begin the Internet e-mail process simply enough by opening a blank e-mail form (see fig. 16.2). Yes, it's the same e-mail form I described in Chapter 5. The ground rules regarding content are the same; you enter an e-mail address, a subject line, and the actual message. There's one difference, though—don't bother using special typefaces, styles, or colors in your document. Everything will be converted to raw, unformatted (ASCII) text when your mail travels through the mail gateway. The use of ASCII text allows for total compatibility with millions of computers, using many operating systems and many kinds of telecommunications software.

 Plain English, please!

Unformatted text, or **raw text,** describes actual letters and numbers without the styling attributes that you apply in a word processing program, such as type size, type style, and so forth. **ASCII text** generally includes just the basic 128-character set without fancy characters such as trademark symbols and other characters you access on your keyboard when you add an Option or an Option+Shift to a character.

Fig. 16.2
Only the address differentiates Internet e-mail from regular AOL e-mail. You include a subject line and your message, and you can write these items in the same way you write any other e-mail.

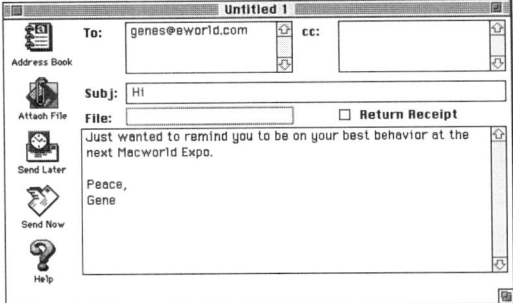

 **The best way to learn the address of an Internet correspondent is** to simply ask the person for it.

How to send Internet e-mail

Sending e-mail over the Internet works the same way as sending normal America Online e-mail to other members. You just type the Internet address of your intended recipient rather than the America Online screen name you normally use to send mail to other AOL members.

Addressing Internet mail is that simple. However, there are a couple of rules, as follows:

- An Internet address never contains any spaces. If someone's mail system does allow spaces at the receiving end, the spaces are automatically replaced by underscores (_) in the Internet address. For example, you might see **john_smith@hugecorp.com**, in which the space between the user's first and last name is closed up with an underscore character.

- Every Internet address must have the user name and domain specified. For our purposes, the **user name** is everything before the **@** symbol, and the **domain** is everything after the **@** symbol. In the domain, a company name is followed by a suffix that describes what type of organization it is. A business, for instance, uses the suffix **.com**, educational institutions use **.edu**, military sites use **.mil**, and government offices use **.gov**.

 Plain English, please!

Domain is a word that identifies the location or company running an Internet site.

The following table shows how you can address Internet e-mail to your friends on other online services. Some additional information about each service has been added to help you address your e-mail for that service. If you follow the format provided here, you can easily address other services in

The world of Internet-speak

Once you get the hang of all those Internet e-mail conventions, the places to put periods and all, there's one more thing to consider: just what do you say to your friends or business associates when they want you to tell them (not write) your Internet address?

Clearly all this "dot" and "com" stuff is meant to be written, right?

Well, you can say it, though it doesn't quite fall *trippingly* off the tongue. Just remember that the @ character is called "at." With that in mind, here's my Internet address:

It's written as **aflgenes@aol.com**, and it's pronounced: "ay-ef-el-gene-ess-at-ay-oh-el-dot-com."

Now try and say that three times, rapidly.

much the same manner. But let me first explain the meanings behind some of those headlines:

- **Location** is the name of the service.
- **Long Address** is the full Internet e-mail address that you'd normally use.
- **Shortcut** is an abbreviation you can use to reach some services.
- **Example** indicates where you insert your own AOL screen name.

Location	Long Address	Shortcut	Example
AppleLink	applelink.apple.com	apple	*name*@apple
AT&TMail	attmail.com	att	*name*@att
America Online	aol.com		*name*@att
BITNET	<institution>.bitnet		*name*@<institution>.bitnet
BIX	bix.com		*BIXname*@bix.com
CompuServe	compuserve.com	cis	*12345.678*@cis
Connect	connectinc.com		*name*@connectinc.com
Delphi	delphi.com		*name*@delphi.com
EasyLink	eln.attmail.com		*62<name>*@eln.attmail.com
eWorld	eworld.com		*name*@eworld
Fidonet	p<point>.f<node>.n<network>. z<zone>.fidonet.org		*name*@p<point>. f<node>.n <network>. z<zone>. fidonet.org
GEnie	genie.geis.com	genie	*name*@genie
MCI Mail	mcimail.com	mci	*name*@mci
Prodigy	prodigy.com		*userid*@Prodigy.com
Well	well.com		*name*@well.com

TIP Some organizations have a private area that uses **CompuServe** e-mail in their address. You can reach these locations using the format **name@organization.compuserve.com**.

Plain English, please!

The **BITNET network** is a service involving various academic computers. The **.bitnet** designation provides an Internet address for these computers.

CAUTION Each online service has its own requirements and limitations about how the offered Internet services work. AOL's Internet Connection contains help text that will help you address your e-mail to other services. As other services change their Internet offerings, these help texts will also be revised.

TIP Business addresses can be found in the book, *Internet Yellow Pages*, by Christine Maxwell and Czeslaw Jan Grycz, published by New Riders.

CAUTION Internet addresses are almost always expressed in lowercase letters. Although this is not an absolute requirement, you should follow this convention for clarity and consistency with existing Internet practices.

Q&A *Help! Why was my Internet e-mail returned by a MAILER-DAEMON? What's that, and what's it want with me?*

If you do not address your Internet mail in the correct format, or it didn't reach its destination for some reason, the message will be returned by AOL's Internet mail computers.

First thing you want to do is look over the message, which spells out the reason why it was returned.

The most common cause is that the address is marked unknown. If this happens to you, verify the original recipient's correct e-mail address (even an error involving one letter or number is enough to bounce the letter). Internet e-mail can travel through a long, circuitous path on its way from AOL's mail server to its destination. Sometimes errors can occur during transmission (a blip on the information superhighway), and sometimes correctly addressed mail is returned for no apparent reason. The best solution (after verifying that the address is correct) is to resend the letter.

How to receive Internet e-mail

To receive mail from the Internet, you need to know your own Internet address. Your address is simply your America Online screen name, with any spaces removed, plus **@aol.com**. If your screen name is John User, for example, your Internet address is **johnuser@aol.com**.

A look at Internet file attachments

The really neat thing about AOL's Internet e-mail is that you can send and receive files in the very same way you send those files to other AOL members. But there are a few things to consider, especially when it involves someone on another service who may be getting the files you send from AOL:

- Files attached to your Internet e-mail are automatically converted to MIME format. In order to read those files, the recipient may need a separate program, but that's something that the recipient may have to check with the other service.

 Plain English, please!

> **MIME** isn't performing without speaking. It stands for **Multipurpose Internet Mail Extensions**. It's a technique used to convert the file to text form, so it can be read on different kinds of computers. 🙰

- If someone sends you a long text message (containing more than 27,000 characters), it will be converted to an attached file. You'll see the first 2,000 characters in the body of the e-mail message, and the full, original message will be attached as a file.

- Tell the person who is sending you files by the Internet not to attach more than one file to the message. Otherwise, you'll have to use another software program (a MIME converter) to change it back to its normal form. Instead, suggest that he make the files into a single compressed archive, using one of the standard Mac compression programs.

 **If you ever need a program that will convert MIME files, check** AOL's software libraries (using the File Search technique I described in Chapter 10). One file that ought to do the trick is *Mpack,* which is a small freeware program that you can download from AOL in just a few minutes.

CAUTION **Graphic files on the Internet do not have to follow America** Online's Terms of Service regarding nude or sexually explicit content. Be sure to examine the article's header or look at the title and purpose of a newsgroup before transferring material from that area to your computer.

A look at Internet mailing lists

Keyword: **Mailing Lists**

Internet **mailing lists** (see fig. 16.3) are e-mail discussions among groups of people on the Internet who share similar interests. Using regular Internet e-mail, information is exchanged in a continuing, interactive fashion with people all around the world. The entire text of these discussions will appear regularly in your AOL mailbox (don't overdo it, or your mailbox will fill up).

Fig. 16.3
Here's AOL's Internet Mailing Lists center.

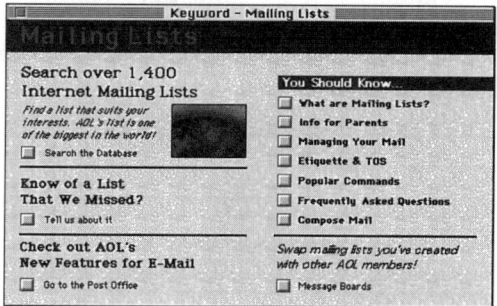

Thousands of Internet mailing lists exist today, encompassing almost every imaginable topic: computer technology, American literature, philosophy, cooking, chess, motorcycling, sports, the environment, rock music, UFOs, alternative lifestyles—take your pick.

The Internet Mailing Lists area has various helpful text articles containing background and instructions on using the Mailing Lists features of the Internet Connection.

To locate specific mailing lists that might appeal to your interests, click the Search the Database button. You'll discover a database of mailing lists you can search by entering descriptive words (see fig. 16.4).

Fig. 16.4
Here's the Mailing List database search window, with the results of your search for mailing lists on the topic of UFOs.

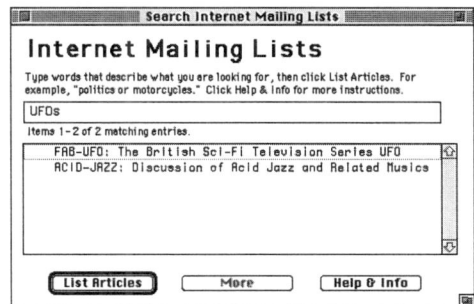

After a list of entries that match your search description appears, click the List Articles button (or press Enter). The items that appear after a successful search from this window contain the descriptions of Internet Mailing Lists available from the matches of your search words entered in the search window (see fig. 16.5).

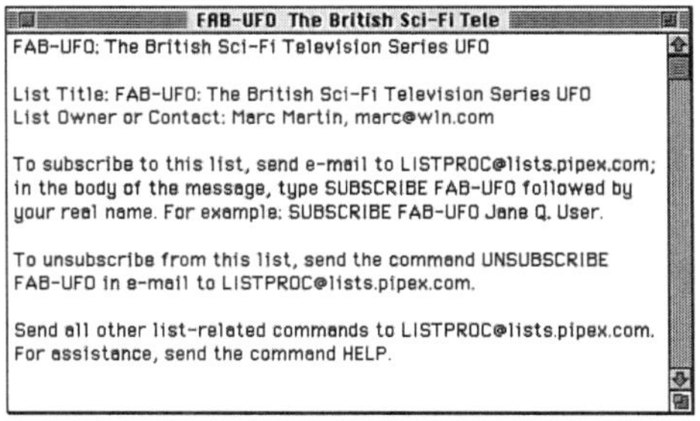

Fig. 16.5
Here's a description of one of the Mailing Lists, containing information on the subject it deals with and how to subscribe.

How to join an Internet mailing list

The descriptions of a mailing list contain instructions on how you can subscribe to the mailing lists that interest you by using your America Online Internet e-mail address. Follow the instructions carefully; they tend to differ slightly from list to list. Remember also to note how you can unsubscribe from any lists you join, in case you change your mind later. Most of these lists generate a large amount of mail and can quickly fill your online mailbox if you don't check in regularly.

CAUTION **Often, these mailing lists are run, not by an individual reading** your request, but by a software program that automates the tasks of establishing and maintaining these mailing lists, and sending the regular mailings to subscribers. Because you are communicating with another computer and not an individual, it's important that you make your requests follow the exact directions in the mailing list subscription.

Here are a few things to keep in mind when joining a mailing list:

- Use the exact commands specified in the instructions you read about joining a mailing list to subscribe and unsubscribe.

- Remember that Internet e-mail might take a couple of days to reach its destination, so be patient about getting a response. Also remember that mailings to subscribers might be sent at infrequent intervals.

- If a mailing list is also available as a USENET newsgroup, you might prefer to use that option. With a USENET newsgroup, you don't have to handle unsolicited e-mail, and you can easily limit reading messages to the ones that interest you within a given time frame, and ignore messages dealing with topics you do not want to see.

TIP **I'll cover USENET in full detail in Chapter 18.**

How to respond to mailing list messages

The material you receive from a mailing list looks the same as any standard e-mail message (see fig. 16.6), and you respond to those messages in exactly the same way. Just choose the Reply option on your mailing list e-mail to incorporate your comments about a particular article in a subsequent group of messages. If you want to post an article to a mailing list, you'll want to consult the original instructions for that mailing list. Normally, this requires composing mail to the list address rather than responding to an individual message.

Fig. 16.6
Here's some typical
e-mail from a mailing
list.

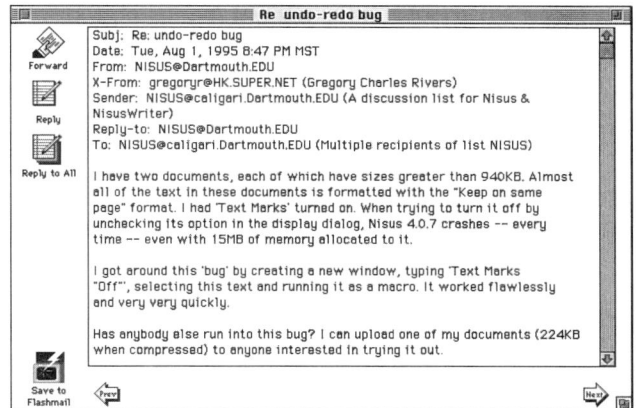

How to leave a mailing list

The instructions you receive when you first join a mailing list generally include online information on how to cancel the mailing list, or unsubscribe. If the mailing list is run by an automated list server computer, you must make your request using the exact format contained in those instructions. Computers are very literal-minded. If the list is run by a person, you can just send a regular e-mail request.

CAUTION **If you change your screen name or cancel your AOL account, be** sure to unsubscribe all of your mailing lists (the mail won't be forwarded). If the list is maintained by a person, you can send whatever mail-forwarding information is appropriate. You'll have to resubscribe to the mailing lists.

What to do if your mailbox is full

There are so many fascinating mailing lists that you will no doubt be tempted to join a number of them. It's not uncommon to overdo it a bit, and you might find your mailbox clogged with messages still unread. FlashSessions can produce huge incoming mailboxes. The best advice is to be judicious about managing your mail so that you aren't overwhelmed.

Presently, your AOL mailbox is limited to 550 items. This number includes not only the mail you have read, but also the mail you have not yet seen. The list of mail you've sent remains in your mailbox for 28 days; mail you've read is deleted after four days (at the time this book was written).

CAUTION **If the number of read and unread mail exceeds 550, the oldest** mail is deleted automatically by AOL's host computer system. By managing your mailbox carefully, you'll avoid losing mail you might want to keep. The amount of time your AOL mail is kept may change from time to time to make the mail server computers run better.

Here are some common-sense tips to help you keep your mailbox down to usable proportions:

- Be sure you subscribe only to mailing lists you really want to read.

- Take note of directions on how to unsubscribe to a mailing list when you join, in case the mailing list doesn't meet your expectations or you find your mailbox getting a little too crowded.

- Check your e-mail regularly to keep your mailbox as small as possible.

TIP **If you've lost directions on how to subscribe or unsubscribe to a** mailing list, simply search for the mailing list, again using the search feature in the Internet Mailing Lists area. The results of your search can be saved and printed for later review.

>

The Lowdown on Internet Newsgroups

● **In this chapter:**

- **What Internet newsgroups are**

- **What Netiquette** *really* **means**

- **How to find the newsgroups you're interested in**

- **How to participate in newsgroups**

For hot-and-heavy discussions about most any subject under the sun (and then some), there's nothing like a USENET newsgroup. . . . . >

America Online's own message boards are one source of information exchange. But for really intense debate you'll want to head for the global Internet network. The discussion boards on the Internet, unlike those on AOL, are not restricted by the boundaries and requirements of a single online service (or even their rules and regulations).

Some of the most interesting parts of the wide world of the Internet are newsgroups, also known as USENET newsgroups (see figure 17.1). **Newsgroups** are popular and active exchanges. Just as with mailing lists, there are newsgroups covering almost any topic you can think of, and then some.

Fig. 17.1
One of the most exciting Internet features is newsgroups, where the action can be hot and heavy.

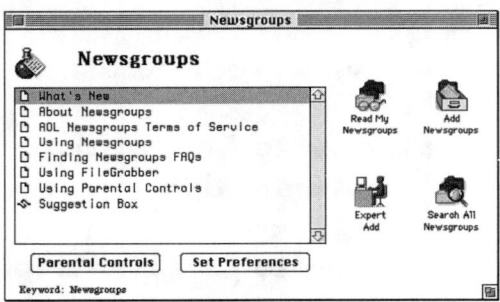

66 *Plain English, please!*

USENET is short for user network, which summarizes the essence of these discussion boards, in which Internet users speak their minds about the subject at hand. 99

How to set up AOL's newsgroup reader

If you've used a newsgroups reader on another online service, you're apt to find some differences because America Online is a graphical service, and many dedicated Internet providers still used text-based software.

66 *Plain English, please!*

A **news reader** is software used to read, organize, and post messages in a newsgroup. AOL's news reader is integrated into its client software, so you can seamlessly switch from a regular message board to a newsgroup without having to access another program. 99

Over the next few pages, I'll show you how how to set up AOL's newsreader for best performance, I'll cover some of the rules of online etiquette, and then you can seek out and participate in some popular newsgroup discussions.

First, let's set your newsgroup preferences

The opening Newsgroups window (see fig. 17.1) has two sets of preferences. There is yet a third set of preferences, but you can't access that until you open a list of messages. This third set is described later in this chapter. For now, look at the two rectangular buttons at the bottom of the Newsgroups window.

First, there's Parental Controls, which can be used to limit access to certain Internet features. See Chapter 7 for more details.

The Set Preferences button produces a collection of preferences you can set (see fig. 17.2). Using these preferences, you can create a signature that automatically appears at the bottom of your newsgroup messages; you can dictate how you want those messages to appear.

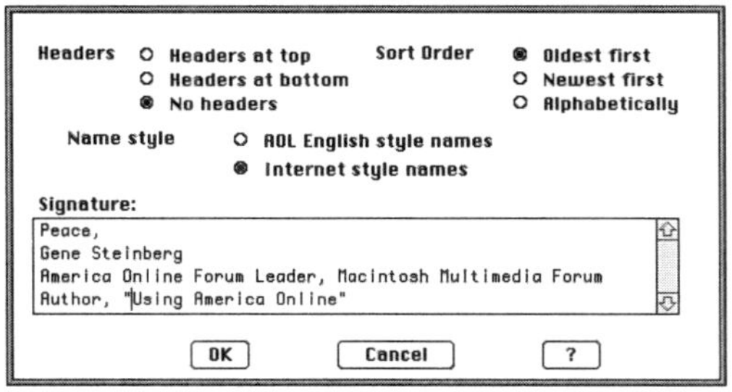

Fig. 17.2
Set your global newsgroup preferences in this dialog box.

How the messages will appear

17 Internet transactions go through a circuitous route, from computer to computer, on their way to America Online. You can choose whether you want to see any of this header information, which displays the long, roundabout path your message takes (you might want to leave it off to keep message windows free of clutter). Here are the header options to choose from:

- **Headers at top.** The path your message travels is included at the top of your message window.

- **Headers at bottom.** The path your message travels is included at the bottom of your message window.

- **No headers.** Ah, that's more like it. The headers are stripped from the messages you see. The header is limited to the date and time the message was sent, the message ID information, and the Internet address of the message's author.

The order of display

In what order would you like your messages to appear? By default, you see the oldest first, and then you move through them, in chronological order, with messages grouped by thread (topic). Here are your choices:

- **Oldest first.** The default setting enables you to read the messages in their normal sequence.

- **Newest first.** This choice might seem like reading the end of a book before the beginning, but if you have a huge number of messages to read through you may find it convenient to look at the latest messages first. This option makes following a message thread difficult, however, because you will see the response before you see the question (sounds similar to what Johnny Carson used to do when he hosted *The Tonight Show*).

- **Alphabetically.** This option groups messages by topic, in alphabetical order.

What's in a name?

The name of a newsgroup follows a specific naming convention, which might seem confusing if you are visiting the Internet for the first time. You have two options:

- **AOL English style names.** For this setting, a newsgroup might be identified as Help with Newsgroups.

- **Internet style names.** When you select this option, Help with Newsgroups is shown as **aol.newsgroups.help**.

The Internet name, despite its odd syntax, is really not difficult to comprehend, but whether to choose this option is up to you. Why not try both methods? You can change your preferences at any time by opening the Set

Preferences window, making your alterations, and then opening your list of newsgroups again. The changes take effect immediately.

TIP **If you are viewing your newsgroups with English-style names, you** can see the actual Internet name by clicking the Internet Names icon at the top of the newsgroup message window. This action brings up a window showing the Internet-name versions.

Internet newsgroups—the ground rules

When you first visit AOL's newsgroups area, you'll want to jump right in and get involved in a discussion board. Before you do so, though, you should learn something about newsgroups in general and about how to introduce yourself to a discussion group. Over the years, the Internet, although largely unregulated and unsupervised, has developed certain forms and conventions.

So here are a few tips, based on hard-won experience on the Net:

- You'll be tempted to plunge in to a discussion that interests you. Don't. Spend a little time reading messages or following the discussions (which experienced Net visitors call **lurking**). Often you'll find a set of FAQs, a set of text files that provide a list of ground rules for a specific discussion group, and responses to typical user questions. After you've developed a feel for the flavor of a particular group, it's time to consider posting a message of your own.

❝ *Plain English, please!*

FAQ is short for **Frequency Asked Questions**, which is usually a list of commonly asked questions and answers about a specific subject or range of subjects. **❞**

- There are literally thousands of newsgroups. The number of messages you are likely to encounter will be in the hundreds of thousands. You can quickly become overwhelmed by the sheer volume of information if you don't pick and choose carefully. To begin with, you should restrict yourself to only a small number of discussion groups, take time to digest the messages, and add more only when you think you can devote the time necessary to follow up on all the information you'll receive.

- When you respond to a message, consider that you are posting a response to not just a single person, but an audience that could number in the millions. If you decide you want to restrict your audience to a single person, send that person e-mail instead. The option to reply to just the author rather than the group is available in America Online's newsgroup reader.

- Before writing your message, carefully choose the appropriate forum. It wouldn't be a good idea to promote the use of a Macintosh in a discussion group oriented toward users of Microsoft Windows, for example, unless you want to risk generating a lot of ill will.

- Show respect and be polite when you post a message. If you disagree with someone's statement, try to stick to the issues and refrain from personal attack. Such attacks are called flaming, and although they might be entertaining on some television talk shows, they are not considered good taste on the Internet.

 Plain English, please!

Flaming is the online equivalent of a shouting match, which involves making personal attacks and using abusive language. It's not considered good online etiquette under any circumstance.

- When responding to someone else's message, quote the relevant portions of that message at the beginning of your response, or before each part of your message that refers to that message (don't quote the entire message). The usual convention is to place an angle bracket (**>**), signifying a quotation mark, at the beginning of each line, as shown here:

```
> I have access to a Mac Centris 610.
> When I try to run Norton Speed Disk,...
> I get System files not supported in System 7...
> Where can I get an update of Norton?
> Is this software now obsolete/upgraded/replaced??????
```

TIP **You don't have to manually quote line by line. Just use AOL's** file-search feature to locate a copy of a program such as Signature Quote in the computing software libraries. Signature Quote is an application that lets you copy the selected material you want to quote and have it converted automatically to the correct format. Then you can quickly paste the formatted material into a message window.

- It is customary to use your Internet address (described in Chapter 16) as your personal signature, but your name and affiliations can be placed there too (see fig. 17.3). Some folks also include their address and phone number, but before you do this, consider whether you feel that you'd want to really give this information out to millions of strangers. Others add a statement or motto that reflects some aspect of their personality. Before preparing your own signature, you might want to see how others do it first.

Fig. 17.3
This is a typical USENET newsgroup signature. The information below the signature shows the long and twisted path taken by that message before it reached its destination.

- Keep your messages short and to the point. You are reaching an audience of millions of people, and you don't want to waste anyone's time because many users pay high charges for Internet access. Try not to **cross-post** (send your message to more than one newsgroup at a time), unless it's really necessary.

TIP **When you create an online signature for yourself, try to keep it** brief (such as your name and, if needed, company affiliation or a short motto). Long signatures, with elaborate artwork, simply waste bandwidth and may upset users who pay large amounts for Internet access.

- Choose a subject title that specifically describes the topic of your message. Type 1 Crash in System 7.1 is more descriptive than System Crash if you are seeking advice on solving a problem in a Macintosh newsgroup.

- Express emotions and humor with care. When you speak with someone in person, your body language and the inflection of your voice reveal whether you are serious, angry, or happy. But in your messages, your words alone must be the mirror of your feelings. Experienced online users express emotions with smileys :). See Chapter 5 for a list of common online shorthand characters (known as **smileys** and **emoticons**).

- Before you respond to a message, take the time to see whether someone else has already answered it. Time on the busy Internet is at a premium, and reading the same sort of message over and over wastes everyone's time, including your own.

How to participate in Internet newsgroups

There are thousands upon thousands of newsgroups that cover interests of all sorts. Many newsgroups overlap in terms of content, too, so you probably will want to select more than a single newsgroup that interests you.

America Online maintains a list of the most popular newsgroups in its own database. Just click the Add Newsgroups icon in the main Newsgroups window. You'll see a directory list, shown in figure 17.4, that displays many subjects of interest.

Fig. 17.4
The first step in locating a newsgroup is to get a list of groups that deal with your favorite subjects.

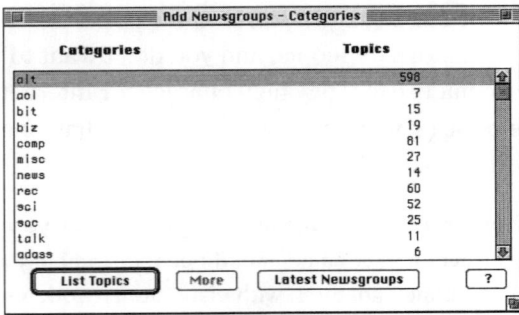

After you've picked a subject, click the List Topics button to bring up a list of newsgroups that fit the description. To find the newsgroup itself, click the list once more, and then you'll see the display shown in Figure 17.5.

Fig. 17.5
Here's a list of
newsgroups catering to
a particular interest.

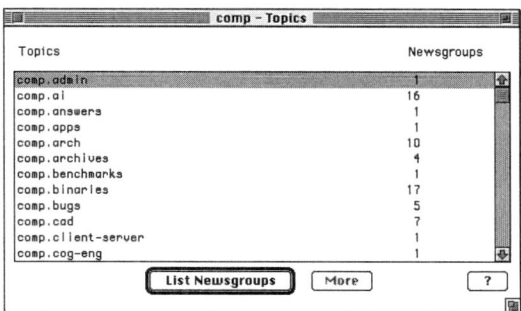

You don't have to join any newsgroup yet, but if you want to dive in you can automatically subscribe to the selected newsgroup by clicking the Add button (shown in the list of newsgroup titles). If you'd rather sample the flavor of a particular discussion group, just click its name and you'll see a list of the available messages, as shown in figure 17.6. You can read those messages, but because you are just sampling the newsgroup for now, you cannot actually post a response to a message or create a topic of your own. To do either, you must actually add the newsgroup to your list.

Fig. 17.6
Before you actually
join a newsgroup, you
might want to look
over some of the
messages.

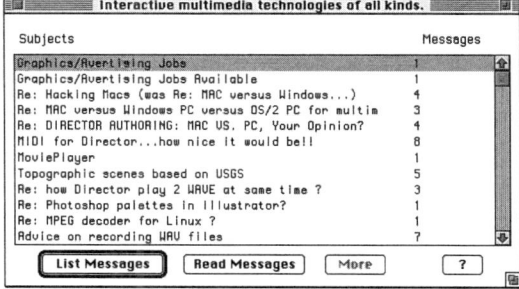

When you've actually added a newsgroup, it appears under the Read My Newsgroups list, which is discussed later in this chapter.

How to find a newsgroup

If you don't find a newsgroup that interests you, perform a more thorough search of the available newsgroups. Click the Search All Newsgroups icon in the Newsgroups area to bring up a search window, as shown in figure 17.7. Enter the subject for which you want to locate a newsgroup in the list field.

Fig. 17.7
Search from among thousands of newsgroups for one that piques your curiosity.

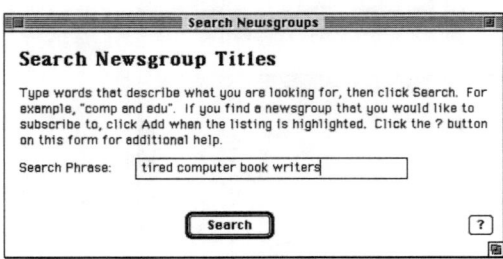

If there is a newsgroup that meets your search criteria (and sometimes you have to refine the phrases a bit or even try related ones), that newsgroup title appears in a window. From there, you can read a capsule description by double-clicking the newsgroup's title. You'll find, however, that many newsgroups do not actually have any description other than the titles themselves, which those newsgroups usually consider sufficient to describe their mission.

Unlike the Add Newsgroups feature, the searching mechanism doesn't give you the ability to sample a newsgroup before adding it to your list. Because you can remove a newsgroup later if you choose, by the simple click of a button, this is not a major shortcoming.

TIP **If you want to search for more than a single item, you should** insert **AND** between words and phrases to separate subjects. You also may expand your search with the word **OR** when you wish to look for one option or another, but not both; and you can exclude an item with the word **NOT** to designate a subject or word you don't want to use in the search result list.

Use Expert Add if you know the name

As with e-mail addresses, the titles of newsgroups are identified by a special syntax, with words generally separated by a period. An example is **comp.sys.mac.advocacy**, which, as the title suggests, is a discussion group with active debates on the subject of using the Apple Macintosh versus other computing platforms. If you know the exact title of a newsgroup, you can bypass the search mechanism or America Online's own list and join by using the Expert Add feature, shown in figure 17.8.

Fig. 17.8

If you know the name of the newsgroup you want to join, enter it here.

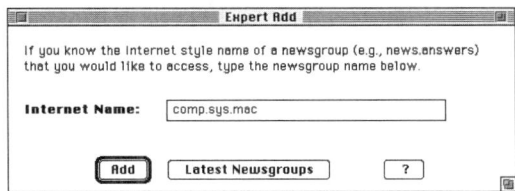

> *If you know the Internet style name of a newsgroup (e.g., news.answers) that you would like to access, type the newsgroup name below.*
>
> **Internet Name:** comp.sys.mac
>
> [Add]   [Latest Newsgroups]   [?]

CAUTION **America Online's Expert Add feature is quite literal. For it to** work, you need to enter a newsgroup's name using the exact spelling and punctuation. Otherwise, the newsgroup won't be located, or, worse, you'll add the wrong newsgroup.

After you've subscribed to the newsgroups that interest you, it's time to read the messages.

How to read your newsgroup messages

Click the Read My Newsgroups icon at the main screen of the Newsgroups area, and you'll see a list of all the newsgroups you've subscribed to, as shown in figure 17.9. When you enter this area for the first time, you'll see a list of popular newsgroups that America Online has automatically included, but you can remove them at any time by highlighting the name of the newsgroup and clicking the Remove button. The Mark Read button enables you to flag the messages in a selected group as read without actually opening the messages themselves (use this feature with caution if you want to read those messages later).

Fig. 17.9

Here are the newsgroups you've joined. You've got lots of reading to do!

My Newsgroups	Unread	Total
comp.sys.mac.comm	6787	6787
comp.sys.mac.digest	32	32
comp.sys.mac.hardware	0	7092
comp.sys.mac.misc	4081	4081
comp.sys.mac.system	6567	6567
comp.sys.mac.wanted	3541	3541
comp.sys.powerpc	6872	6872
misc.forsale.computers.mac	0	4328
rec.audio.high-end	1527	1527
rec.audio.opinion	2189	2189

[List Unread] [List All] [Mark Read] [Remove] [More] [?]

Before you begin to read the messages in your selected newsgroups, you'll want to review the section on Netiquette earlier in this chapter. Take some time to read the messages themselves. The first time you read the messages, you might find there are literally thousands in a single newsgroup alone. But because the messages are grouped by topic (also known as **message threading**), as shown in figure 17.10, you'll easily be able to pick the messages you want to read.

Fig. 17.10
Newsgroup messages are threaded, or grouped, according to topic.

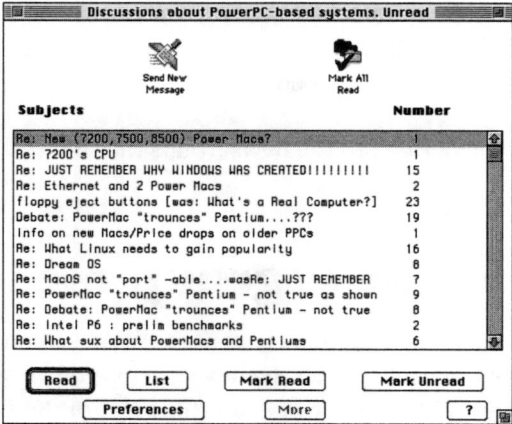

After you've read all the messages in a single thread, the next message you bring up (by clicking the Next button) takes you to a new thread. If you want to bypass that subject, just close the message window. You can then look over the directory of unread messages for another topic you want to follow.

How to follow a message thread

All newsgroup messages are normally sorted by date and then by topic. You can choose to display messages in a different order using the Set Preferences feature described previously. But in this description, the messages will be referred to in their regular order.

❝ *Plain English, please!*

The process of organizing messages into topics is known as **threading**. It enables you to read messages and responses about a single topic without having to read through messages on other subjects. **❞**

After you've read all the messages in a single thread, the next message you bring up (by clicking the Next button) takes you to a new thread. If you want to bypass that subject, just close the message window. You can then look over the directory of unread messages for another topic you want to follow.

TIP **Because messages in a single thread are often posted at widely** varying times, you might actually find two or more separate lists for messages concerning a single topic.

Setting message preferences

Another set of newsgroup preferences covers the time frame of messages shown when you open a message window. It's very similar to the Find Since feature that you use on a regular AOL message board (see Chapter 5). By clicking the Preferences option in a newsgroup message window (see fig. 17.11), you'll have options that will serve you now and in the future.

Fig. 17.11
Choose the time frame under which messages will be displayed, as well as other options.

☐ More button (Pauses to allow cancel during long messages)
☐ (Future expansion)
Ignore messages with these words in the subject :

This feature will be available in a future newsgroups ver

Ignore messages from these users:

This feature will be available in a future Newsgroups ver

Show messages no more than [1] days old.

[Save]   [Cancel]

At the time this book was written, some of the message preferences hadn't been activated. The sole option that was available was the one at the bottom, where you can select the time frame in which messages are displayed. This option can save you the drudgery of having to pore over thousands of accumulated messages during your first visit to a newsgroup or when visiting a newsgroup after a few days' absence from AOL.

CAUTION **The message-board options you choose apply only to the indi-**vidual newsgroup in which you select them. Preferences must be selected separately for every newsgroup to which you subscribe.

Q&A   ***Help! I selected the option to show messages for no more than a day or so, yet I'm still seeing thousands of messages displayed after I click the Save button and close the preference window. Why?***

You need to reload the message list on your computer. Here's how:

1 Close the window containing the message list that appears when you select Read messages.

2 Open the Read My Newsgroups window (if it's not already open), and then double-click the newsgroup window you just closed.

You'll then see only the unread messages posted within the time frame you set on your message preferences.

See it all with the List All feature

When you first open your personal newsgroup list and select a topic, double-clicking the topic name or pressing the Enter key brings up a list of unread messages. To review messages you've read previously, click the List All button instead, which brings up a display of all recent messages available in that newsgroup, whether or not you've read them.

How to reply to a newsgroup message

After you've read the messages in your favorite newsgroup, no doubt you'll be tempted to respond to a particular message. Use the Reply button to add your message to the existing thread so that others will see your response also. There are two ways to respond to a message. First, click the Reply button, which brings up the screen shown in figure 17.12. If you want the author of the original message to receive a reply by e-mail, check the box at the lower left corner of the message window.

The second option is Reply to Author, which enables you to send your response as e-mail instead. You still have the choice of having the same message posted in the newsgroup, by clicking the check box in the Reply to Author window.

Fig. 17.12
The Reply window is where you respond to someone who has written a newsgroup message.

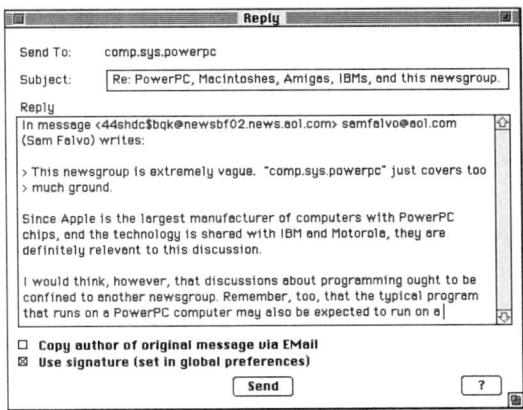

The Use signature (set in global preferences) check box automatically adds the signature you set in the newsgroup preferences box to your message. If you prefer not to use this signature or to use a different signature, click the check box to disable this option.

About cross-posting

Although cross-posting the same message to different newsgroups isn't always a good idea, some of the messages to which you respond are already posted in more than once place. If you respond to any of these messages, you'll see the message shown in figure 17.13. There is nothing you can do to change the route of the response, so just click the OK button.

Fig. 17.13
The response you're posting will appear in more than one newsgroup.

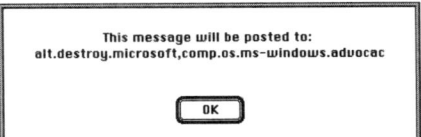

How to post a newsgroup message

If you are not responding to a message in a particular thread and you want to create a new topic, click the Send New Message icon at the top of a message window. This action brings up a blank message window, into which you can insert the topic and then the body of your message.

After you've finished reading the messages in your selected newsgroup and responding to the ones that interest you, click the Mark All Read icon at the top of the directory of available messages. That way, you won't be presented with the same list of messages the next time you visit your newsgroup.

Q&A **Help! The message I posted still hasn't shown up in the newsgroup I sent it to. What's wrong? Where did it go?**

The Internet e-mail and messages you send must pass through a number of computer networks before they make their way to your newsgroup or to the recipient of your message. Your message can sometimes get to the other side of the world in a matter of minutes, yet other times it may take a day or two to arrive. This is common, and you should be patient and give the message some time. In a very few cases, a message does get lost in cyberspace, but because the systems are quite reliable that doesn't happen very often.

CAUTION When you are in the Read My Newsgroups window, before you actually select an individual newsgroup to browse through, using the Update All As Read icon marks all messages in all the discussion groups on your list as having been read. Be careful when you choose this option; otherwise, none of the messages in those newsgroups will be available for reading unless you select the List All option. The latter option forces you to plow through literally thousands of messages (even ones you've read before).

If the newsgroup has no unread messages

If you've read all the messages in a newsgroup and closed the message window, and then you decide you want to add a message of your own, here's what to do:

1 Double-click the directory list for that newsgroup, which brings up a sequence of two messages, shown in figure 17.14 and figure 17.15. You must click the OK button of the first message to see the second.

2 If you want to add a new message of your own, click the OK button, which brings up a standard blank newsgroup message window.

3 If you decide not to prepare that message, click the Cancel button.

Fig. 17.14
You're notified that no unread messages are available.

> You have no unread messages
> for the selected newsgroup.
>
> [OK   ]

Q&A ***Help! I'm getting offensive messages from the Internet. What do I do?***

America Online's Terms of Service, of course, do not apply to members of other services (although they do govern your conduct on the Internet, so be careful). But if you get objectionable or threatening material, you often do have a way to protect yourself. The easiest way to deal with this situation is to check the sender's return address, especially at the domain or location of the service that person is using (such as **@<service>.com**).

If you received the material as e-mail, you can use AOL's forward feature to send the offensive message in e-mail form directly to the folks who administer that service—in this case, it would be **postmaster@<service>.com**. If the material was contained in a message posted in an Internet newsgroup, select the entire message, choose Copy from the Edit menu, and insert the message into the body of an e-mail form, along with your own request that the problem be dealt with.

Many Internet-based services have rules and regulations for their users, and they do not consider such conduct any more acceptable than you do. They will act against that member in accordance with the rules covering their service.

Some services may not object to a message unless its content indicates a possible illegal act. Over the years, I've encountered a very few Internet-only services who care only if the messages aren't being received; not what's contained in the messages.

Fig. 17.15
Decide whether you want to post a new message.

Secrets of AOL's File Grabber

Some newsgroup messages are too large to display in a message window. Others consist of a file instead of a message. In either case, AOL's File Grabber feature will sort this all out for you. When you open such a message window, you'll get the message shown in figure 17.16.

Fig. 17.16
The message is too long, or it consists of a file rather a message. What action should you take? Click Download File.

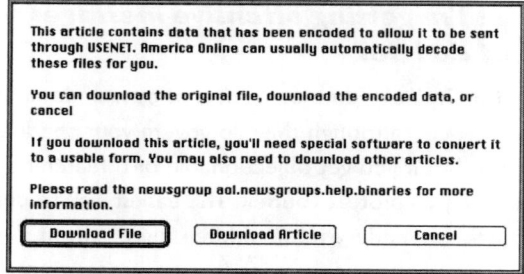

> This article contains data that has been encoded to allow it to be sent through USENET. America Online can usually automatically decode these files for you.
>
> You can download the original file, download the encoded data, or cancel
>
> If you download this article, you'll need special software to convert it to a usable form. You may also need to download other articles.
>
> Please read the newsgroup aol.newsgroups.help.binaries for more information.
>
> [Download File]   [Download Article]   [Cancel]

When you click the Download File button, AOL's File Grabber will work behind the scenes to translate the file to its original form. Then you'll get a dialog box asking where you'd like the file to be downloaded to. The rest of the process is more or less the same as downloading a file from AOL's regular software libraries.

A favorite newsgroup list

Literally thousands of Internet newsgroups are active at any one time. New ones are always being introduced, and others are being discontinued. When you first visit AOL's Newsgroups area, you'll find a list of several newsgroups automatically included in your list (some of them are oriented toward educating you further about Internet practices). Over time, you can change or add to this list.

18
Unmasking the World Wide Web

● **In this chapter:**

- ● **The elements of a web page**

- ● **How to use AOL's Web browser**

- ● **How to surf the Web**

- ● **How to deal with common problems**

You read about it everywhere—the **World Wide Web.** *Let's see what it's all about.* . . . . ▶

I f you've read about the Internet in previous chapters, you've discovered that it's an exciting and sometimes intimidating "place" to visit. Except for AOL's fancy graphic windows, everything on the global information superhighway is text-based. Even graphic files consist simply of text, unless you download them or run them through one of those handy decoder programs.

The World Wide Web (often simply referred to as the **Web, or WWW**) is something different. It adds full-color pictures, and sometimes sound, to the otherwise drab Internet interface, which explains why Web access is becoming one of the fastest growing Internet services. The Web is not only a constant source of information about a huge range of subjects, but also an area where you can observe the creative efforts of a growing number of computer artists.

To understand how the Web works, I want to describe a Macintosh program that Apple Computer has provided free with every new Mac since 1987.

I'm referring to HyperCard (see fig. 18.1), an extremely flexible program that stores document windows called **cards** in files known as **stacks**. To move from one card or stack to another, simply click an icon, a label, or even a section of text, and you're zoomed there!

Fig. 18.1
Apple's HyperCard program gives you a taste of navigating through the World Wide Web. (Notice the Home button, for example.)

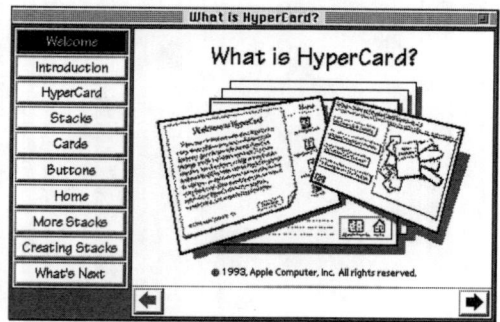

Although the technique isn't terribly different, when you access a page on the World Wide Web (the equivalent of a card in your HyperCard stack or even the Help item in the Window menu of a Mac application), you are not necessarily moving to another part of a single file, but often to another item, located on another computer, in another part of the world. Further, the entire process is transparent; you never see the complex, sometimes convoluted path the data must travel before it reaches your Mac.

Hello, Web site!

Before we take apart a web page, let's visit one. And that requires opening America Online's browser program, which is a separate program that works with your regular AOL software. (I'll tell you how to get it and install it later.)

 Plain English, please!

A **browser** is an application that can locate documents on the World Wide Web. These documents, known as **pages,** are retrieved by the browser program, which then translates them into a form that's readable by your computer. **99**

 **Q&A** *I want to access the World Wide Web. Where do I get this browser program?*

AOL's Macintosh Web browser is a separate program, and it has to be installed separately. To get a copy, use the keyword **Upgrade**, which takes you to an area where you can download AOL's web browser. The area is free of online charges, so you don't pay for the time you spend there. All you have to do is click the Download Now button to transfer the file to your Mac's hard drive.

Entering the World Wide Web from AOL on your Macintosh is simple. The keyword **WWW** (or just clicking the World Wide Web icon at AOL's Internet Connection department) does the following:

The best way to install the Mac Web browser

Since the Mac Web browser is a separate program, AOL has developed a way for the browser program to talk to your AOL software using a technique called **Apple Events,** which is part of Apple's System 7. In order for the programs to work best together, you should install as follows:

1 Install regular AOL software. Do not launch the program yet.

2 Install WWW browser software.

3 Check inside your AOL application folder by double-clicking it to make sure that a folder titled Online Browser is there. (If not, run the WWW software installer again).

4 Launch your AOL software, and go through the initial logon or update process, as described in Chapter 1.

- The AOL browser program is launched.

- AOL's home page is accessed and displays on your Mac's screen after a few minutes (see fig. 18.2).

- If the page doesn't come up, just click the Home icon at the top of the web page document window.

Fig. 18.2
America Online's
WWW home page
guides you to many
other Web sites. Simply
click any icon that
interests you.

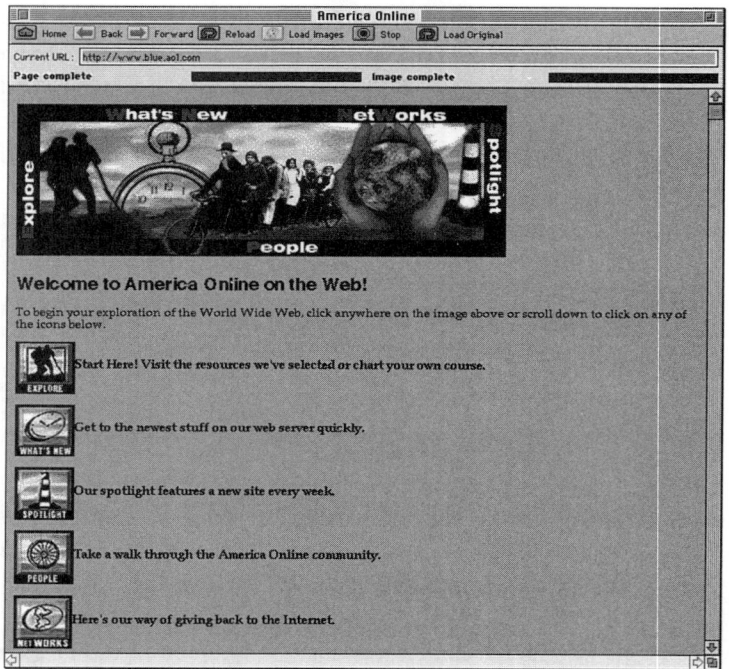

How to get from here to there

Traveling around AOL's home page is just a matter of clicking once on the labeled icon or on an underlined title. Either step will magically transport you to another WWW page that's linked to that site.

This process of moving from one page to another is done behind the scenes. AOL's WWW browser will look up another page or site address, known as its **URL**.

Plain English, please!

URL is short for **Uniform Resource Locator**. The URL information you enter is a shortcut for the location of the site. Here's the format of a typical URL (which happens to be the AOL home page we've just connected to): **http://www.blue.aol.com**

Before going any further, let's dissect that URL to see what it's made of:

- The letters **http** are short for **Hypertext Transfer Protocol**, which is the technique developed by the architects of the World Wide Web to locate and access Web sites.

- The colon (**:**) and the two slashes (**//**) inform the software that the information that follows is the actual Internet address of the site being accessed (**www** stands for World Wide Web).

- The last extension added to this particular Web site, **.com**, identifies it as a commercial enterprise. If the extension is **.edu,** it's an educational institution. You'll find more information about Internet site-naming conventions in Chapter 15.

 *CAUTION* **Be sure to enter the exact URL information shown to visit one of** these sites. Even a single incorrect character will result in failure. If you cannot find a particular site using the information provided in this and the next chapter, you can contact that source directly for additional assistance or use one of the search tools described in this chapter for up-to-date information.

If you want to visit another Web site, simply enter the URL or site address in the Current URL list field; or choose Services, Open URL and enter an address in the dialog box that appears.

Then press Enter, and AOL's Web browser will attempt to access the site. If the browser is successful at finding the site (and usually it is), the image of the new site will begin to appear on your Mac's screen in just a moment or two. It will always take a little while for the entire page to be displayed, depending on the speed of your AOL connection.

CAUTION   **To use both the regular AOL Mac software and the WWW browser,** you need at least 5M of free RAM. This is in addition to the amount of RAM your Mac uses for system software (including any system extensions you are using). If you don't have that amount of RAM available, consider a memory upgrade before visiting the World Wide Web.

Q&A   *Why has my Mac browser's link gone down?*

To connect to a Web site on your Mac, it isn't enough to be running your AOL Web browser and your AOL software. You must also be logged on to AOL. If you log off, get disconnected, or if AOL's Internet access is interrupted, you'll get a message to that effect. You will also see the flashing icon of the Web browser application on your Mac's menu bar.

To remove the message, just click on it and then check to make sure that your AOL application is running and that you are logged on to AOL. If you are logged on at the time this message is seen, log off immediately and then log on again. If the problem continues, you might want to try using the World Wide Web at a later time.

Q&A   *Why does it take so long for Web images to appear on my computer's screen, especially compared to the images I see on AOL?*

There are a couple of reasons. First of all, the images retrieved by AOL's Web browser are sent from a remote computer, and the transmission process is not as efficient as it would be on AOL's host computers.

Also, the speed at which you connect to AOL is a major factor in the time it takes for a Web page's image to appear. At the very least, you need a 14,400 bps modem and 14,400 bps AOL connection to get adequate speed on the World Wide Web. The new generation of V.34 (28,800 bps) modems are worth considering if there's an AOLNet access number in your city. If you are limited to a 9600 bps modem or access number, or something slower, my suggestion is that you use the World Wide Web feature judiciously because you will be disappointed with its performance.

Let's get past that home page

Once you've hooked up to a Web site's home page, you can easily navigate to other pages by clicking an icon or underlined text. You need not know the URL to locate the additional pages—that's the beauty of those behind-the-scenes links used by the browser to move from one page to another.

How to make a hot link

As you see, moving from one Web site to another is simple. You just enter the correct URL, and press Return or Enter to send AOL's browser on the path to the page you've selected. The Next and Previous buttons will take you directly to pages previously retrieved. (The Next button, of course, will only function if another page was retrieved after the one you're currently viewing.)

 **TIP** **You can navigate directly to a specific Web page, other than a** home page, if you know its full URL (including the name of the actual page). For example, **http://www.blue.aol.com/preview/ welcome.html** accesses AOL's own Web site, and the part of the address following the **.com/** takes you to a specific page at that site.

As you visit Web sites, you will find places you want to return to from time to time. AOL's Mac Web browser lets you create an address book of your favorite sites, a **hot list,** to enable you to revisit sites easily. To add the Web site you've just accessed to that list, simply choose Services, Add to Main Hot List. The Web site shown on your Mac's screen will be added to a list like the one shown in figure 18.3 (where I've already included some of my favorite sites).

Fig. 18.3
You can create a list of your favorite WWW sites with a few short steps.

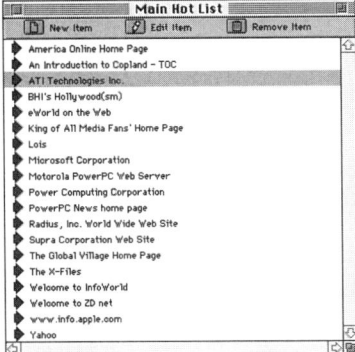

 **TIP** **If you're into keyboard shortcuts, here's one to instantly add your** open WWW page to the Main Hot List. Simply type **Command + Option + H**. Your Main Hot List will be instantly opened, and you'll find the selected page added to the list.

Because Web site addresses can change from time to time, you might want to change an item in your hot list. To do so, follow these steps:

1 Choose Services, Hot Lists and select Main Hot List. (If you've made another hot list that you want to edit instead, choose that one.)

2 Click the entry you want to edit to select it.

3 Click the Edit Item icon.

4 Make your changes and click OK to save those changes.

If you want to remove an item from the hot list, follow these steps:

1 Choose Services, Add to Main Hot List.

2 Click the entry you want to edit.

3 Click the Remove Item icon or choose File, Cut.

4 When the dialog box appears asking you to confirm that the item is to be deleted, click the OK button to remove that site from the hot list.

5 If you change your mind and want to leave the entry intact, just click the Cancel button.

You aren't limited to one hot list. As your Web browsing becomes more intense, you might choose to create a hot list for different categories of Web sites: perhaps one for computer-based sites, another for entertainment, and another for education. To make a new hot list, simply choose Services, Hot Lists and select New Hot List. This will bring up a standard Mac Save As dialog box, where you can name your new hot list.

Your new hot list is edited in exactly the same way as your main hot list, with one exception: you can only select your newly created hot list by choosing Services, Hot Lists. The Add to Main Hot List command will only access your main hot list listing.

What else can I do with the Mac Web browser?

Besides addressing Web sites and building hot lists, there are other features available in AOL's Web browser via icons or menu bar commands. First, I'll run down the control icons shown below the title bar in the main browser program window (see fig. 18.4). If an icon is grayed out, that function is unavailable.

Fig. 18.4
Control the way WWW images are displayed using these handy icons.

- **Home.** Click to return to AOL's home page.

- **Back.** Click to return to the previous page.

- **Forward.** Click to go to the next page.

- **Reload.** Click to reload the current Web page onto the program's document window.

- **Load Images.** Click to reload graphic images on the selected Web page.

- **Stop.** Click if you want to halt the process of retrieving a Web page.

- **Load Original.** Click to reload the original selected page from a site.

These commands are probably sufficient to cover most of your WWW needs; they'll allow you to quickly navigate to your favorite sites without delay and easily switch from page to page. I'll cover just a few more here that may help you use the browser more effectively. You can explore the rest of the commands at your leisure.

Edit menu

The commands in the Edit menu are almost identical to the ones you find in any other Macintosh program, with URL added. It allows you to select URLs shown in the Current URL page, and paste them in a hot list or even in another document. You can also use the browser's search functions to locate specific items in a formatted original HTML document.

The one command in the Edit menu that you'll want to look over further is Configure. Configure allows you to adjust specific settings of your browser application. Many of the preferences concern communications and file-translation protocols. The one preference I do want to describe in more detail is accessed by clicking on the Web icon (see fig. 18.5).

Fig. 18.5
You can set global
WWW preferences,
most of which you'll
want to leave
unchanged.

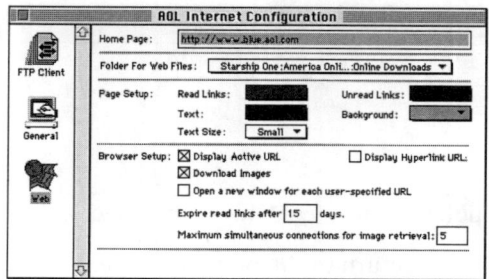

This set of preferences includes the name of AOL's home page. If you prefer to activate another WWW site as a default, you can enter that in the Home Page field.

There are three other options you'll want to review:

- **Folder for Web Files.** This popup menu allows you to choose a folder for storing all the files you download from Web or FTP sites. By default, it's set to the same folder that contains your browser application. In the example, I selected my standard AOL Downloads folder instead; this allows me to keep all of my downloaded files in one location.

- **Page Setup.** This series of preferences lets you establish colors for specific WWW page displays and choose the size of the text that is displayed on that page.

- **Browser Setup.** These preferences are used to provide basic defaults for retrieving images from the World Wide Web. The default options will serve for most users.

Services menu

The options in the Services menu allow you to use the major features of the browser program (see fig. 18.6). The Open URL and Hot List functions are described in the previous section.

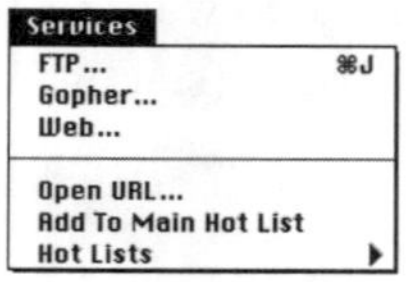

Fig. 18.6
Use the browser's
Services menu to access
the program's features.

Here's how the rest of the commands work.

- **FTP.** This command lets you access the browser's own FTP function (see fig. 18.7). The screen shown here appears when you click the More Options button (which adds all of the selections shown beyond the first line).

 **TIP** **AOL's regular FTP area (keyword FTP) is a better and easier to use** choice for downloading files. That area offers automatic anonymous logons and a much more informative file directory, which includes the actual dates the files were posted at the remote site.

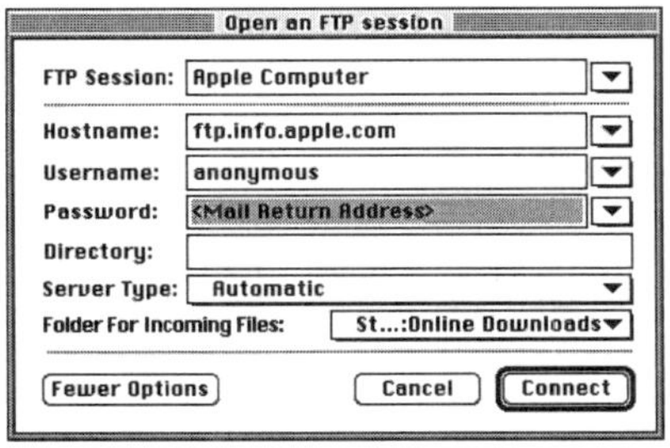

Fig. 18.7
AOL's Web browser has its own FTP feature; remember, this screen is being shown with the More Options button clicked.

```
═════════ Open an FTP session ═════════
FTP Session:  │Apple Computer              │▼│
Hostname:     │ftp.info.apple.com          │▼│
Username:     │anonymous                   │▼│
Password:     │<Mail Return Address>       │▼│
Directory:    │                            │
Server Type:  │ Automatic                  ▼│
Folder For Incoming Files:    │ St...:Online Downloads▼│

( Fewer Options )          ( Cancel ) ( Connect )
```

Here's the easy way to connect to most FTP sites:

1 Enter the name of the site you want to reach as the Host name.

2 Enter anonymous as your User Name.

3 Enter your AOL-based Internet address (**name@aol.com**) as your password.

You can also define the precise folder to access, if you prefer. In situations that require restricted access, you can enter a custom name and password. After you've filled in the blanks, click the Connect button to get to your site.

When you've connected to your chosen site, you'll see a file transfer window that actually lets you retrieve or send files to the remote FTP site (see fig. 18.8, which was made after clicking through several file directories). To transfer a file, simply click the file's name to select it, and then click the Copy button to transfer it to either your own computer or the remote site.

TIP   **If you need to find an FTP site address, you should visit AOL's** regular FTP gateway (keyword: **FTP**). Then click the Search icon on the main screen, and enter the name of the company or educational institution you wish to find. You'll see a list of matches, if any, along with actual FTP addresses.

Fig. 18.8
Choose files to transfer
via FTP. You will often
have to step through
several levels of file
directories to get to
the ones you want to
download.

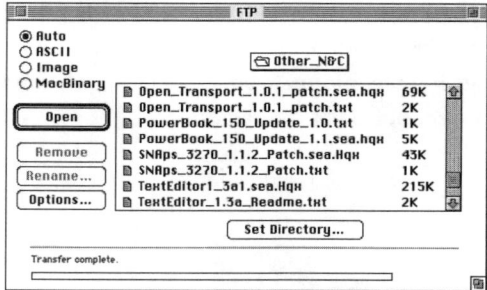

CAUTION   **Before you attempt to transfer a file to a remote FTP site, you** might want to contact the site administrator to determine if you have access privileges to send files. There will often be a text file of some sort at a site explaining how to contact the folks who run it. Sites that offer anonymous access often will not permit users to send files.

- **Gopher.** This command lets you access a Gopher site directly if you know its address. Most of the time, though, you'll get more efficient performance by using AOL's own Gopher and WAIS database search feature (keyword: **Gopher**).

TIP   **AOL's Mac Web browser will transparently go to FTP or Gopher** sites that are directly accessed through a WWW site. You won't have to enter a separate site address to access them. All that's necessary is to click a picture or underlined text—the same technique you use to go to another WWW page. When you choose a file to download via FTP from a Web site, you'll see a progress display window showing the status of your file download, similar to the one you see when you download software via AOL's regular software.

And the AOL menu?

The last menu on AOL's web browser, the AOL menu, offers you just two functions. The first, Connect, is used if you are not presently logged on to AOL. It will log you on using the screen name that has previously been selected in the Setup and Sign On window. Also, it opens the AOL program if it hasn't been launched. The other option, Switch to AOL, does precisely what it describes: it switches you to the regular AOL program.

Speeding up Web access

Under any circumstances, the World Wide Web can tax the fastest computer's CPU with its roster of photos, sounds, and animation. As convenient and as useful as WWW access is, don't expect speedy performance. Sometimes, heavy network traffic will slow image displays to a crawl, and there's nothing you can do about it—other than trying to log on to AOL at a different time or using a different access number. But there are ways to make AOL's Web software perform better. Here are a few considerations:

- Get a faster modem.

- Find a faster access number. Use the keyword **Access** to get a list of connection numbers. Because AOL's new AOLNet network, with 28,800 bps access, is expanding, you'll want to check occasionally for newer phone-connection choices.

- Get a faster computer. It goes without saying that Macs and PCs are getting faster and cheaper. If you have an older model, it might be time to look at a new computer equipped with a PowerPC microprocessor. These new models can outperform older models by a huge factor.

- Give a program more RAM. Click once to select AOL's software and the Web browser software icons (the programs must not be running when you perform this operation), then choose Get Info from the Finder's File menu (see fig. 18.9). Enter a higher preferred memory setting, usually in increments of 500K or higher.

Fig. 18.9
Enter a higher memory setting in the Get Info window. In this example, using System 7.5, make the setting in the Preferred size field.

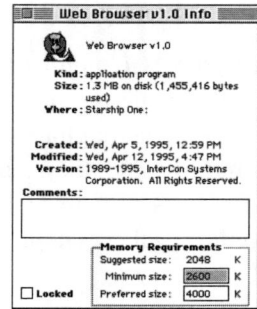

 **CAUTION** **To give your Mac WWW browser software a greater dose of RAM,** you need to have enough free memory. If your computer has less than 8M of RAM, it might be time to consider a memory upgrade.

- Turn off the option to show graphics. This choice is available as part of your multimedia preferences, which is represented by an icon that you can select from the Personal Choices window (keyword: **Personal Choices**). It's a last resort, and is recommended only if you have serious performance problems viewing graphics, but it's worth a try.

 **TIP** **Some AOL departments offer access to a Web site by double-**clicking a directory listing or clicking once on an icon. The areas that offer this capability usually have an icon labeled Top Internet Sites or something similar. You can also access a WWW site during your online session by using Command+K to bring up the keyword window, and entering the URL as the keyword. Once you click Go, the WWW browser will be opened (if necessary), and you'll be magically transported directly to that site.

19

Getting Started on the Web

● In this chapter:

- Some of the most popular Macintosh Web sites (and a few others)

- A quick way to search for additional Web sites

Now that you know how to get on the World Wide Web, you'll want to find some fun places to visit while you're there . . ❯

n the last chapter, I unmasked some of the elements of the World Wide Web. I explained how you can install and use AOL's WWW browser to access all those color sites. A few popular World Wide Web sites were described to illustrate how particular features of the software are used.

There are literally thousands of sites from which to choose on the World Wide Web, covering every conceivable category—from your favorite forms of entertainment to areas where you can read about the latest products from your favorite computer manufacturer. This chapter is devoted to listing just a few of the popular Web sites along with their **URLs** (locations). You can easily visit these sites by entering the URL information (precisely as shown) in AOL's Web browser (or just by a keyword). You navigate through these sites by clicking the underlined titles or descriptions, which provide quick access to the named areas.

TIP **Some Web sites offer the ability to display material in text or** graphic form. If you don't have a 14,400 bps or faster modem (and an AOL connection to match that speed), choose the text option where possible to improve performance and reduce the time it takes for material to appear on your computer.

CAUTION **To visit one of the WWW sites described in this chapter, be sure to** enter the exact URL (Web site address) information shown. Even a single incorrect character will result in failure to access these locations. The author and publisher are not responsible for errors, however, so if you cannot find a particular site using the information provided, you can contact that source directly for additional assistance or use the Yahoo search site, described at the end of this chapter, for up-to-date information.

Just a few favorite Mac sites (and some other good stuff)

Since I started surfing the Web, I've built up a list of sites I like to revisit often. I'm going to share a few of those locations with you (plus a few others some friends have suggested). The selections that follow were chosen arbitrarily and are only meant as a guide to get you started. No doubt you'll find others equally compelling during your online travels.

Apple Computer, Inc.

URL address: **http://www.support.apple.com/**

Apple Computer has established an attractive visual display (see fig. 19.1) that enables you to learn about its full array of products—ranging from its popular line of personal computers to its operating system and other software products. You'll be able to tap the resources of Apple's huge technical information library, so you can learn first-hand about dealing with common problems and finding quick solutions.

Fig. 19.1
Apple Computer's Web site offers information about new Apple products, software updates, and technical information.

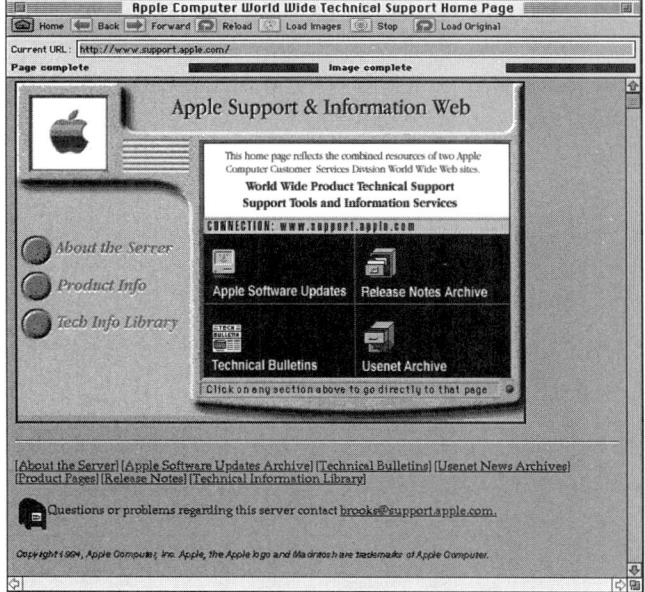

 **TIP** **Remember that visiting a Web site doesn't just involve reading** text and looking at pretty pictures. It represents a valuable resource for software, and you might actually find that downloading from a Web site seems easier than rummaging through various folders or directories to locate the files you want.

 **Q&A** *Help! How can I get to the World Wide Web sites you describe in this book?*

The Web is a fluid place, and sites are always being added, removed, and changed. If a site address shown in this book is no longer correct, use the Yahoo search site, described at the end of this chapter, to locate a site's correct URL.

Microsoft

URL address: **http://www.microsoft.com**

Microsoft's Web site is valuable to both Mac and PC users because Microsoft's software is so popular on both computing platforms. You'll find this site (see fig. 19.2) a helpful resource for further information about both Windows-related issues and matters concerning popular productivity software, such as Excel and Word.

Fig. 19.2
Microsoft's Web site offers support and information on their products.

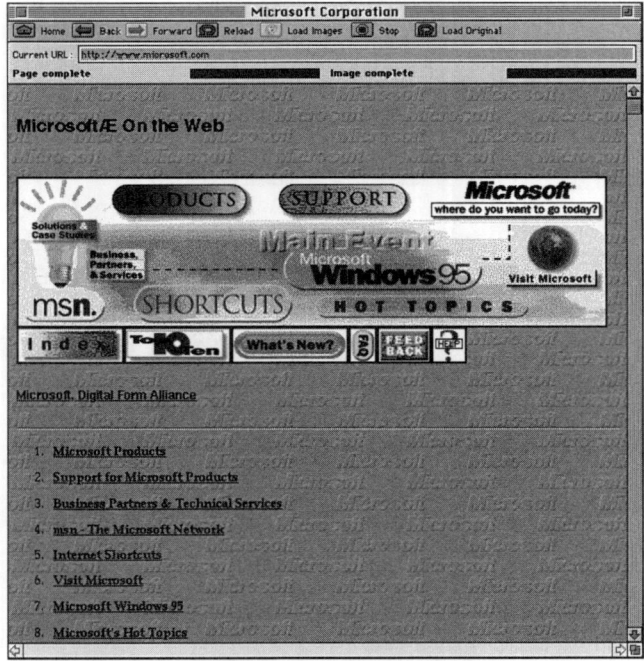

Novell, Inc.

URL address: **http://www.novell.com**

Novell (see fig. 19.3) is the well-known publisher of networking software for both the Macintosh and the Windows environments. Novell is also the publisher of WordPerfect, which is available in versions for DOS, Mac, and Windows. The company's Web site takes full advantage of the terrific graphics you can create on the World Wide Web.

Fig. 19.3
Pay a visit to Novell's Internet-based support facility.

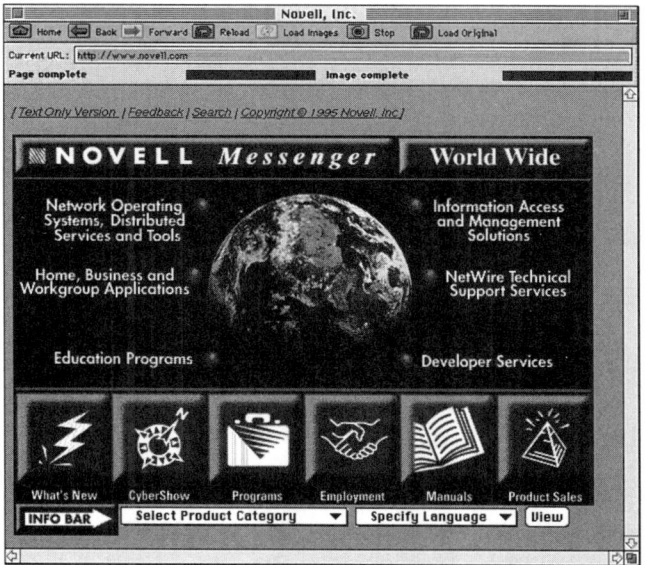

Software Ventures Corporation

URL address: **http://www.svcdudes.com/**

Software Ventures (see fig. 19.4) is a publisher of telecommunications software for both the Macintosh and the Windows environments. This Web site is designed to offer helpful technical information, updates for modem drivers and other utilities needed by the program, and ways to interact with the publisher to help you solve your own telecommunications problems.

Fig. 19.4

Get support for telecommunications software from Software Ventures.

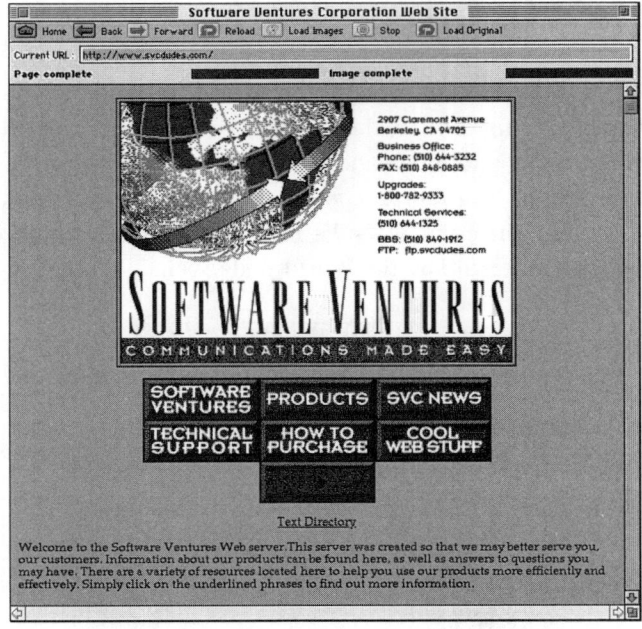

Ziff-Davis

URL address: **http://www.ziff.com**

Many of you are probably regular readers of some of the various Ziff-Davis computer magazines, such as *MacUser*, *PC User*, *MacWeek*, and *PC Week* (see fig. 19.5). The publisher's Web site offers a colorful repository of the latest material from all of these publications. If you want to read more about the newest software from Microsoft or a hot announcement about a new computer from Apple, navigate through the Ziff-Davis site.

Fig. 19.5
The popular Web site run by Ziff-Davis offers text from many of its computer magazines and software for you to download.

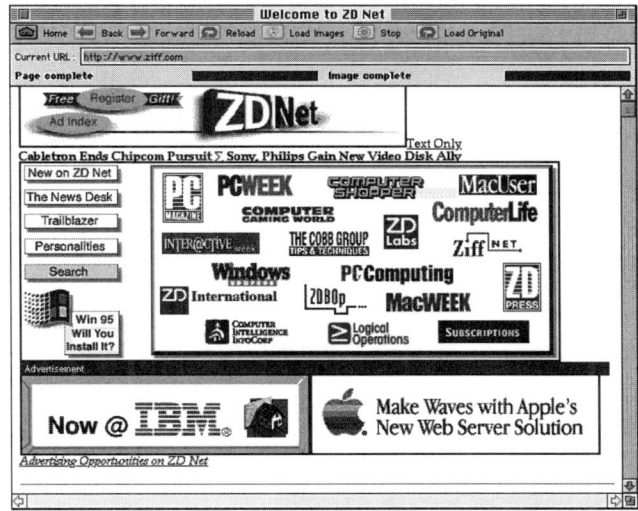

The Howard Stern Show

URL address: **http://krishna.cs.umd.edu/stern/**

What can you say about one of the most controversial figures in broadcasting? Howard Stern (see fig. 19.6), the self-proclaimed King of All Media, has been praised and vilified (sometimes by the same people at roughly the same times) for a radio show that can be irritating, controversial, exciting, funny, or none of the above. This site is run by Howard's fans to report on his activities and those of his sidekicks.

Fig. 19.6
Where radio has never gone before: *The Howard Stern Show.*

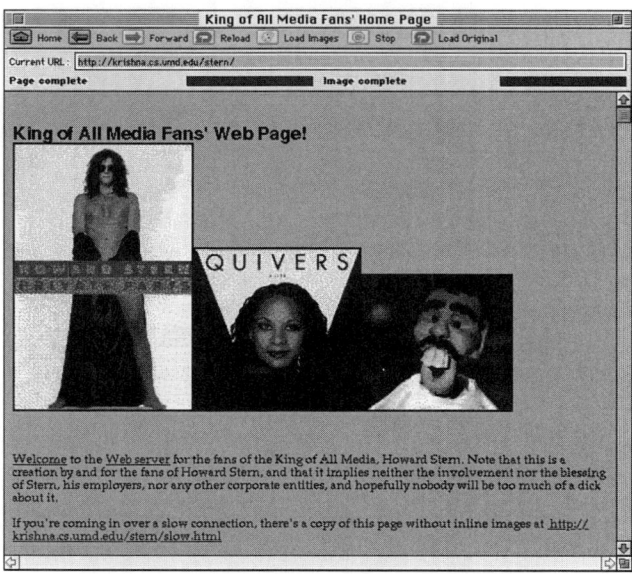

Star Trek Voyager

URL address: **http://voyager.paramount.com/VoyagerIntro.html**

Star Trek Voyager's Web site offers information about past episodes, the cast and crew, and the strange and wonderful beings who appeared on the show. It also enables you to experience some of the finest moments of the program, and it offers insights into new developments (such as possible movie projects). The site shown here, by the way, is one of several devoted to various *Star Trek* programs.

Fig. 19.7
Star Trek Voyager's
holographic doctor
takes you on a tour of
this Web site.

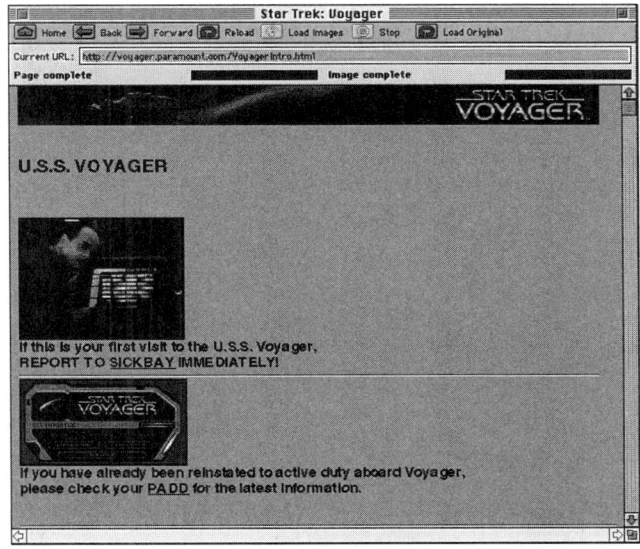

The Young and the Restless

URL address: **http://www.digimark.net/wow/yr/**

The plot of the typical television soap opera is often difficult to describe in a pithy paragraph or two, so I won't even try. *The Young and the Restless* (see fig. 19.8) has been on the air for more than 20 years. It involves the lives of dozens of characters whose activities intermingle in many related (and sometimes unrelated) story lines. At this site, you'll find a complete description of some of the most popular story lines, learn about the doings of your favorite characters, and locate descriptions about what you might expect in future shows.

Fig. 19.8
Fans of *The Young and the Restless* will find a lot to read about here.

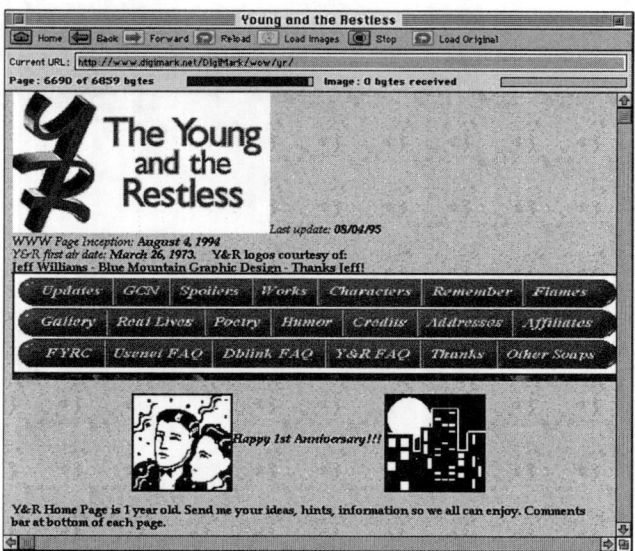

The X-Files

URL address: **http://www.rutgers.edu/x-files.html**

The Fox television program *The X-Files* (see fig. 19.9) has garnered a level of interest that is reminiscent of Star Trek "fan-dom." The show details the exploits of two FBI agents who choose to investigate weird or unusual cases that might involve UFO visitation or psychic phenomena (ghosts and things that go bump in the night). This Web page describes everything from show plots to background information on the stars of the program.

Fig. 19.9

Learn about the most popular episodes of The X-Files and even download a sound file that contains the show's theme.

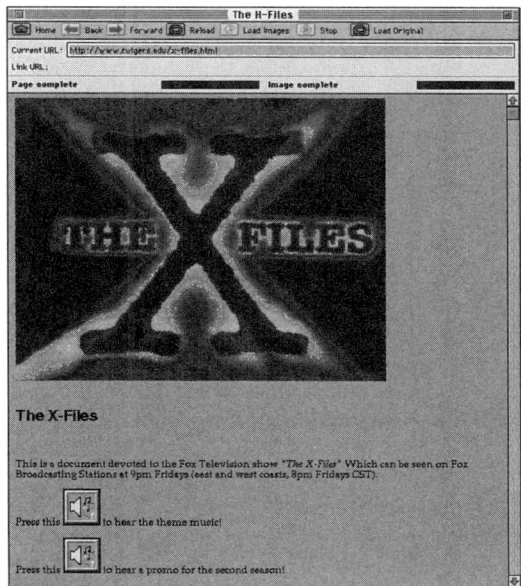

The Central Intelligence Agency

URL address: **http://www.ODCI.gov**

What's this? A Web site devoted to the CIA? You won't find any top-secret information here, but you will find online publications about the agency's mission and place in the world (see fig. 19.10). One useful resource is the *Factbook on Intelligence*, which you can read while visiting this Web site. It tells of the CIA's early history, provides a basic overview of its purpose in the world, and informs you about the setup of its headquarters—or at least as much as can be described without compromising national security. The *Factbook* is indexed by topic, and just clicking the appropriate item brings up additional information. One topic worth reading about is entitled "Key Events in CIA's History."

Fig. 19.10
Learn about the CIA
by visiting its Web site.

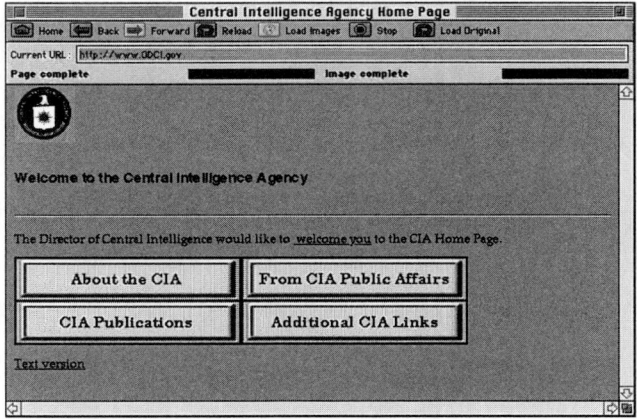

Finding Web sites on your own

The above selections are but a few of thousands of Web sites that can be found across the world. How do you find a particular site or find out if a particular business or educational concern has a Web site?

Fortunately, this is becoming easier to do because more and more representatives of such firms include their URLs on their business cards and stationery. You also find WWW listings in popular magazines and newspapers. Press releases announcing new products or services will also mention the Web site address somewhere in the text.

Q&A *Why do I get a* `Fatal Error` *message when I try to access a WWW page?*

Take heart: The message doesn't mean your Mac has crashed, or that you have encountered a really serious problem. Most of the time, you get that error when the page you are trying to reach isn't available, or you've entered the URL site address information incorrectly. When you get this message, recheck the URL and make sure that every character is accurately entered. Remember, there are no word spaces, for example, in an URL. If you've confirmed that the URL is correct, you might want to recheck the source from which you got that site location to make sure the address hasn't changed. Or maybe you should just try again. Sometimes network glitches (or simply a system problem on the site's own server) along the Internet will make a site easily available one day, and unavailable the next.

Paying a visit to Yahoo

URL address: **http://www.yahoo.com**

If you want a convenient way to look up additional sites, pay a visit to the Yahoo Web site (see fig. 19.11).

Fig. 19.11
You can use Yahoo to search through a directory of thousands of Web sites.

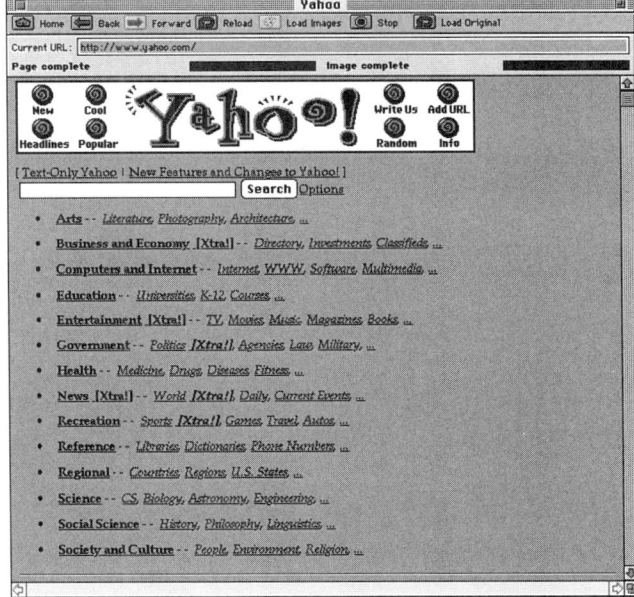

Not just a casual pursuit

The Yahoo search site is a classic case of a hobby blooming into a real business. It was started by two undergraduate students, David Filo and Jerry Yang. They created the search database for their own personal use so they could keep tabs on their favorite Internet sites.

The site has mushroomed into a huge Internet searching facility that tracks literally thousands of Internet sites worldwide. Also, it has corporate sponsors, which is why you'll see ads displayed on various Yahoo pages. Although the name, Yahoo, is reported to stand for Yet Another Hierarchical Officious Oracle, Filo and Yang maintain that they chose the name because they regard themselves as yahoos.

The tale of the creation of Yahoo has drawn the attention of the national news media. Stories about it have appeared in *USA Today* and other newspapers.

You'll find using Yahoo's Web facility similar to searching for data on America Online. If you want to find sites dealing with a specific topic, simply click the underlined item representing the category, or click the Search tool (see fig. 19.12). After you find the area that you want to visit, click the underlined reference to go directly to that site.

Fig. 19.12
This is an efficient way to search for other Web sites that might warrant further exploration.

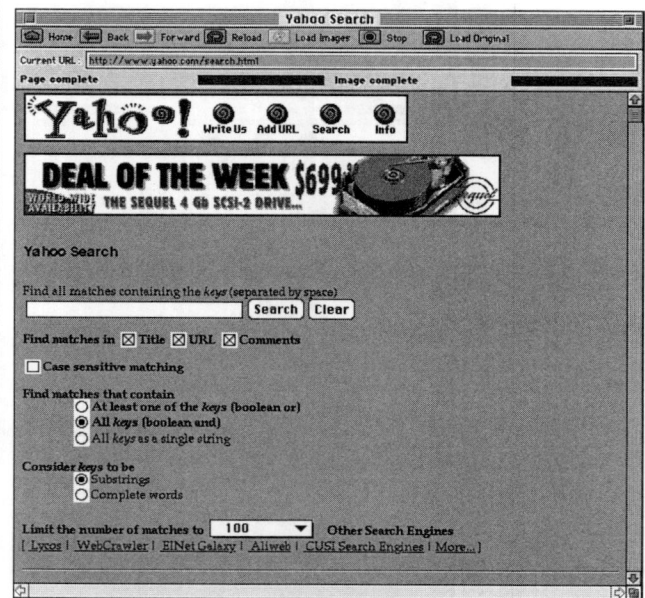

More search tools

America Online provides links to other popular WWW search tools at its own site, which you can reach via the URL address: **http://www.blue.aol.com/ preview/search.html.** When you enter that site address (or just choose the Search icon from AOL's regular Preview page), you'll see the selections shown in figure 19.13.

Fig. 19.13
AOL offers a selection
of Web sites that
provides an extensive
range of search tools.

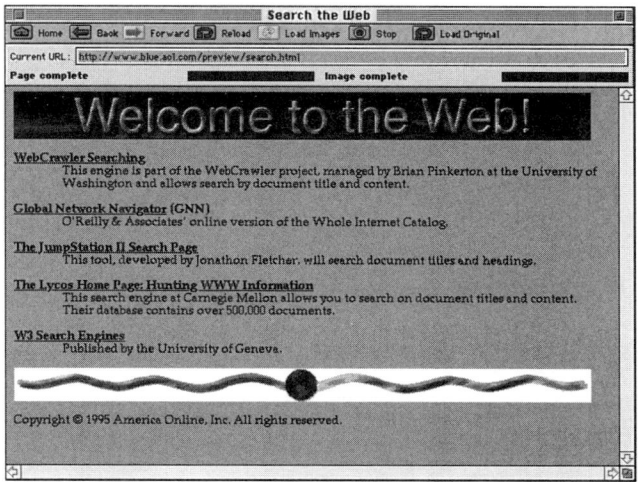

Clicking each of the items shown on this page will provide a different tool for
seeking information on the Internet.

Here's a quick summary of what's offered at these sites:

- **WebCrawler Searching.** This site allows you to locate a specific site
  by its name and topic. It also provides a Top 25 Sites listing and helpful
  advice on how to locate sites that may interest you. (AOL was so
  impressed with this search tool, by the way, that it bought the product.)

- **Global Network Navigator.** This is the online version of The Whole
  Internet Catalog, and it lists a large number of sites by subject. By
  clicking on a subject, you get a list of sites meeting that criteria. The
  next step, clicking on the site's name, gets you a one-paragraph description and the option to go right to that site to see it for yourself.

- **JumpStation II Front Page.** Here's another valuable search tool that
  helps you quickly locate sites that may interest you. Before you give it a
  try, you'll want to review some of its text documents to learn all about
  the search procedures.

- **The Lycos Home Page.** Clicking on this entry takes you to Carnegie-Mellon University's Web site, which lets you search a database of over 500,000 documents.

- **W3 Search Engines.** This may be the best search tool in AOL's list. It gathers a number of search engines into one handy interface, listing the most popular sites, a text entry field, and a Submit (request) button that lets you access that particular search function to locate the site or information you seek. The illustration shown here (see fig. 19.16) depicts only a few of the search functions you can access from this site.

Fig. 19.16
W3 Search Engines provide a big selection of search tools to help you locate the information you want.

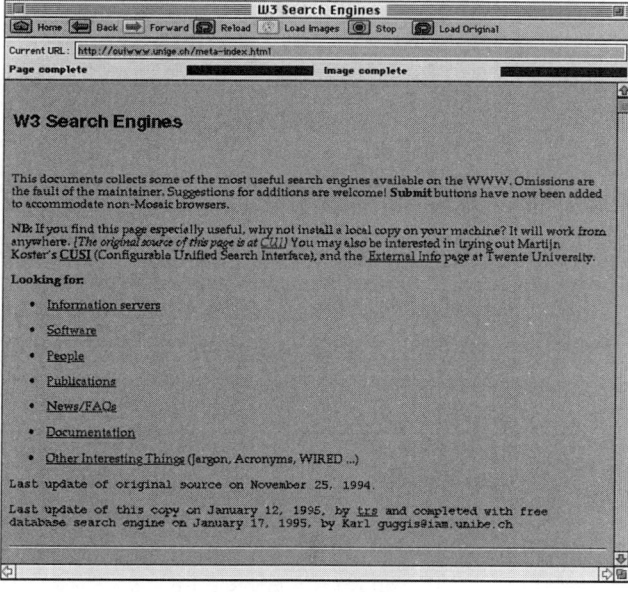

Index

PLUG YOURSELF INTO...

THE MACMILLAN INFORMATION SUPERLIBRARY™

Free information and vast computer resources from the world's leading computer book publisher—online!

FIND THE BOOKS THAT ARE RIGHT FOR YOU!
A complete online catalog, plus sample chapters and tables of contents!

- **STAY INFORMED** with the latest computer industry news through our online newsletter, press releases, and customized Information SuperLibrary Reports.

- **GET FAST ANSWERS** to your questions about Macmillan Computer Publishing books.

- **VISIT** our online bookstore for the latest information and editions!

- **COMMUNICATE** with our expert authors through e-mail and conferences.

- **DOWNLOAD SOFTWARE** from the immense Macmillan Computer Publishing library:
    - Source code, shareware, freeware, and demos

- **DISCOVER HOT SPOTS** on other parts of the Internet.

- **WIN BOOKS** in ongoing contests and giveaways!

TO PLUG INTO MCP:

WORLD WIDE WEB: **http://www.mcp.com**

FTP: ftp.mcp.com

Complete and Return this Card
for a *FREE* Computer Book Catalog

Thank you for purchasing this book! You have purchased a superior computer book written expressly for your needs. To continue to provide the kind of up-to-date, pertinent coverage you've come to expect from us, we need to hear from you. Please take a minute to complete and return this self-addressed, postage-paid form. In return, we'll send you a free catalog of all our computer books on topics ranging from word processing to programming and the internet.

Mr. ☐   Mrs. ☐   Ms. ☐   Dr. ☐

Name (first) ☐☐☐☐☐☐☐☐☐☐☐☐☐☐   (M.I.) ☐   (last) ☐☐☐☐☐☐☐☐☐☐☐☐☐☐

Address ☐☐☐☐☐☐☐☐☐☐☐☐☐☐☐☐☐☐☐☐☐☐☐☐☐☐☐☐

☐☐☐☐☐☐☐☐☐☐☐☐☐☐☐☐☐☐☐☐☐☐☐☐☐☐☐☐

City ☐☐☐☐☐☐☐☐☐☐☐☐   State ☐☐   Zip ☐☐☐☐☐ ☐☐☐☐

Phone ☐☐☐ ☐☐☐ ☐☐☐☐   Fax ☐☐☐ ☐☐☐ ☐☐☐☐

Company Name ☐☐☐☐☐☐☐☐☐☐☐☐☐☐☐☐☐☐☐☐☐☐☐☐☐

E-mail address ☐☐☐☐☐☐☐☐☐☐☐☐☐☐☐☐☐☐☐☐☐☐☐☐☐

1. Please check at least (3) influencing factors for purchasing this book.

Front or back cover information on book .... ☐
Special approach to the content .... ☐
Completeness of content .... ☐
Author's reputation .... ☐
Publisher's reputation .... ☐
Book cover design or layout .... ☐
Index or table of contents of book .... ☐
Price of book .... ☐
Special effects, graphics, illustrations .... ☐
Other (Please specify): _____ ☐

2. How did you first learn about this book?

Saw in Macmillan Computer Publishing catalog .... ☐
Recommended by store personnel .... ☐
Saw the book on bookshelf at store .... ☐
Recommended by a friend .... ☐
Received advertisement in the mail .... ☐
Saw an advertisement in: _____ ☐
Read book review in: _____ ☐
Other (Please specify): _____ ☐

3. How many computer books have you purchased in the last six months?

This book only .... ☐   3 to 5 books .... ☐
2 books .... ☐   More than 5 .... ☐

4. Where did you purchase this book?

Bookstore .... ☐
Computer Store .... ☐
Consumer Electronics Store .... ☐
Department Store .... ☐
Office Club .... ☐
Warehouse Club .... ☐
Mail Order .... ☐
Direct from Publisher .... ☐
Internet site .... ☐
Other (Please specify): _____ ☐

5. How long have you been using a computer?

☐ Less than 6 months   ☐ 6 months to a year
☐ 1 to 3 years   ☐ More than 3 years

6. What is your level of experience with personal computers and with the subject of this book?

	With PCs	With subject of book
New	☐	☐
Casual	☐	☐
Accomplished	☐	☐
Expert	☐	☐

Source Code ISBN: 0-7897-0593-1

7. Which of the following best describes your job title?

Administrative Assistant .... ☐
Coordinator .... ☐
Manager/Supervisor .... ☐
Director .... ☐
Vice President .... ☐
President/CEO/COO .... ☐
Lawyer/Doctor/Medical Professional .... ☐
Teacher/Educator/Trainer .... ☐
Engineer/Technician .... ☐
Consultant .... ☐
Not employed/Student/Retired .... ☐
Other (Please specify): _____ ☐

8. Which of the following best describes the area of the company your job title falls under?

Accounting .... ☐
Engineering .... ☐
Manufacturing .... ☐
Operations .... ☐
Marketing .... ☐
Sales .... ☐
Other (Please specify): _____ ☐

9. What is your age?

Under 20 .... ☐
21-29 .... ☐
30-39 .... ☐
40-49 .... ☐
50-59 .... ☐
60-over .... ☐

10. Are you:

Male .... ☐
Female .... ☐

11. Which computer publications do you read regularly? (Please list)

_____
_____
_____
_____
_____
_____
_____
_____
_____

Comments: _____
_____
_____

Fold here and scotch-tape to mail.